BERING

BERING

The Russian Discovery of America

ORCUTT FROST

YALE UNIVERSITY PRESS / NEW HAVEN & LONDON

Published with assistance from the Annie Burr Lewis Fund. Research for this book was partially funded under grants from the Alaska Humanities Forum, the National Endowment for the Humanities, and Alaska Pacific University.

Designed by Mary Valencia.
Set in Fournier type by Binghamton Valley Composition.
Printed in the United States of America by Vail-Ballou Press.

Library of Congress Cataloging-in-Publication Data

Frost, O. W. (Orcutt William), 1926–
Bering : the Russian discovery of America / Orcutt Frost.
p. cm.
Includes bibliographical references and index.
ISBN 0-300-10059-0 (alk. paper)
1. Bering, Vitus Jonassen, 1681–1741. 2. Explorers—Russia—Biography. 3. Alaska—Discovery and exploration—Russian. 4. Northwest Coast of North America—Discovery and exploration—Russian. 5. Arctic regions—Discovery and exploration—Russian. 6. Kamchatskaëiia çekspediëtìsiëiia (2nd : 1733–1743) 7. Kamchatskaëiia çekspediëtìsiëiia (1st : 1725–1730). I. Title.
G296.B4F76 2003
917.9804'1'092—dc21
2003009889

10 9 8 7 6 5 4 3 2 1

Frontispiece: Bust of Vitus Jonassen Bering, reconstructed from skeletal remains by V. N. Zvyagin and colleagues, Institute of Forensic Medicine, Moscow (photograph by Sten Olander; courtesy of the Horsens Museum, Denmark)

To the memory of my parents:

ORCUTT WILLIAM FROST SR. (1901–1974)
AGNES HARRIET WILLIAMS FROST (1902–2001)

Contents

Illustrations

Illustrations are reproduced courtesy of the individuals, publishers, and institutions named in the captions. Where no acknowledgment is given, the item is the author's. "Efimov" followed by a number refers to the map number in A. V. Efimov, ed., Atlas of the Geographical Discoveries in Siberia and Northwest America in the Seventeenth and Eighteenth Centuries *(Moscow, 1964). All Efimov maps have been redrawn.*

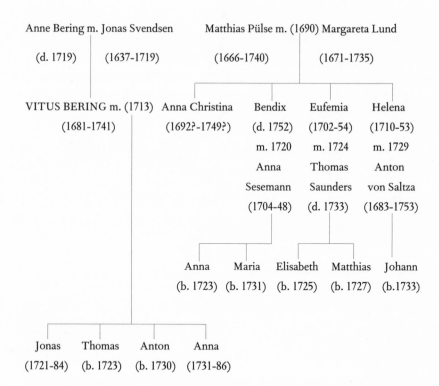

Figure 1. BERING FAMILY TREE.

Preface

Vitus Jonassen Bering is one of the world's great explorers between the epochs of Columbus and James Cook. Peter the Great appointed Bering commander of the First Kamchatka Expedition, 1725–30; and Empress Anna Ivanovna reappointed him to lead the Second Kamchatka Expedition (sometimes called the Great Northern Expedition), 1733–43, which he did not survive. These extremely ambitious land-and-sea expeditions are important for three reasons: they consolidated and expanded Russia's empire from Siberia to North America; they pioneered the geography of Siberia and the North Pacific Ocean; and they opened California and the Pacific Northwest to a new era of European trade and settlement. They also contributed to scientific knowledge of the flora and fauna of the North Pacific Rim through Georg Wilhelm Steller's observations on Kayak Island, in the Gulf of Alaska; on Nagai Island, in the Shumagin Islands; and on Bering Island, off the Kamchatka peninsula.

That peninsula was pivotal for each expedition. It was the destination of journeys across Siberia, and it provided a home port on the North Pacific Ocean for voyages to the Icy Sea (Arctic Ocean) in 1728 and to North America in 1741. The peninsula provided timber for the ship that Bering built on the Kamchatka River during the first expedition. For the second expedition it provided another home port that has since become a principal city (Petropavlovsk-Kamchatka) and a base for fishing fleets.

Just as Ferdinand Magellan's voyage across the South Pacific in 1519–21 gave rise to a "South Sea" (or "Mer du Sud," as in Fig. 20), so Bering's crossing of the North Pacific in 1741 gave prominence to a broad northern sea, or a northern extension of that South Sea. These discoveries, together with the European finding of the Americas (whether as island or continent) between Europe and Asia, greatly enlarged geographers' concepts of the world and obliterated forever the old theological concept of the world as consisting of three continents, Europe, Africa, and Asia, separated by a "middle sea" (Mediterranean), with Jerusalem at the center.

It is almost incomprehensible nowadays that geographers before the eighteenth century speculated wildly about the relationship of Asia and America, whether there was a small sea between them or merely a strait or channel. From Marco Polo's account of his travels, a Venetian geographer in 1562 mistakenly understood "Ania" to be a "Strait of Anian" north of China rather than to the south of China, as Polo evidently intended. To the Bering expedition this strait was understood to be "the channel" extending between Asia and America well south of the present Bering Strait (Fig. 20).

Whereas the Bering expeditions gave European cartographers a fairly accurate outline of Siberia and of North America immediately north of California, they left to the end of Captain Cook's third voyage in 1778 the accurate mapping of both the Bering Sea and Bering Strait.

It was Bering's sea voyage from Kamchatka to North America that precipitated the rush of Russian fur traders to both the Commander and Aleutian islands and eventually to south-central Alaska and northern California. That rush was occasioned by the sight of sea otter pelts brought back to Kamchatka by survivors shipwrecked and stranded for nine months on Bering Island, one of two chief Commander islands. The rush led to the monopoly in 1799 of the Russian-American Company and its rule of Russian America (Alaska) until its sale in 1867 to the United States.

The reported presence of Russians in North America prompted Spain to extend its settlements in California from San Diego to San Francisco by 1776. If expeditions are judged by the extent of territory and seas they explored and by their subsequent outcomes, then the two great expeditions commanded by Vitus Jonassen Bering have rarely been matched in magnitude and result in modern world history.

Any account about Bering understandably has its focus on his two expeditions. They were the culmination of his career in the Russian Imperial Navy; they dominated the last sixteen years of his life, when he was usually either on expedition or making preparations for an expedition; and they are an important chapter (one often omitted) about Russia's history of expansion into North America from 1741 to 1867. Any biography of the explorer should also include his relationship with two individuals who joined him on part of his second expedition. One was Anna, his wife and the mother of their four children, a woman to whom he was devoted and who had, to all appearances, a very companionable and influential bond with him. The other was Georg Steller, his physician on the voyage to America, a relatively young man who shared his cabin aboard ship, cured him of scurvy, and contributed significantly to the survival of the expedition after it was shipwrecked on Bering Island.

This book may surprise scholars and knowledgeable readers. Bering here is not the man pictured in some earlier histories concerning the expeditions. He is not the corpulent fellow seen there in portraits supposedly of him. Surely no obese person could have made the trek across Siberia as Bering did, not once but three times. He did not of course go alone. He had hundreds of people with him for the transport of many thousands of pounds of provisions (meat, flour, and butter) for the voyages and tens of thousands of pounds of equipment (cannon, rigging, and sail) for the building of ships on Russia's Pacific frontier. Bering was muscular, presumably from a lot of heavy lifting. Thanks to forensic reconstruction of skeletal remains, this great explorer as he looked, and as Anna Bering and Georg Steller knew him, is revealed in the Introduction.

As for Anna Bering, readers of English will meet her for the first time, especially in Chapter 6. (She made a notable appearance in 1997 in personal letters written in German, translated into Danish, and published in Denmark under the title *Kommandøren og Konen*, or *The Commander and His Wife*.) In her ambitions she was clearly a good match for her husband. What they sought in their lives was ultimately neither cash nor fame. It was the (unrealized) reward of a country estate where they might spend their final years with their children and then pass it on to them as an inheritance.

Steller, like Bering, is not presented in this book as he often appears elsewhere—not as a habitually virulent individual who was somehow a scientific genius but unhappily a social misfit. A key to his character and achievement was his Lutheran Pietism. He was a loner, supremely self-assured and highly motivated to serve the expedition but often in his own divergent way. For example, he desperately wanted more time (preferably all winter) in America to describe America's natural history, but Bering reluctantly allowed him but ten hours on Kayak Island, where the expedition's first landing off America occurred. Consequently, Bering had what today might be called a "management problem" with him. More seriously, Bering underestimated at first the potential value of his physician's services. The dramatic story of Steller's changing role during the second expedition begins in Chapter 7.

There is another reason why Steller is a prominent figure in this biography. Bering's last known substantial writing is his progress report about the Second Kamchatka Expedition, dated April 18, 1741. Thereafter until his death on December 8 of that year, including the months that encompassed the entire voyage to America, two of the most useful sources about Bering are Steller's journal of 1743 and his report of November 16, 1742. Steller is sometimes mistaken and frequently outspoken and judgmental, but during 1741 he alone makes detailed observations about several dramatic events that focus on Bering. With rare exceptions, other expedition records, logbooks, reports, and journals mention Bering uncritically. Such records also mention him only briefly and infrequently.

This book grew in three stages. It was first an account of those ten hours that Steller spent on Kayak Island (Chapter 9)—the puzzle of where he landed, where he went, and what precisely he did. It then occurred to me that those ten hours, to be properly understood, needed the context of the entire Second Kamchatka Expedition.

Finally, it seemed desirable to include as well the story of the First Kamchatka Expedition to give Russian America its genesis through Peter the Great. So a story of ten hours on a remote island on July 20, 1741, became in the end the story of a very long journey across two continents and a vast uncharted ocean to reach a third continent, all over a period of seventeen years: a journey that was a colossal undertaking, given the varied modes of travel and the problems of supply. No wonder Vitus and Anna Bering yearned for a settled life.

It has also taken me seventeen years to complete the research and writing of the story. I began with Steller and concluded with Bering. I have gone into many byways, such as the preparation of a new edition of Steller's journal of his voyage with Bering from Kamchatka to North America; the organization of an international conference at Alaska Pacific University, Anchorage, to celebrate the 250th anniversary of the Bering voyage of 1741; publication of the proceedings of that conference; and the publication of a translation (by Katherine L. Arndt) of a book in Russian concerning recent excavations of the Bering expedition camp on Bering Island. Also I attended Bering and Steller exhibitions in Denmark and Germany and visited the hometowns of Bering and Steller, respectively Horsens, on the Jutland Peninsula, and Bad Windsheim, near Nuremberg.

In my research and writing I have endeavored to take nothing for granted, neither conclusions about Bering in the studies of specialists nor occasionally the accuracy of translations from German, Latin, or Russian primary sources. Whenever information was lacking, especially about landing sites on islands, I made repeated visits to those islands— Kayak, the Shumagins, and Bering—during summer months to ascertain site locations and to visualize settings of episodes in the Bering story. In 1997 and 1999 I visited the site of Bering's Harbor of the Apostles Peter and Paul at Petropavlovsk-Kamchatka. In 2002, on a small cruise ship, I followed Bering's voyage of 1728 from the mouth of the Kamchatka River to the Bering Strait.

With the exception of Petropavlovsk-Kamchatka, I am impressed by how little the land has changed over the centuries in all these remote places, still largely uninhabited as part of the establishment of modern ecological preserves or, especially in northeastern Asia, as a result of inclement weather, declining resources, or desolate landscapes.

It seems incredible, especially in our time of jet travel and instant e-mail connections, that Vitus Bering and Georg Steller traveled over as much as half the northern hemisphere under the most trying conditions of climate and uncharted seas. Their stories are endlessly fascinating. They had differing talents, personalities, and motivations. With contrasting perspectives, they plunged into the challenges and consequences of first contact, European and Native American. Above all, their stories continue to come alive as they reveal themselves as never before in discoveries made through archaeological excavations and through analysis of newly found personal letters and other documents.

My objective has been to present a creditable account of Vitus Jonassen Bering and his expeditions against the backdrop of the political changes that occurred during the reigns of Peter the Great and the five other Romanov rulers who followed him between 1725 and 1743.

Chronology of Events

Dates of events occurring before 1918 in Russia, including Siberia and North America, are Old Style (O.S.), based on the Julian rather than the Gregorian calendar. Also, dates are based on civil rather than nautical time, which was used in the logbooks of the St. Peter and St. Paul. (Nautical dates are from noon to noon.) Dates after 1918 are New Style (N.S.).

1581—Beginning of the Russian conquest of Siberia.

1587—Tobolsk founded; later capital of Siberia.

1632—Yakutsk founded on the Lena River.

1637—Birth of Jonas Svendsen, Bering's father, in Scandia, won by Swedes in 1645.

1639—Russian detachment reaches the Pacific Ocean at the Sea of Okhotsk.

1648—Okhotsk founded. Semyon Dezhnev sails through the Bering Strait.

1649—Anadyr (Anadyrsk) founded; Russian outpost closest to North America.

1652—Irkutsk founded near Russia's border with China.

1675—Death of Vitus Pedersen Bering, royal historian of Denmark, for whom Vitus Jonassen is named.

1681: Aug. 5—Vitus Jonassen Bering baptized in Horsens, Denmark.

1689—Peter becomes co-ruler of Russia with his stepbrother, Ivan. Treaty of Nerchinsk by which China prevents Russia's use of the Amur River route to the Pacific Ocean.

1696—Bering signs on as ship's boy for a voyage to Tranquebar, India. Ivan's death.

1703—Beginning of the construction of St. Petersburg.

1704—Bering joins the Russian navy as sublieutenant.

1709—Russians defeat Swedes at Poltava.

1710—Peter establishes the Ruling Senate.

1713: Oct. 8—Bering marries Anna Christina Pülse in Viborg, Russia.

1719—Bering's parents die at Horsens.

1721—Peter proclaimed emperor. The Holy Synod replaces the Patriarchate. The Peace of Nystad ends the Great Northern War against Sweden.

1724: Feb. 26—Bering retires from Russian navy.

Oct. 3—Bering rejoins Russian navy as captain first class.

Dec. 29—Bering is appointed commander of First Kamchatka Expedition.

1725: Jan. 28—Peter dies, succeeded by Catherine I, his wife.

Feb. 6—Bering leaves St. Petersburg for Tobolsk, capital of Siberia.

1727—Catherine I dies, succeeded by Peter II.

Aug. 16—Bering's *Archangel Gabriel*, built on the Kamchatka River, reaches 67°24'N above Bering Strait.

1729—Peter II dies, succeeded by Anna Ivanovna, Peter's niece.

1730: Feb. 28—Expedition returns to St. Petersburg.

Apr. 30—Bering proposes a second expedition.

1731—Itelmens on Kamchatka peninsula rebel against the Russians.

1732: Apr. 17—Empress Anna Ivanovna orders that Bering's proposed second expedition (not officially named) be carried out.

June 12—Senate approves an academic contingent for the expedition.

Aug. 21—Mikhail S. Gvozdev anchors *Archangel Gabriel* off America (Seward Peninsula).

1733: Apr. 29—Vitus and Anna Bering with their two youngest children leave St. Petersburg.

1734: Feb. 27—Bering and Anna leave Tobolsk for Irkutsk and Yakutsk.

October—Bering establishes his headquarters at Yakutsk.

1737 August—Bering arrives at Okhotsk from Yakutsk.

1740: July 2—Construction of *St. Peter* and *St. Paul* completed at Okhotsk.

Aug. 13—Georg Steller arrives at Okhotsk.

Aug. 19—Anna Bering and children leave Okhotsk for St. Petersburg.

Sept. 8—*St. Peter* and *St. Paul* leave Okhotsk en route to Kamchatka.

Oct. 17—Anna Ivanovna dies; succeeded by Ivan VI, an infant.

1741: Mar. 20—Steller joins Bering on Avacha Bay, Kamchatka.

Apr. 18—Bering completes his report about the second expedition.

May 4—Sea council decides to sail southeast by east from Avacha Bay.

June 4—*St. Peter* and *St. Paul* begin voyage from Kamchatka to America.

June 20—The two ships are separated in a gale.

July 15—*St. Paul* (Capt. Chirikov) sights North America at 55°21'N.

July 16—Bering sights America from the sea south of Mount St. Elias.

July 18—Chirikov sends eleven men ashore to obtain fresh water.

July 20—Bering reaches Kayak Island, sends a boat (with Steller aboard) for fresh water and a second boat to explore a bay north of *St. Peter*'s anchorage.

July 24—Chirikov sends four men ashore to assist men sent six days earlier.

July 27—Chirikov decides to return to Kamchatka; fifteen men sent ashore presumed ambushed and dead.

Aug. 20—Scurvy afflicts twelve seamen of *St. Peter,* Bering among them.

Aug. 30—Landings made for fresh water on Nagai in the Shumagin Islands. Nikita Shumagin dies of scurvy and is buried on Nagai.

Sept. 4—Two Aleuts, each in a *baidarka,* salute *St. Peter:* the expedition's first meeting with Native Americans.

Sept. 9—*St. Paul* meets Aleuts off Adak Island.

Sept. 24—Scurvy returns to *St. Peter.*

Oct. 10—*St. Paul* reaches Avacha Bay.

Nov. 6—*St. Peter* enters Commander Bay, Bering Island.

Nov. 25—Coup d'état in St. Petersburg; Peter the Great's daughter Elizabeth becomes empress.

Dec. 8—Death of Bering. Lt. Sven Waxell assumes command.

1742: Aug. 14—Departure from Bering Island on rebuilt smaller ship.

September—Anna Bering reaches St. Petersburg.

Nov. 15—Waxell's report to Admiralty College.

Nov. 16—Steller's report to Senate.

1743—Date of Steller's manuscript journal of his voyage with Bering.

Sept. 4—Anna Bering receives news of her husband's death.

Sept. 25—Senate terminates the Second Kamchatka Expedition.

1746: Nov. 12—Steller dies in Tyumen, Siberia.

1754—Publication of G. F. Müller's map showing Russian discoveries.

1758—Publication of Müller's official history of the Bering expeditions.

1794—Arrival of first Russian Orthodox (celibate) priests, Kodiak Island.

1799—Monopoly granted to Russian-American Company.

1824—Arrival of Ivan Veniaminov, married parish priest, Unalaska district.

1966—Bering monument erected on Commander Bay hillside by "residents of Kamchatka."

1979—Russian archaeologists begin excavation of Bering expedition camp.

1988—Publication of *The Komandorskii Camp of the Bering Expedition* in Russian (English ed., 1992), report of archaeological findings.

1991: Aug. 3—Danish archaeologists discover Bering's grave.

1992—Completion of forensic reconstruction of Bering's image and Bering's reburial.

1997—Publication of Bering family letters in *Kommandøren og Konen* (The commander and his wife), Copenhagen.

INTRODUCTION

History has not been kind to Vitus Jonassen Bering. He has never been the subject of an adequate biography because almost nothing has been known about his family. Also, his reputation has suffered because the Russian government continued to maintain its secrecy concerning the Second Kamchatka Expedition for a dozen years after Bering died. Unfortunately, Bering had not yet written a report about the sea voyage of that expedition, and since his death there have been long silences about his important role in Russia's history, silences broken at rare intervals by stories that are often untrue and even slanderous. Out of France in the middle of the eighteenth century, for example, came the surprising rumor that Bering, having died on an island off Kamchatka, did not reach North America at all. A century later a Russian scholar declared that the commander was the "moral subordinate" of a Russian officer who served under him. In the twentieth century an American historian concluded that severe criticism by government officials in St. Petersburg so discouraged Bering that he lacked the initiative to assume command of his ship bound for America; and a popular American journalist speculated that Bering was accused of rounding up young women in Yakutsk, Siberia, for his own harem.[1] This last story is all the more remarkable given the commander's advancing years, his reputed poor health, and especially the presence of his wife and their two small children with him in the town.

Another blow to Bering's reputation since the mid–twentieth century has been the repeated publication of an image purportedly of him in an eighteenth-century oil painting.[2] The man in the painting has puffy cheeks and perhaps jowls and a double chin. In other words, he appears to be obese. This image has seemed to confirm stories about the commander's stupor, lethargy, and indecisiveness. Besides, how could he win the respect of seamen if he was so fat that he could not readily move about a ship?

But now at last, against all odds, there has been a surprising, favorable turn in his reputation, prompted by his recent rising—literally, with help—from his grave.

On August 2, 1991, a small Danish party arrived at the summer camp of what was known as the "Bering 91" Russian-Danish Archaeological Expedition on Commander Bay of Bering Island. The Danes were four archaeologists with an entourage of an interpreter, a geographer, a photojournalist, a television producer, and a representative of descendants of the Bering family living in Denmark. There were twenty-two Russians, including notably the expedition leader and a forensic physician, along with numerous scientific specialists and their assistants.[3]

The day was a momentous occasion, the start of an international effort to locate Bering's grave. Russians expected that the objective, if successful, would take a long time to reach. But on the very first day of their work, the day after they arrived, the Danes went directly to a particular spot, dug a short trench, pulled back the turf—and *there it was*, a small cemetery, unmarked. It had been there for two and a half centuries, relatively undisturbed, on the flattened top of a low sandy ridge that had been covered with grassy vegetation. To all appearances these Danes went right to the place where one of the world's great explorers, Captain-Commander Vitus Jonassen Bering of the Russian Imperial Navy, presumably lay buried. When the sod was pulled aside, the rectangular outlines of several graves were revealed by depressions of settled sand and earth. Surely one of these graves would prove to be Bering's, for they were next to house-pit sites of the 1741–42 winter camp, and the Danes (not the Russians)[4] knew that Georg Steller, Bering's physician, had written in his journal that the commander was buried close to this camp.

If the Danes were elated by the discovery now before them, some of their Russian colleagues were utterly aghast. They had not expected that the Danes would find the grave site so soon. Before the Danes arrived, some of the Russians had worked for several weeks, very systematically making a soils survey. Within grids they had taken samples and tested them for phosphates that might have leached out from bones over the centuries.[5] They had tried to tell the Danes where they should start, but the Danes paid no heed. They knew exactly where they wanted to work.

On their aircraft en route to Bering Island, with topographical maps in hand, they had already pinpointed the spot where they supposed they could most profitably dig. It had to be "close by" Bering's winter camp. It had to be in ground easily dug in late autumn by weakened, half-starved men. It should be in an open area where snow would likely blow away. It should have a generally east–west orientation, favored for burials by Christian seafarers of the eighteenth century. It should be a solitary place over which men would not trample in going from their dwellings to obtain fresh water from the nearby Commander River or to their wrecked ship on the shore of the bay. An extension of the ridge on which Russian archaeologists had excavated and reconstructed dugout dwellings of the Bering winter camp in 1979 and 1981 met all those requirements. These underground dwellings, huddled together, were about as close to the meandering river as the grave site projected by the Danes, a bit farther to the north. They had hypothesized that on the same sandy ridge the living and the dead, in separate spaces, once lay together. Two kinds of "graves," one kind larger and deeper with a pit for fire—and, yes, with a way out.

Here is another surprise: Steller in his journal, with macabre humor, had called their dwellings "graves" before actual graves were dug—close by.[6]

Bering and his men had found America and were coming home, twice stopping at islands for fresh water. Then, without warning, storms pounded them for days with unceasing fury. Their ship, with sails furled, drifted unpredictably, pummeled by waves that hit like shot from a cannon, then rose and dropped as men sick with scurvy shrieked with pain or cried in despair. The ship creaked agonizingly with every rapid rise

to the top of a wave's crest. It then fell abruptly into the black depths
between towering waves. The ship's navigator declared that in all his
fifty years at sea he had never experienced such storms. Steller expected
that at any moment the ship would shatter and sink.[7]

Just as suddenly as storms came upon them, they vanished. Repairs
were made. There were still some able-bodied men who could manage
sail. Some days favorable winds swept the ship swiftly along for hours
at a time. Hopes revived despite daily deaths from scurvy. When it was
announced that the Kamchatka peninsula of the Asian mainland was
near, land did appear. Men who were very sick rolled out of their beds
and crawled on the deck to see it. Brandy that had been squirreled away
was quaffed in celebration. Some men began to identify points of land
on the horizon. That land was Kamchatka. It was surely Kamchatka.

The ship entered what seemed to be a broad inlet. The fog was too
thick to be sure. Then the ship tacked to run out of the far side of the
presumed inlet, but contrary winds beat it back. Sail was damaged.

Two senior officers, Sven Waxell and Safron Khitrovo, asked Bering
to call a sea council. Anyone able to enter the commander's cabin was
invited to participate. Abed with scurvy and unable to control the proceedings himself, Bering spoke first. He urged a decision to sail on to
home port. When his adjutant, Dmitry Ovtsin, spoke up in agreement,
Waxell and Khitrovo took charge of the council and drove Ovtsin out.
Then they proposed that the ship be run into a bay to the west to seek
rescue ashore.

Some men asked if the land were really Kamchatka. Khitrovo declared that if it were not, "he would let his head be chopped off."[8]

No one challenged him. A vote was taken. Several men abstained,
but the outcome was decisive: the ship was to be anchored in the bay.

Khitrovo's remark was remembered later as marking the beginning
of a new tragedy. Once the ship was at anchor, all men were eventually
ferried ashore. Search parties were sent out. No help was found anywhere. The dying continued. Winter with its heavy snows was upon
them. There was a growing realization that their worst fear was coming
true. They were stranded on an island.

The graves uncovered, the Danes were about to proceed with excavation when suddenly one Russian came up (they scarcely knew these
Russians yet) and with a show of authority ordered them to stop. They

did not have permission to dig, he said. But of course they did. It was given very explicitly in a letter. The previous spring the Moscow Adventure Club had invited the Danes to participate in a search for Bering's grave. For their financial support—it was considerable—they had been granted the task of locating the burial site. If they found it, they had permission to excavate it, with the proviso that they would turn over all skeletal remains to the Russians for scientific study and reconstruction.[9]

The Danes had been invited because Bering had been born a Dane. Three of the archaeologists were from Horsens, Bering's birthplace. Their leader, the director of the Horsens Historical Museum, had invited a fourth archaeologist from the National Museum in Copenhagen.[10] The occasion for the dig was the 250th anniversary of Bering's death.

Within ten days the excavation was finished. Six dead were recovered. In the center of the grave site were two individuals, a tall, slender man with a tiny tin cross upon his chest and another man with head propped up because the coffin that dignified him in one of the deeper graves was too short to contain him fully laid out. These two could be tentatively identified, the first as Andreas Hesselberg, the navigator, and the second as Bering, because his was the only coffined burial.

According to records of the Bering expedition, eight other men had died and were buried on the land. Some of the first were probably buried on the beach of the bay; if so, their remains will probably never be recovered because of flood tides and gradual subsidence of the land. It is also possible that the meandering Commander River, in changing course many times over the years, had eroded away whatever sandy ridge in which some of the other dead may have been placed.

Once all the skeletal remains found in the grave site had been brushed clean, strengthened with glue, and sectioned and boxed for removal, people of Nikolskoye, the only village on the other side and other end of the island, became alarmed when news reached them that *their* Bering had been found and was about to be taken away by ship from *his* island (Fig. 2). They were mollified only when, in the city of Petropavlovsk-Kamchatka, it was agreed that Bering and his companions in death would be returned to the island one year hence with a military guard for appropriate reburial.[11]

In Petropavlovsk-Kamchatka, founded by Bering in 1740, each individual skeleton was minutely described in a laboratory of the district

Figure 2. STATUE OF VITUS JONASSEN BERING, NIKOLSKOYE, BERING ISLAND. THE FACE IS MODELED ON AN EIGHTEENTH-CENTURY OIL PAINTING.

museum. The descriptions, once reviewed by a commission hastily called together, were attached to certificates signed by the commission members. Finally the remains were bagged, boxed, and flown in a single day all the way to Moscow and its Institute of Forensic Medicine of the Ministry of Public Health. Here began Bering's sabbatical, which produced a revelation that would change forever the assessment of his life and achievement.

That revelation was stunning. Reconstruction of his appearance from skeletal remains revealed a man resembling a world champion weight lifter. Indeed, so muscular was he that the principal Russian forensic physician concluded that Bering, even late in life, "could not but distinguish himself among those around him by his obvious physical strength." He had very evidently carried heavy loads from his youth. His weight (about 168 pounds) was ideal for his height (5 feet, 6 inches).[12]

Other findings concerned his health. It is commonly assumed that the immediate cause of Bering's death was scurvy. Yet his teeth were found to be intact and their condition good, ruling out scurvy: one of the surest signs of death from scurvy is loose or lost teeth. Though the scurvy he suffered during the homeward voyage might have weakened his physical condition at his advanced age of 60 years, the immediate cause of his death was heart failure, indicated by the swollen ankles Steller observed. Bering evidently did have several complaints—neck pains, headaches, and flat feet, none of which was life-threatening. A year's medical examination of his remains in Moscow resulted in a highly favorable judgment that, everything considered, Bering had been "attentive to his health, actively withstanding extreme conditions of life."[13]

This new information about Bering's physique and general health sharply contradicts prevailing, often defamatory views. Bering in the years 1738–40 has been described as "crushed," as between "two millstones." It has also been supposed that early in 1741 Bering "collapsed" and, "sunk into a state of physical and mental apathy," seemingly "lost all interest" in the business of the voyage.[14]

Some scholars hesitate to affirm that Bering's grave has been found. It is true that that eighteenth-century oil painting has the name "Vitus Bering" at its base and that it was found in Russian archives. If the portrait were of the commander's great-uncle, Vitus Pedersen Bering, the royal historiographer in Denmark, why was the painting found in St. Petersburg? Another consideration concerns those who died on Bering Island that fall and winter of 1741–42. Of the fourteen men who died there, only six have been found in their graves. Could not Bering be buried somewhere else? Who then is the real Bering? Is he the man in the painting or the man in the coffin found near house pits on the island? There has not been much debate over this question, but a magnificently illustrated volume titled *Die Grosse Nordische Expedition* (The Great Northern Expedition), published in 1996, includes pictures of both Berings, stating that the forensically reconstructed image is "probably" Bering's.[15]

Now, no one can say absolutely that Bering has been found. But the evidence is convincing.

Steller's journal is the only expedition record that indicates the location of the grave. His day-by-day account of the voyage and stranding was revised and dated 1743. One English translation (1925) of his German reads, "We buried his lifeless body . . . near our dwelling." Another (1988) is similar: "We buried his corpse . . . close to our dwelling."[16] The grave site and the winter camp were found to be side by side. Steller was an eyewitness.

Of the six graves in the site, only one had a coffin, and this particular grave was deeper than most of the others. It was obviously given exceptional care and respect.

The coffin boards were larch, probably from Kamchatka. Able-bodied men to make a coffin were in short supply at a critical time well within the period of dying on the island, from November 6, 1741, to January 8, 1742. According to Steller, the beach was then at first "depressing." Most men were immobile, unable to stand unaided. Men lay helter-skelter on the beach, some crying, some cursing. They were harassed by Arctic foxes scurrying about, emboldened to bite into the living and the dead. House pits could not be readied quickly enough and the sick had to be led or carried a half mile to them, first along the beach and across the shallow mouth of a small river and then upstream to the low sandy ridge below a high bluff. Fifty men were in a constant state of hunger. Many could hardly eat, even if they had food. Their gums were swollen over their teeth.[17]

So it was a struggle to bury the dead. Some corpses remained on the beach unattended (except by foxes) for days at a time. But for the man for whom a coffin was made and a grave dug fairly deep, there was but the interval of a single day between his death and his very decent burial. Who could he be but Bering?

All this evidence is circumstantial (coffin, depth of grave, prompt burial) or imprecise ("close by" the camp). The best scientific evidence is the determination of age by tooth wear and by other bone studies. Russian analyses tend to confirm the identity of the two men. Steller reports that Hesselberg was 70 years old at the time of his death. Analysis of the teeth of the man presumed to be him fixes the skeleton's age at death between 65.7 and 70.7 years. Moreover, there was found on the chest of this same individual a small tin cross that only a Protestant or Roman Catholic Western European would wear. This cross could belong to only Hesselberg or Bering. They were both Lutherans, the only Protestants among the fourteen men who died on the island. There were apparently no Catholics. Bering lived 60.4 years. Analysis of the teeth of the man in the coffin yields an age between 56.4 and 61.4 years at death.[18] Of all the men who had been on the ship, only Hesselberg was known to be older than Bering.

Who are the other four men buried on both sides of the commander and his navigator? Again Steller's journal is helpful. It reports that Bering "lies between his adjutant, a commissary, and [two] grenadiers." Three of these men are easily identified from a list of the dead reported by Waxell.[19] The only man who had formerly served as an adjutant was the assistant navigator, Nikita Khotyantsov, who died the day Bering was buried; that is, December 9. The commissary was Ensign Ivan Lagunov, the last to die, on January 8, 1742. From Steller's statement it is apparent that these two men are on one side of the two Lutherans (Steller was probably thinking only of those who died *after* Bering, so he omits Hesselberg's name). Though Steller had the idea that two grenadiers were on the other side, only a single grenadier died on the island, on December 17. He was Ivan Tretyakov. The fourth man's name is not known.

Because the graves to the south (toward the camp) are well spaced and the first—presumably Khotyantsov's—is about as deep as Bering's, it is presumed that they were prepared for the two officers, whereas the other graves on the north side, both very shallow and crowded against each other and the coffined burial, appear to be for the grenadier and the other unidentified person. Presumably the ornamented silver Russian Orthodox cross, well preserved and slipped behind the head of the individual in the southernmost grave, belonged to one of the two officers who were Orthodox.

Here then is the lineup of the men buried in six graves in a row from south to north, with the age range determined for each individual and with date of burial:

Ivan Lagunov, 55.5–60.5, commissary, January 8, 1742
Nikita Khotyantsov, 49.5–54.5, former adjutant, December 9, 1741
Andreas Hesselberg, 65.7–70.7, navigator, November 22
Vitus Bering, 56.4–61.4, commander, December 8
Ivan Tretyakov, 50–55, grenadier, December 19
Unknown, 40–45

Thus Steller's journal, the archaeological excavations, and forensic studies of skeletal remains combine to identify the grave of Vitus Jonassen Bering. With such evidence the identity of his remains can hardly be doubted.

The uncovered physical remains reveal that Bering was still strong and healthy up until the very last months of his life, and the documentary record supports the argument that Bering was an effective leader during that time. Although he had some misgivings about his performance in Siberia (the expedition there was too large and complex), he remained confident of his abilities and was determined to carry out his duties.

The discovery of Bering's personal letters written early in February 1740 affords fresh insight into his feelings. In a letter to the gymnasium professor who cared for and supervised the education of his two older sons, he says, "We rejoiced not a little" over reports of progress and proficiency. He then requests private lessons in Russian for his second son, Thomas. In a long letter to an esteemed friend, the Austrian minister in St. Petersburg, he is jovial in response to his friend's teasing, appreciative of hospitality given Jonas and Thomas, candid about alternatives for Jonas's future, and grateful for the news that his friend will "graciously intervene" in advocating Bering's further promotion to rear admiral.[20] In these and other letters to his sons there is not the slightest hint of a man caught between millstones. Rather, the letters show control over his family affairs, good humor, and hope for the future.

If, on the eve of his sea expedition to America, Bering were "broken" and ailing, his own words do not betray such handicaps. In a cover letter for a long report addressed to Empress Anna and dated April 18, 1741, he concludes with these words: "We, your humble servants, will be sailing from Avacha Bay [Kamchatka] this spring, if God permits, as soon as the sea is free from ice. No time will be wasted. During the voyage, we will follow Admiralty instructions and *do our utmost*." As for his health, his physician, Steller, declares that when Bering recovered from scurvy in early September 1741 "he was able to get out of bed and on deck and to feel *as vigorous as he had been at the beginning of the voyage.*"[21]

Was Bering determined? Was he fit? Testimony in the affirmative is limited, but it is significant in the absence of persuasive testimony to the contrary.

The entire available documentary record shows that Bering was an effective leader who normally projected strength and confidence, remaining above petty quarrels, jealousies, and favoritism. Though his wit could be quick and devastating, his aura of power and vigor typically won him the advantage of being deliberate in decision making, ever mindful of his instructions from superiors in St. Petersburg and consultations with leaders around him. His command of two of history's largest and longest land-and-sea expeditions demonstrated administrative ability under the most trying conditions. Peter the Great wisely chose him for the first expedition, which gave him unrivaled experience to lead a much larger second expedition. Now that Bering's remains have been exhumed and studied, he can be newly appreciated as he was—a man's man and the empire's man.

In September 1992 the Russian historian Leonid Pasenyuk had an opportunity to view Bering's remains in the Petropavlovsk Museum. In his books on the Commander Islands he had criticized Bering for "sluggishness, timidity, even lack of professional skills." Having viewed the remains and feeling deeply the revelations they contained, he had a sudden impulse and asked permission to hold Bering's skull in his hands. Permission was granted and he took the skull. Instantly there came a moment of éclairecissement, of epiphany.

To Bering he uttered two heartfelt words: "Forgive me."[22]

On September 15, 1992, six coffins, with a uniformed guard of honor, arrived in Commander Bay on the Coast Guard frigate *Kedrov*. Two days earlier a military ceremony had been held in Lenin Square, Petropavlovsk-Kamchatka, with the coffins paraded on gun carriages. In addition to officers of the Russian Pacific fleet, those present included the vice governor of Kamchatka, a delegation led by the mayor of Horsens, Denmark, and the Danish ambassador to Russia.[23] In the service of reburial these worthies witnessed an end to two and a half centuries of history, from the discovery of the island to recognition of a hero who, as empire builder, was a heavy lifter for Russia.

The coffins were lowered into a compact grave site in a new location on the slope of the bluff several hundred yards above the site of the 1741–42 camp and cemetery. Here they are directly below five wooden panels, set just above ground level, listing the names of the men who died during the Bering expedition. Here they are also at the same elevation as the Bering monument, a high steel Latin cross above a cast-iron plaque set in the ground with the inscription (translated):

1681–1741

To the great navigator
Captain-Commander VITUS BERING
from the residents of Kamchatka
June 1966

The monument and new grave site overlook a panoramic view of the bay and river valley (Fig. 3).

The new grave site is separated by two steel crosses, a Latin cross above Bering with Hesselberg directly below and a Russian Orthodox cross over the four Russians buried in two rows parallel to the Protestant burials. The nearly square site is bounded by low steel posts supporting a single heavy chain.

The old cemetery, again overgrown with grassy and bushy vegetation, awaits eventual ruin as the Commander River continues to change

Figure 3. VITUS BERING MEMORIAL, COMMANDER BAY, BERING ISLAND
(FROM *THE KOMANDORSKII CAMP OF THE BERING EXPEDITION*
[ALASKA HISTORICAL SOCIETY, 1992]).

course and as the bay gradually creeps inland on a broad front and the land continues to subside slowly. The old winter camp itself, thoroughly excavated and marked by irregular holes, also awaits obliteration. The memorials set on the slope will be silent witnesses as nature re-creates itself. Bering will be, for the foreseeable future, above it all.

PART ONE

CROSSING SIBERIA

VITUS BERING SIGNS ON WITH RUSSIA

In the Russian service Vitus Jonassen Bering traversed three vast contiguous geographical areas of the Earth—European Russia, dominated by autocratic rulers; Siberia, open to riches in furs and maladministration; and the North Pacific Ocean, mysterious, remote, and stormy. In the eighteenth century, Russian America was often a year—or a shipwreck—away from authority in European Russia.

At the beginning of this century Peter the Great was that authority. He managed war, business, and the church. He clipped wings—and beards—at will. No one could oppose him, not for long. No one could hide, not his own son and presumptive heir, not the head of the church. For having defied his father and run out of the country with his sweetheart, Aleksei, the son, though returning as a penitent, was tortured to death. The last patriarch of the Russian Orthodox Church could only wail: "Where shall I go from your spirit and how shall I flee from your face? Everywhere your sovereign power reigns over me; it is impossible to hide from it." This patriarch, Stefan Yavorsky, was abruptly deposed in 1718 and replaced by an ecclesiastical college. To this college, soon known as the Holy Synod, Peter assigned a chief procurator, or informer. In this way he effectively "reformed" the church on a Protestant model: there would be no patriarch or pope to challenge his authority.

As Christian sovereign, he ruled according to his own will and at his own discretion.[1] But of course he could not make a lot of decisions, especially when he himself was off to war. In 1708 he decentralized the government into ten provincial administrations. In 1711 he created a "ruling senate" to be set over them to act on his behalf, chiefly to gain support for war through taxation and recruitment.

One of the provinces posed a particular problem. Siberia, extending from the Ural Mountains to the Pacific Ocean, was twice the area of the other nine provinces combined. Peter himself was never there. He looked to Western Europe, actually visiting Amsterdam, London, and Paris. But over the Urals he sent Prince Matvei Petrovich Gagarin as the first governor general of Siberia. This governor, hanged in 1721 for bribery and corruption, was one of many Siberian officials who paid Peter his taxes in order to pay themselves a fortune. A German visitor in Siberia, Friedrich Christian Weber, remarked that in four or five years such officials could amass sufficient wealth to build palatial stone houses for themselves, while some natives they overtaxed had to abandon their cottages and run away.[2]

Siberia was simply another country, too vast to be administered and too rich in fur-bearing animals not to be exploited to the detriment of the resource. The natives hunted the sable and fox, and the Russians "hunted the natives." The state collected, as best it could, a tax or tribute in sables from natives and a tithe in sables from merchants.[3] The big loser was the sable, and in many areas the native was not far behind. So it is not surprising that in the eighteenth century Earth's largest nation never gained anything approaching control over or around the Earth's largest body of water. Not that imperial Russia did not try. In 1741 it reached the Gulf of Alaska, halfway around the northern hemisphere from St. Petersburg, relying on the skills and experience of Western Europeans in leadership roles.

Bering's loyalty is not seriously questioned. But evidence now available provides grounds to assert that he as well as other Western Europeans in the Russian service ignored imperial regulations because they could, far away from Moscow and St. Petersburg on Russia's Pacific frontier or on the North Pacific Ocean itself.[4]

Bering, appointed commander by Peter the Great late in 1724, was greatly tempted because of three dominant influences in his life: his ambition, his marriage, and the nature of his service to Russia. By his very name he represented the fading aspirations of an illustrious Danish family. On him was bestowed the name of his mother's uncle, who had died in 1675, six years before he was born. This great-uncle was Vitus Pedersen Bering, royal historiographer and a poet known as "the Danish Virgil." The epithet is significant. For just as Rome had Aeneas as its legendary founder, Denmark had its heroes and its glorious past. Indeed, until the seventeenth century, Denmark was the foremost nation of Northern Europe.

In the early centuries of the Christian era, the Danish homeland was centered in Scandia, on the southern Scandinavian peninsula (now a part of Sweden). As Angles and Jutes migrated to England (Angle-land) in the fifth and sixth centuries, Danes also moved westward, occupied the Jutland peninsula, and, after numerous raids, settled in that northern part of England known as the Danelaw. One Danish king, Canute the Great (995?–1035), became ruler of all England and Norway as well as Denmark. Though Normans subsequently replaced Danes as rulers of England, Denmark gained control of other lands south of the Baltic Sea, became Christianized over two centuries, and in 1104 had an archbishop as head of a national church. On the eve of the Protestant Reformation, Denmark had more than seventy monasteries with estates that brought them great wealth. Landowners with surplus butter, bacon, and horses became merchants and ship owners. The kingdom acquired colonies in Africa and India. Tranquebar, on the southeast coast of India, was a busy Danish port from 1620 and received its first Lutheran missionaries in 1706.

But by this time Denmark had become the loser in wars against Sweden. Jutland was pillaged. In 1645 Scandia, including the town of Halmstad (Fig. 4), Bering's father's birthplace, was lost irretrievably. For Denmark the seventeenth century brought painful decline and diminution. It had a stronger navy, but Sweden had superior armies, better military strategists, and the best iron produced anywhere in Europe. Even as a boy, Vitus Bering, as well as many of his countrymen, could see little future in Denmark. It was time to travel, to see the world. A ship—any ship—was the best way out, and in 1696 Bering shipped out. He rarely returned to his native town of Horsens, a small Baltic port on the east side of the Jutland peninsula, where he was baptized August 5, 1681, in the Lutheran church.[5] He left his father, Jonas Svendsen

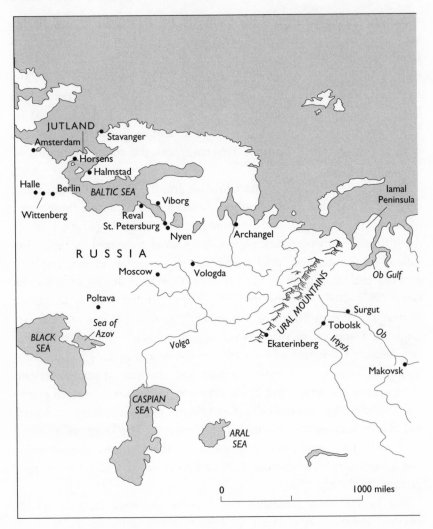

Figure 4. BERING'S SIBERIA, 1725–30, 1733–43.

(1637–1719), a customs inspector and churchwarden, and his mother,
Anne Pedersdatter Bering. When Jonas was born in Halmstad, it was
still a part of Denmark. In Horsens he already had three children, two
sons and a daughter, before he married Anne. The family was not poor.
Both of Jonas's sons attended the University of Copenhagen. The elder,
named Jonas for his father, won royal appointment as clerk of court on

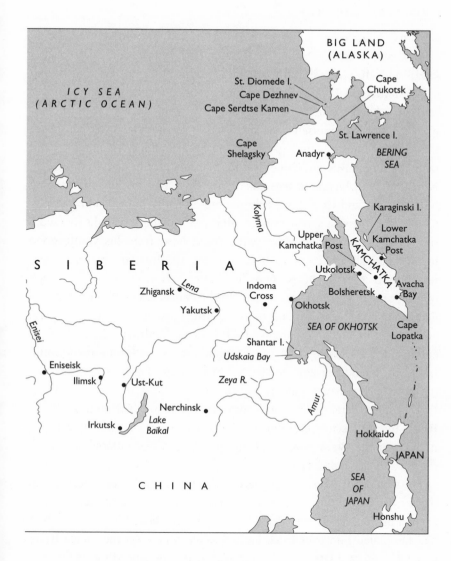

tiny Amager Island, located southeast of Copenhagen. The younger son, Svend, started out as a student of theology but was arrested for participating in a riot. His sentence was commuted to fifteen years of service in exile as customs collector and harbormaster in Tranquebar, India. When he shipped out in 1696, he was not alone. Vitus, only 15 years old, signed on as ship's boy.[6]

During the next eight years Bering began to fulfill the promise of his name as a student of navigation, serving under Danish and Dutch captains, completing officers' training in an Amsterdam navigation school, and reaching India, the Dutch East Indies, and other distant lands. The Russian admiral Cornelius Ivanovich Cruys, meeting Bering in Amsterdam in 1704, considered him qualified for the beginning officer rank of sublieutenant. Born in Stavanger (now in Norway, then in Denmark), Cruys had himself been recruited in Amsterdam in 1697 by Peter the Great's embassy and given the task of building, equipping, and manning a new Russian Baltic fleet for war against Sweden. In this Great Northern War, Denmark was allied with Russia against its longstanding bitter enemy, and Cruys probably had no difficulty in persuading Bering to join the Russian naval service. Bering, "out of gratitude to God," says Steller, "used to mention with praise how, from his youth, good fortune had always come to him." Joining the Russian Imperial Navy was indeed a stroke of fortune, for Bering advanced steadily through officer ranks. He was promoted to lieutenant in 1707, to captain-lieutenant in 1710, to captain of the fourth rank in 1715, third in 1717, and second in 1720.[7] Apparently he fought no battles at sea. In 1705 he commanded a schooner delivering building materials for a fort on Kotlin Island to defend the new city of St. Petersburg. The fort later became the port of Kronstadt and the site of Peter's Imperial Naval Academy. In 1711, after Peter's disastrous campaign against the Turks on the Pruth River, Bering rescued the ship *Munker* from the Sea of Azov by running it through the Black Sea, the Bosporus (past Constantinople), and all the way to the Baltic Sea.

He would not have had any greater opportunity for advancement in the service of another nation. The Russian Imperial Navy was new and expanding rapidly. It was Peter the Great's creation, his passion. Ships had fascinated him ever since he had sailed a boat on the Yauza River as a teenager and later, as a young tsar, had experienced the White Sea on a Dutch yacht built for him and delivered to the port of Archangel. It was not enough for Peter to skim over the water. He had to manage sail, steer, and captain his vessel.[8] In 1697–98, on his first trip abroad, he studied Dutch and British ships. In his own navy, as well as in his army, he assumed a subordinate rank commensurate with his competence and experience, ostensibly an example to fellow Russians who, after him, would literally learn the ropes.

Who would command and who would teach? Foreigners, of course. Peter had consorted with them from boyhood days in the German suburb of Moscow. An old Dutch merchant, Franz Timmerman, had taught him to sail. Peter could see that it was more expedient to recruit foreigners to serve Russian institutions than to send large numbers of Russians to study abroad. The advantages were immediate. His new Moscow School of Mathematics and Navigation was up and running as soon as its British instructors arrived. The Russian Imperial Navy was fully operational as soon as Admiral Cruys had obtained ships and signed on officers who were already seasoned veterans in fleets of the Danes, Dutch, or British.

For Bering and other Western Europeans, advantages were also immediate in rank and pay, and eventually, for the favored few, in aristocratic titles and enserfed estates. But there were also anxieties. Would Russia prevail over Sweden? Would Russia remain accommodating to immigrant experts after their students had become expert?

Meanwhile there was the question whether Russian controls over foreigners would become intolerable. In the Russian Imperial Navy control was in the hands of a relatively inexperienced seaman, Fyodor M. Apraksin, as lord high admiral. He was a drinking companion and trusted friend of Peter himself. Perhaps more ominous was the shadow of Peter—the tsar might be outranked as a naval officer but he was still the tsar. There was, moreover, the sea council peculiar to the Russian navy. Any senior officer could request a council, which a captain would be obliged to call, and at which the captain could be outvoted by his officers—clearly a check on the authority of a foreign commander. Finally, foreign expedition leaders, especially during 1733–43, were required to make a pledge of secrecy. Discoveries were not to be divulged by any means to persons residing outside Russia, or in fact to anyone unauthorized to know within Russia, "on pain of severe punishment," until those discoveries had been officially promulgated.[9]

All too soon and all too well Bering became familiar with the pain. He was a member of the court-martial of none other than Vice Admiral Cruys. Cruys's offense? "Not having embraced the opportunity of taking or destroying two Swedish ships in 1712" and also "when, in the chase of three Swedish ships of war in 1713, his own ship having struck a rock . . . not going on board another ship to hoist his flag and pursue the enemy." The sentence? Cruys "was by this court adjudged to lose his life, but his Majesty had mitigated the sentence to banishment in Kazan." The mitigation was fortunately short-lived, for when the Admiralty chancellery was reformed in 1717–18 and renamed the Admiralty College, Apraksin was of course named president and the knowledgeable but chastened Cruys was named vice president. Such proceedings led by Apraksin, with the tsar in attendance, were no joke. One foreign naval recruit who was sentenced to banishment suffered a mental break-down and soon died.[10]

Just as meetings of a sea council usually had Russians in the majority, membership on a court-martial was dominated by Russians. In the case of Cruys, Admiral Apraksin presided with the tsar at his ear and elbow. With them were Captain-Commander Aleksei Menshikov and two Rus-sian lieutenants. Foreigners deliberating were Captain-Lieutenant Be-ring, Captain Peter Sievers (a fellow Dane), and two other captains whose names, Nelson and Cronenburg, suggest that they were recruited respectively from England and Holland or Germany.[11] In any event, the Western Europeans were outnumbered 5 to 4, but more obviously they were also outranked. What voice did they have? No doubt the trial was an object lesson for them as well as for Cruys.

Most daunting for many foreigners in the Russian service was the religious divide. By tradition Russians were Orthodox, and by conviction the Orthodox—and only the Orthodox—were inheritors of heaven. As God ruled in heaven, so the tsar or tsarina was God's viceregent on Earth. It followed that Muslims, Jews, Catholics, and Protestants were all heretics. The Russian Orthodox Church taught that Moscow was the third—and last—Rome. The first Rome theologically went astray in the contention that its pope ruled over the temporal as well as the spiritual sphere. The second Rome, Constantinople, was lost to the Turks in 1453. The third Rome, Moscow, which ruled over all Russia, was idealized as the harmonious union of church and state, with the tsar as Christ's successor.

Thus the line dividing Christendom was theologically a gulf between Western and Eastern Europe, and those who crossed over from west to east at the turn of the eighteenth century were at least vaguely aware of Orthodox patriarchal fulminations leveled against them. Patriarch Joachim (d. 1690) issued this warning: "May our sovereigns never allow any Orthodox Christians in their realm to entertain any close friendly relations with heretics and dissenters—with the Latins, Lutherans, Cal-vinists and godless Tatars. . . . Let them be avoided as enemies of God and defamers of the Church." His successor, Adrian (d. 1700), particularly inveighed against "newly introduced foreign customs."[12]

Such discord in the boasted "symphony" of church and state ended predictably. The beardless Peter, who introduced foreign innovators and innovations, dealt decisively with those who criticized his conduct as head of the church. For he understood the sources of his power and his weakness. On the one hand, his Christian lordship was supported by a gift taken over from the Mongols—absolute power to tax on demand solely at his pleasure aristocrats who held land and serfs. His weakness, despite the vastness of his realm, was a combination of thin, cold, relatively unproductive soil and a hierarchal system that discouraged initiative, experimentation, and rapid economic and scientific advance. Peter's solution to this problem was not to model Russian society on some Western European nation but to scrape up practically all available capital by taxation to build up and modernize his army and navy with imported Western technology and leadership.

The war against Sweden marked the culmination of his success. He sucked in and swallowed up the Swedish armed forces at Poltava (1709) and proceeded to wear down the enemy by land and sea to win the prize of a large window on the Baltic Sea through the Peace of Nystad (1721). His new capital of St. Petersburg was now protected by the acquisition of the port of Viborg and the Karelian isthmus to the northwest and the Baltic states to the southwest. Russia, allied with Austria, became a counterpoise to France and England in a newly aligned balance of power in Europe.

Peter, playing catch-up, found himself nearly ahead. But the price he paid was not just in rubles. It was in compromise of Orthodoxy and in the increasing threat that foreigners would supplant Russians in leadership positions throughout the state. The German suburb in Moscow had existed, it is true, since the time of Ivan the Terrible, and "Germans"— that is, German speakers—living there were granted liberty of conscience and the privilege of having their own Lutheran pastors and church. With Peter as tsar there came a heavy influx of Lutherans, who were no longer sequestered in a single colony. "Mixed" Orthodox-Lutheran marriages became commonplace. Finally, with the Peace of Nystad, Peter found himself to be the "spiritual father" of predominantly Lutheran Baltic states. Perhaps most distressing to many Orthodox was Peter's sending his first wife, Eudoxia, to a nunnery and eventually marrying his mistress, Catherine, of uncertain European origin and raised as Lutheran. Although she obligingly converted to Orthodoxy, her succession as Empress Catherine I indicated further drift toward Western influence in imperial decision making.

How close was Bering to these developments? It is hard to say because little is known about his early years. It is probable that he knew and befriended Heinrich Johann Friedrich Ostermann, son of a poor German Lutheran pastor, who joined the Russian service in the same place (Amsterdam) a year earlier (1703) and might indeed, as Cruys's secretary, have prepared the enlistment papers that Bering signed.[13] Now known as Andrei Ivanovich, Ostermann rose rapidly as Peter's interpreter and foreign minister, serving Russia well as negotiator with the Swedes in achieving peace. Bering most likely had a network of Western European friends and acquaintances because of his connections through the Admiralty in St. Petersburg.

These ties were strengthened after Bering's marriage to Anna Christina Pülse. They became husband and wife on October 8, 1713, in the Lutheran church in Viborg, already taken from the Swedes in 1710. Anna was the eldest child of a wealthy German-speaking Swedish family. Her father, Matthias Jacob (1666–1740), was a merchant born in Nyen, a prospering town of several thousand German-speaking Swedes five miles upstream on the Neva River from the future site of St. Petersburg. Her parents married here in 1690. Anna and her brother, Bendix, were probably born there before the family moved to Viborg from Nyen in 1702, the year before the Russians captured the town on the Neva River and defended it from Swedish attack in the first naval action in which Peter the Great himself took part.

Later in life Anna had a habit of understating her age. If she were as young as she claimed, she would have been only 8 years old on her wedding day. In the absence of birth or baptismal records, it seems likely that she was born within a few years after her parents' marriage; that is, about 1692, or eleven years after the birth of her husband, Vitus. (Her two sisters also married considerably older men.) If she were born in 1692, she would have married at 21 years and given birth to the last of nine children (only four survived childhood) at 39 years.[14]

There has been confusion about Viborg, Russia, and Viborg, Denmark, because Bering's forefathers were outstanding citizens of the Danish Viborg. His namesake, Vitus Pedersen, the royal historiographer, was born there. Peder P. Bering, his mother's father, was pastor there, and another Bering of the same generation, another Peder P., became mayor of the Danish Viborg.[15]

During the war with Sweden, Anna probably did not see much of her husband. He was captain of various ships, engaged primarily in lightering. In 1715 he captained the *Pearl* from Copenhagen around western and northern Scandinavia to Archangel, where he then captained a newly constructed ship, the fifty-two-gun *Selafail*, all the way from the shipyard in Archangel to Reval (Tallinn), at the mouth of the Gulf of Finland.[16] On one occasion in 1716 he was called upon to join a Russian fleet assembled off Norway. Another time he was the ranking officer at Reval, where Anna could join him.

But by the end of the war, his own parents having died in Horsens in 1719, he identified his future with his wife and her family. A major disappointment, for Anna as well as for her husband, was his failure to be promoted again in 1721 in recognition of his war service. Many of his colleagues were so recognized. Indeed, he complained that men who had served under him were now promoted over him.

But the Admiralty was not directly responsible for a humiliating personal blow that overtook Anna and Vitus Bering within a few more years. Thomas Saunders, a British recruit and relative newcomer to the Russian service, became engaged to marry Eufemia Pülse, Anna's sister. Saunders was already a rear admiral in the Russian Imperial Navy. By virtue of his rank, Saunders was not only Bering's superior but, unlike Bering, entitled to the courtesies and privileges of the nobility. The marriage, which took place in Viborg on January 21, 1724, was very likely a coup for the Pülse family, but for Anna, as senior to her siblings, it was an unacceptable reversal of fortune.

In 1713 she married Bering as a captain-lieutenant. In 1724 he was still but a captain second class. To her it was contrary to the proper order of things that, with Eufemia's marriage, she should be socially subordinated to a younger sister and that her husband, after twenty faithful years in the Russian navy, should be professionally subject to a brother-in-law with only five years in the same navy.

Letters she wrote sixteen years later (the only ones she wrote to her family and friends that are known to have survived) reveal Anna as a woman who is artfully domineering in the family sphere and cleverly insinuating and flattering in the wider world of favor and preferment. Anna was never one to conceal her feelings, as she admitted. Eventually she and her husband came to a decision. To preserve their honor and status, they decided, Bering had no choice but to submit a request for retirement from the navy. He did so on January 20, just one day before Eufemia's wedding.

On February 26 his resignation was accepted with the generous proviso that he was granted the rank of captain first class in retirement and that he was given two months' pay to cover the expense of his move to his "own country."[17] Thereupon, with their two sons, Jonas, 3 years old, and Thomas, almost 1, the Berings left St. Petersburg for Anna's home in Viborg.

The next six months were without doubt the lowest point in the marriage of a most ambitious couple. What would Bering do? At 42 years, he had a young wife, two small sons, no prospects, and no pension.

Five months of relative inactivity in Viborg were sufficient to convince Bering that he had made a serious mistake. On August 18 he appeared for an interview at the Admiralty College and formally requested return to active service. Apraksin, as president of the college, officially granted his request the same day.[18] (Apraksin had already conferred with Peter, now emperor.) For the time being, with Eufemia now making her home in St. Petersburg, Anna remained with her children in Viborg.

Bering thus began a second career in the Russian navy—and one that distinguished him above all his naval colleagues.

CHAPTER TWO

NEVER ON LAND HAD SO MANY GONE SO FAR

On October 2, 1724, Bering was back in the navy, retaining in active service the rank of captain first class. He was assigned to the Baltic fleet as commander of the ninety-gun *Lesnoe*. By this time both his brother-in-law and Danish colleagues in the Admiralty were almost surely aware of an impending new command for which Bering could be a strong candidate.

During the Great Northern War and for several years thereafter, Peter the Great had put off organizing a major expedition to produce accurate maps of his vast realm east of the Urals, which would permit him to extend and secure his empire well ahead of further exploration by Western European seafaring nations. The English, Dutch, and French were consumed by a passion to discover a northern passage from the Atlantic to the Pacific Ocean for the benefit of their trade. By Russian imperial edict of 1619, Western European nations were forbidden entry into the Icy Sea (Arctic Ocean) east of the Yamal Peninsula. This earlier action largely protected Russia's exploitation of valuable furs (chiefly sable and fox) east of the Urals. Peter knew that it was only a matter of time before the English would once again, after Sir Francis Drake, explore the North Pacific Ocean; or the Dutch follow up north of Japan, after the 1643 voyage of Maerten Gerritsen Vries; or the French, who in Paris in 1717 had proposed to Peter that *they* send an exploratory expedition to northeast Asia. Peter realized that there were yet potentially valuable lands between Kamchatka and Spanish America, both islands and continental coasts. What members of the French Academy wanted to know and a Russian expedition could discover was the nature and extent of the lands of northeast Asia and the geographical relationship between Asia and America. If there were a navigable northwest or northeast passage, Russia with its modern navy was ready to claim and use it.

After the Peace of Nystad, Peter was preoccupied with converting part of his navy to a merchant fleet and devaluing the ruble (which, incidentally, reduced the pay of surplus naval officers who, like Bering, then held a rank below captain first class). Consequently, discussions about a special government expedition were informal and sporadic; actual planning was put off until late in 1724, when Peter first realized that he was very ill.

Then suddenly that planning became very rushed. On December 23, 1724, Peter ordered the Admiralty College to act. First of all, it was to identify land surveyors who had worked in Siberia. Then it was to identify a qualified lieutenant or sublieutenant to go with the surveyors to Kamchatka; find a shipwright—a student or apprentice—who could build one or two decked ships on Kamchatka, together with four young assistants, a quartermaster, and eight seamen; and find one or two sailmakers, rigging, and four cannon. Two navigators should know the sea "north toward Japan."[1] Peter envisioned a party of about twenty men, all of them young and vigorous with the possible exception of surveyors and navigators, whom he expected to be familiar with Siberia and the Pacific Ocean. It is especially significant that his first concern was for surveyors who could produce reliable maps. Such mapmaking had recently been ongoing in European Russia through the Naval Academy in St. Petersburg. For example, Mikhail S. Gvozdev, who later made a landfall on the American continent, was a student of land surveying at that institution until 1721, when he was assigned to the Russian army in Novgorod to survey rivers. Then in 1727 he was sent to Siberia.[2]

Within a few days the Admiralty College responded to Peter's order in writing, listing nine surveyors for Peter's consideration. Three lieutenants and two sublieutenants were named as officers considered well qualified and two captains were recommended as commanding officer, proposed specifically by "Vice Admiral [Peter] Sievers and Rear Admiral [Naum] Senavin." The captains recommended were Bering and K. P. von Verd (van Werden), of Dutch and Danish parentage. This statement followed: "Bering has been in East India [the East Indies?] and knows conditions, and Verd has been a navigator." Not noted was Verd's extensive mapping experience. For three years he had served Russia by charting the Caspian Sea.[3] Clearly the statement favored Bering, whose name was listed first.

Peter himself made one further comment about staffing. On the Admiralty's response he made a marginal note: "It is very necessary to have a navigator and assistant navigator who have been to North America."[4] Clearly, then, Peter expected that North America might be found. Perhaps he assumed that a navigator's firsthand knowledge of British, French, Spanish, Dutch, or Danish colonies in North America would be advantageous in any meeting with a ship of Western European origin or in dealings with Native Americans.

Bering had been to North America. In the extensive seafaring of his youth, he reportedly served on Danish whalers in the North Atlantic and visited Western European colonies in America and the West Indies. Indeed, in Bering's teasing of Steller years later, he challenged his naturalist's knowledge of plants in the sea around such islands as Cape Verde and Bermuda.[5] The implication is that Bering knew these places because he had been there, whereas Steller was knowledgeable about them only through his reading.

On December 29 Peter appointed Bering commander of what became known as the First Kamchatka Expedition. Peter probably had four good reasons for his choice: Bering was known to be popular with subordinates because he was cautious, dependable, and even-handed; he had extensive experience in the transport of goods during the Great Northern War; he had already sailed as far as the East and West Indies; and he was favored by the Admiralty College.

On the same date, Peter appointed two lieutenants to assist Bering: Martin Spangberg (also spelled Spanberg and Spangsberg), a fellow Dane who very likely had also been to American colonies, and Aleksei Chirikov, promoted to lieutenant from sublieutenant. Born in 1698 near Esbjerg, on Jutland's west coast, Spangberg was noted for his toughness, tenacity, and seamanship. He was five years older than Chirikov, who had but a single year of experience at sea, in the Baltic fleet. In 1715

Chirikov had transferred from the Moscow School of Mathematics and Navigation as one of ten top students to enroll in the new Naval Academy in St. Petersburg. In 1722, a year after graduating, he was assigned to teach in that academy. Vice Admiral Saunders (Bering's brother-in-law) praised him as the academy's "most skilled" instructor.[6] Whereas Spangberg was apt to be temperamental, rough, reckless, and minimally literate, Chirikov was smart, diplomatic, and thorough. If Spangberg could weather a storm, Chirikov could make astronomical observations and write a polished report.

By January 8, 1725, personnel for the expedition had been selected, chiefly from Russia's Baltic fleet. Instead of the approximately twenty men that Peter had envisioned earlier, there were now thirty-four, including thirteen sailors and nine artisans. The Admiralty decided that only essential equipment and supplies likely to be unavailable in Siberia should be carried from St. Petersburg. These included six anchors (each weighing about 360 pounds), eight cannon, twenty-four guns, compasses, sounding leads, hourglasses, rigging, sail, canvas, and a chest of medications.

On January 7 Bering had permission to go to Viborg "to attend to his affairs." In addition to arranging adequate financial support for his family from his salary during his absence, he is likely to have sought advice from his merchant father-in-law, Matthias Pülse, concerning trade goods he might take with him into Siberia. The commander had the privilege of taking baggage commensurate with his rank and position.[7] Even Bering's annual salary marked him as standing well above his two officer assistants: he got 480 rubles, they only 180 each.

Other affairs would be personal, such as concerns about where he would be going (he could not tell Anna much because not much was known) and, more to the point, how long he would be gone. The plan was to allow two years to get to his destination—wherever that was—and one year more to get back. Such a long separation—probably longer than they had ever been away from each other, even in wartime—would be difficult. But they had this consolation, evident in later letters: both knew that the expedition, however risky, was a necessary gamble for their future and their children's future in Russia. For them the upward mobility of their family was paramount, and for that purpose almost no sacrifice could be too great.

What land route would Bering take to Kamchatka? The best way, a southern route from a tributary of the Lena River south toward the Amur, offered the only major river route leading generally east to the sea. But this route was foreclosed in 1689 by the Treaty of Nerchinsk, whereby China first succeeded in curtailing Russian expansion into the Amur River Valley, a costly setback for Russia. For in 1643 Vasily Poyarkov had navigated the great river 2,700 miles to its mouth and another 600 miles at sea north to the mouth of the Okhota River. Between 1649 and 1653 Yerofei Khabarov had led two expeditions into the Amur Valley, where two Russian forts were subsequently built, Nerchinsk in 1659 and Albazin in 1665, the latter lost by terms of the Treaty of Nerchinsk. Russia lost (until 1858) not only the sole major river route to Kamchatka and the Pacific Ocean, but also a convenient potential agricultural base for its continuing eastward expansion.

There remained the inland route down the Lena River to Yakutsk (founded in 1632), bypassing Irkutsk (1652), near the border with China. From Yakutsk the route followed the footsteps of Ivan Moskvitin and his party over the coastal mountains and down to the mouth of the Okhota River. Here there was established in 1648 the tiny settlement of Okhotsk, whence in 1716 a sea route had been charted across the Sea of Okhotsk to the mouth of the Bolshaya River, on the southwest coast of Kamchatka.

This inland route from St. Petersburg to Kamchatka offered two major provisioning stops: Tobolsk (founded in 1587), a small city whose chief administrator was the governor of Siberia; and Yakutsk, a small town and fur-trading center with a district governor. Intermediate points between Tobolsk and Yakutsk were forts with indeterminate resources: Yeniseisk (1618), Ilimsk (1631), and Ust-Kut (1631), all on major river routes. The most critical unanswered questions concerned the route beyond Yakutsk: How would the heavily laden expedition get over the coastal mountains? How serviceable was the ship that crossed the sea to Kamchatka? What resources were available on Kamchatka for transporting cargo across the peninsula? Where would timber be found for shipbuilding on Kamchatka?

Peter was dying. On January 16 he was stricken severely by an infection of the urinary tract. For several days, resting in bed, he continued to summon Ostermann and other ministers to his bedside. On January 22 his pain had such force that he received the last rites. The next day Peter admitted Apraksin and ordered him to protect foreigners in St. Petersburg. On the 26th Peter at first seemed to rally but then suffered such pain that he involuntarily cried out. On the 27th Archbishop Feofan Prokopovich was at his side. The next morning Peter died. Through the twelve days of Peter's final agonies, Catherine was always with him.

His death ended firm control and direction of Russian domestic and foreign policy. His successors had comparatively brief reigns. Russian aristocrats jockeyed with the foreign-born administrators Peter had recruited, chiefly from northwest Europe. A mere child and even an infant were among successors who were titular heads of state. Under these circumstances, Bering as expedition commander was to experience delays, wavering support, and at times uncertain direction from St. Petersburg or Moscow. Scholars even today cannot agree on the purpose or purposes of the First Kamchatka Expedition. Was it to map the route to Kamchatka and the northeast extremity of Asia? Was it to seek a land bridge between Asia and America? Or did Peter intend Bering to find America and describe whatever he could learn about that continent? The answers to such questions lead to various judgments. Nor surprisingly, most specialists who write about the first expedition criticize Bering for failing to do enough.

As empress, Catherine pledged continuation of Peter's projects. On January 24, just four days before Peter died, Chirikov had left St. Petersburg with twenty-six men and twenty-five sledges pulled by horses over well-traveled roads en route to Vologda, 411 miles away. Bering and Spangberg remained behind to receive detailed instructions from the Admiralty College, orders from the Senate to the governor of Siberia to give all assistance needed so that "the enterprise will lack nothing," and Peter's orders from Empress Catherine I.[8]

Those orders consisted of two specific tasks and a third conditional task. Bering was "to build one or two ships with decks" in Kamchatka or some other place. He was to sail "along land which lies to the north." He was, finally, "to search for the place where that land might be joined to America, and from there proceed to some settlement belonging to a European power." If he sighted a European ship, he was to "find out from it what the coast is called, and write it down." Then he was to "go ashore, obtain accurate information, locate it on a map," and return to St. Petersburg.[9]

There has been much scholarly speculation concerning the second and third tasks. What "land . . . to the north" did Peter have in mind? What conception did he have of "the place" where it joins America?

Finding America and then proceeding all the way to Acapulco, at that time Spain's northernmost port on America's Pacific coast and hence the European settlement on the west coast of North America nearest Kamchatka, would have been a stunning achievement, especially given the distances involved. But Peter's instructions required only that he "search for" a place that is "joined to America." To search is not necessarily to find. Accordingly, once the search is made and it proves unsuccessful, then everything else in Peter's orders concerning European ships and America is provisional. Bering then was not ordered to find America, and Peter probably had only a vague notion about a place where North America might be connected, or nearly connected, to Asia.

From Ivan Lvov, commandant at Anadyr, 1710–14, he had received a sketch map showing in outline several new features of land and sea (Fig. 5).

Prominently across the middle of this map is the location of the "Anadyrsk" (Anadyr) fort on the Anadyr River, which flows into the "Anadyrsk Sea" (Bering Sea). What surely caught Peter's attention are three landforms north and east of this sea: (1) a miniature "Nos Anadyrskoi" (Chukotsk "Cape," actually a peninsula), off which in a channel (Bering Strait) are shown (2) two long parallel islands (Diomede Islands greatly enlarged) and, farther east, (3) a long, fingerlike peninsula identified as "Big Land," emerging from the north and running well south of the twin islands. Peter might well ask, "Is this Big Land a part of North America?" It might have been Lvov's map that suggested to Peter the need to explore this region.

Peter also had the first map depicting the actual shape of Kamchatka, made in 1721 by the surveyors Ivan M. Yevreinov and Fyodor F. Luzhin (Fig. 6). Peter had sent them to Kamchatka in 1719 "to make an accurate map of everything." The Kamchatka River, Penzhina Bay, "Japanese Islands" (the Kurils), and Yakutsk are all shown with remarkable accuracy. On neither Kamchatka nor the Kurils did they get even a hint

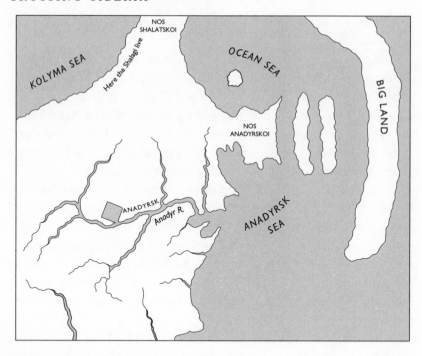

Figure 5. LVOV MAP: NORTHEASTERN ASIA (BASED ON EFIMOV NO. 55).

about a link between Asia and America. A third map that Peter acquired had been made by Philipp Johann Tabbert von Strahlenberg (Fig. 7), a Swedish prisoner of war, during his residence in Tobolsk, 1711–21. It shows the long finger of the Lvov map as an unnamed island and another land east of Kamchatka as "Company Land." Kamchatka itself, badly misshapen as depicted, erroneously extends to the southeast.

Whatever maps Peter sent to Johann Baptist Homann, the Nuremberg mapmaker, it appears that for his composite map of northeastern Asia (Fig. 8), completed before his death in July 1724, he ignored (or did not have) the Yevreinov-Luzhin map and combined features of the Lvov-Strahlenberg maps. For there appears on Homann's map almost a replica of Lvov's map. The landform appearing as an elongated finger open in the north suggests the possibility of land connections between Asia and America. Farther south on the same map is Kamchatka, resembling the peninsula on Strahlenberg's map, and across a narrow channel to the east is Strahlenberg's Company Land, much enlarged but un-

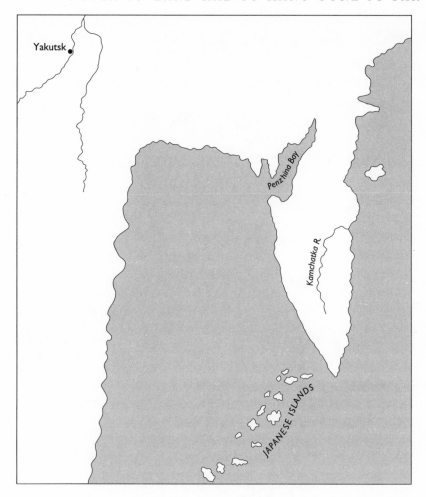

Figure 6. YEVREINOV-LUZHIN MAP: KAMCHATKA (BASED ON EFIMOV NO. 61).

named, suggesting the existence of an American continent very close off the mouth of the Kamchatka River.

This Homann map is a puzzle. If Peter supplied it to Bering, what on it was to be understood as "the land . . . to the north"? Was it the finger open at the top or was it the bulbous mass just east of Kamchatka? Neither possibility makes much sense. If it were the first, in the far north of the Icy Sea, what is the likelihood that Bering would meet

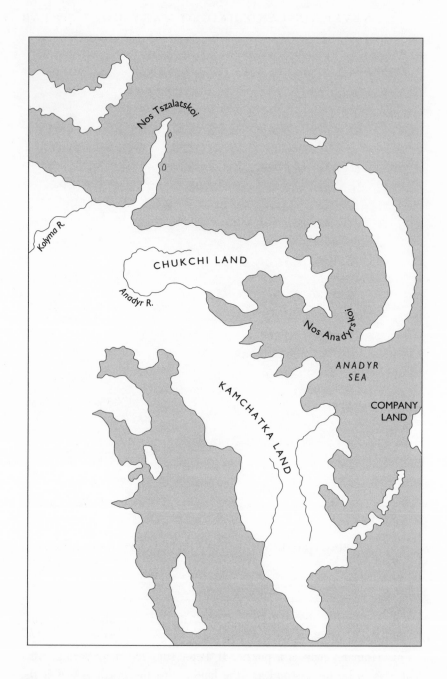

Figure 7. STRAHLENBERG MAP: EASTERN SIBERIA (BASED ON EFIMOV NO. 74).

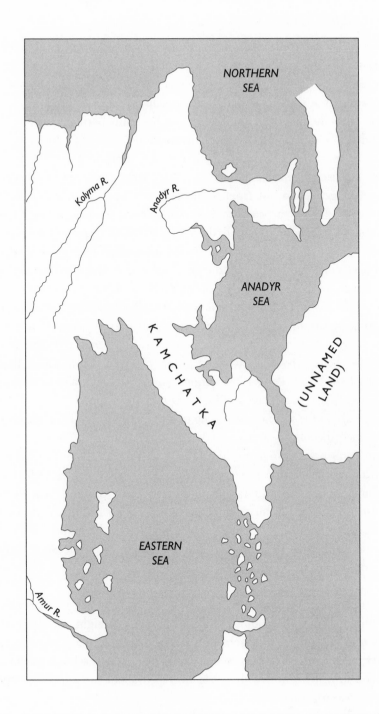

Figure 8. HOMANN MAP: NORTHEASTERN ASIA (BASED ON EFIMOV NO. 58).

there, or along some coast from there, either a European ship or a European settlement? If it were the second possibility, why would Peter not call it "the land . . . to the east"? Also, would not this land be missed altogether if a ship constructed on Kamchatka were to proceed to the north from the mouth of the Kamchatka River (as Bering actually did)? So what is the meaning of Peter's instructions?

They make little sense in relation to the Homann map. There is a third eminently sensible possibility: that Bering was sent forth on a mapmaking mission not from Kamchatka but from Tobolsk.[10] For this reason he did not proceed to Kamchatka from St. Petersburg by sea around what is now known as the Cape of Good Hope and across the Indian Ocean to the Pacific. He would have taken that route if Peter had been concerned only with the geography of Asia and America along the Pacific's northern rim. No, Bering's mission was to map the way from Tobolsk to Kamchatka and from Kamchatka to the Icy Sea. Any sighting of islands or the American continent was incidental to the mission. Bering was not simply to use some existing map but to make a new and better one. This was the primary purpose of the First Kamchatka Expedition. Peter's instructions assume that, literally as a matter of course, the route across Siberia would be mapped. They pertain specifically to the second part of the task of charting Russia's imperfectly known northeastern seaboard, understood as "the land . . . to the north." Bering was not sent out specifically to find America, but if he did find it, the third instruction was applicable. (Obviously Peter, as well as his contemporaries, had no concept of the immensity of the North Pacific Ocean.) The First Kamchatka Expedition, though it did not primarily concern the finding of America, was a prelude to the highly ambitious Second Kamchatka Expedition, whose centerpiece was indeed the extension of empire to North America.

On February 6 Bering and Spangberg left St. Petersburg with six men and eight sledges; they joined Chirikov at Vologda eight days later. On March 16 the combined detachments reached Tobolsk. They had traveled 1,763 miles over a low pass of the Urals. It was the easiest segment of the journey. With horses they had averaged about forty-five miles per day. It was a good start.

But then the expedition was still small, still very manageable. For chiefly three reasons it grew quickly at Tobolsk. First, Bering counted on adding recruits and provisions as he needed them. There was no point in transporting what he could later acquire as he moved ahead. Second, with winter and good roads ending, he now needed boats instead of horses, and he had to have more men to build them and to carry goods over portages. Finally, in Tobolsk he sought out men who carried news from Kamchatka. A lieutenant returning to St. Petersburg told Bering that the *Vostok*, a small ship at Okhotsk, needed repairs, that natives on Kamchatka were hostile to Russians, and that in the absence of horses, timber for construction of a ship on the Kamchatka River had to be carried by men and dogs.[11]

At first Bering had requested that twenty-four soldiers from the Tobolsk garrison join the expedition. Then, after meeting the lieutenant from Kamchatka, he increased his request to fifty-four. But the governor could spare only thirty-nine. Yet this number alone more than doubled Bering's manpower. Still, he needed many more men for travel on Siberia's river system and for shipbuilding on Kamchatka. He wanted sixty carpenters and seven blacksmiths and their necessary tools, but the governor informed him that half the number he requested would have to be added at Yeniseisk, his next major stop.

Bering had hoped that the entire expedition would be completed within three years and that he could reach Yakutsk the first year. But now at Tobolsk he suffered delays. On April 23, the Irtysh River ice broke. It was time to go, but travel funds did not arrive until May 12, and four flat-bottomed riverboats, forty feet long with mast and sail, were not ready until two days later. Once under way, Bering sent the naval cadet Peter Chaplin ahead with nine soldiers to deliver orders at each fort. In this way Bering attempted to reduce the time of the journey.

Between the Ural Mountains and the coastal range fronting the Sea of Okhotsk, Siberia is a broad, fairly flat series of watersheds, sloping gradually northward to the Icy Sea from the mountain ranges of Central Asia. Major rivers flowing to the north have tributaries that serve, with portages, to connect river systems and to accommodate commerce in furs and Chinese goods moving generally from east to west. The expedition was following a well-established, century-old river highway. Methods of transport were also well established. Forts along the way could readily serve merchants traveling in small groups. Two major problems faced Bering: the large numbers of men he needed to recruit for transporting the expedition's freight and the great distance between Tobolsk and Yakutsk.

They were off to a fast start down the Irtysh to the great river Ob. When winds were favorable, they sailed midstream through the night to take advantage of the two-mile-an-hour current. Occasionally, when the weather was disagreeable because of snow or freezing temperatures, they stopped for shelter and warmth at a tiny village nestled within the forest above the riverbank. After a week on the Irtysh, they halted for a day above the junction with the Ob River to make rudders for the boats for the long haul up two rivers.

Now the hard work began, the test to see if the expedition could make up for lost time. Ahead of them they had to cross two river systems, the Ob and Yenisei, before going down to Yakutsk on a third, the Lena. On May 25 they entered the Ob. Now oars and barge poles were used as they hugged the shore to avoid the full force of the current. Sometimes, especially with headwinds, each boat crew landed to pull the boat from shore with tow lines. Sometimes a crew got far ahead and waited for the others to catch up, usually at a village.

On May 30 the expedition reached Surgut, a Russian fort founded in 1593. Here Bering first experienced a rude Russian administrator. The expedition needed guides who knew the rivers ahead of them. Bering formally presented his letter requesting them. The administrator glanced at it and peremptorily threw it to the ground.[12] Bering was learning that remote forts such as Surgut could be a law unto themselves; imperial or gubernatorial orders were of no concern to them.

After a month on the Ob, the expedition reached the Ket River and proceeded eastward up this long tributary. It became increasingly narrow and shallow as the travelers approached Makovsk (founded in 1618). This fort was the gateway to an easy portage of forty-six miles toward the town of Yeniseisk (1618), trading center of the Yenisei River basin. Here the expedition found itself as unwelcome as at Surgut. Not only was a request for men to help unload the boats refused but the administrator cursed Bering. The next day (June 20) the same man berated some of Bering's soldiers standing guard, saying, "You are all swindlers and you should be hanged."[13] But at last Bering obtained horses and carts for use on the portage.

At Yeniseisk the expedition got the men requested, but Bering complained by letter to the governor that "few were suitable, and many were lame, blind, and ridden with disease."[14] Happily, here the surveyor Luzhin joined the expedition, and here the renowned Siberian explorer Daniel G. Messerschmidt shared information he had acquired.

On August 12, well behind schedule, the expedition left Yeniseisk with another four riverboats. These followed the shore of the Yenisei a short distance to the Upper Tunguska (later named the Angara) and then up that tributary for some five hundred miles to the mouth of the Ilim. Here it was necessary to secure shorter, flat-bottomed boats from Ilimsk (1631). After they arrived from the fort some eighty miles upstream, they were lightly loaded. Then the boatmen picked up at Yeniseisk returned to that town in the riverboats. Chirikov and a small detachment remained to guard leftover freight until sleds, also delivered from the fort, could be used.

Most men of the command rowed up the Ilim, portaging around rapids on the way. They arrived at Ilimsk on September 26, three days before the river froze up. From here it was another eighty miles overland to Ust-Kut, on the Lena River. Bering sent Spangberg and a third of the men ahead to Ust-Kut to build boats for passage to Yakutsk in the spring. Leaving Chirikov in charge at Ilimsk, Bering traveled to Irkutsk to consult with the vice governor there, who had formerly served at Yakutsk. He was concerned about the best way to get over the mountains between Yakutsk and Okhotsk. There was no established trail, rivers were shallow, and getting tons of accumulated supplies overland could be a horrendous task. In Irkutsk, Bering got his best preview of the terrible conditions he faced in letters from Chaplin, who was waiting for him in Yakutsk. Rivers from there were so low that boats would need to be short, with shallow drafts even when fully loaded.

From Ust-Kut it took little more than two weeks to go 1,200 miles down the Lena River to Yakutsk. They all reached the town of 4,000 inhabitants in June, Bering and Spangberg on June 1 and Chirikov on the 16th. It was imperative to leave town as quickly as possible to reach Okhotsk before the start of another winter. But practically nothing was ready. No horses. And Chaplin's appeal to the Yakutsk district governor got him only fifty workers to help manage the boats.

Bering was furious. Only when he threatened the governor with responsibility for the expedition's failure did he get 69 more workers, together with 660 Yakut horses and drivers.

On July 7 Spangberg's was the first detachment out of Yakutsk. He had the Herculean task of transporting seventy-six tons of anchors and cannon as well as fifty tons of flour. For such a formidable cargo he was assigned 205 men and thirteen flat-bottomed boats. On July 27 Fyodor Kozlov, the apprentice shipbuilder, was the second out of Yakutsk with a small party to ride on horses over the mountain range to Okhotsk, where he was to cut hay, dry fish, and begin construction of a ship. On August 16 Bering and Chaplin left with light loads on seventy-seven horses, twenty-nine of which carried the commander's baggage. Chirikov was to follow the next spring with whatever supplies of flour he could get.

The overland parties met staggering obstacles. Horses died for lack of grass. Rivers were forded as often as six times in a single day. Corduroy roads had to be built over boggy terrain. There were days, Chaplin said, when they progressed slowly "like pebbles" in the swift low water of a stream. Bering wrote, "I cannot put into words how difficult this route is."[15]

Years later some priests traversed the 685 miles between Yakutsk and Okhotsk and described the horrors of the trip: "It can be said that for our sins we suffered on the Okhotsk Road ten tortures similar to those of Egypt: rabid horses, quagmires where land turned to water; nocturnal darkness amidst thick woods; branches threatening us with blindness; hunger, cold; mosquitoes; gadflies—truly *biting* flies; dangerous river crossings; and sores on the horses."[16] This priestly description clearly concerns a summer crossing, when horses could survive.

In the face of wind, cold, and snow at higher elevations, three men in Bering's party died and forty-six deserted, stealing some of the remaining horses with the provisions they packed. Only a remnant of the overland parties reached Okhotsk in October. For two months there was no news of Spangberg's whereabouts.

Spangberg left men behind to guard cargo strewn over a desolate winter landscape. The rivers were at first full of rapids. Towing heavily loaded boats with ropes was so slow and fatiguing that his men could not attain even a mile a day. He lost forty-seven men by September 21. Some he dismissed and others deserted. Then by the end of the month the boats became locked in ice, so he had to build a winter shelter and storehouse, leaving eight men as guards. Next he built sleds. Now he had to threaten men with flogging to get them to carry cargo from the boats to the sleds. With eighteen tons of goods on ninety sleds, men started pulling in mid-October. For nearly three weeks they endured blizzards and snow up to the waist. Four men too weak to pull were left in a hut built for them. Soon the remaining men started leaving cannonballs, one cannon, and kegs of gunpowder behind. In December the starving began. They ate a dead horse. Spangberg, with two men, left his party to plunge ahead forty miles to Yudoma Cross, a winter camp so named because a cross had once been erected in that place by the Yudoma River. Until provisions that Bering had stashed there were carried back to them, Spangberg's men stayed alive by chewing on any bit of hide they had—saddlebags, straps, breeches, and boots. Four men died before the first sleds reached the Cross three days later. Here Spangberg left Luzhin and the navigator George Morrison with only three days of food. The Cross was aptly named.

With those who could still walk, Spangberg set out for Okhotsk from the Cross. They still had forty sleds, but they were now desperate, knowing that once again their food was running out. On December 29 nothing was left to eat except dead horses found by chance on the trail. Once again Spangberg and two men plunged ahead, walking day and night, pulling sleds with the most essential items—government funds, geodesic instruments, carpentry tools, and medicines. On January 6 they stumbled into Okhotsk. On January 16 sixty more stragglers arrived, some very ill. Bering sent out three winter rescue parties. The first, led by Chaplin, in February and March found four dead men, including Luzhin and Morrison, at Yudoma Cross. They saved seven other men and recovered cargo left on the trail. The second party, led by a corporal in March, could not stop a rebellion by twelve Russians who grabbed knives and axes, declaring, "We do not want to die like the others did, so we are going straight to town [Yakutsk] and you can't stop us."[17] The third party in April picked up all remaining goods at Yudoma Cross. It had been a terrible winter. Bering reported that local people claimed it was the worst winter in memory.

In Okhotsk, a community with only eleven huts, lack of food became critical. Bering's men seized 432 pounds of flour "on credit" from the inhabitants. The salmon run in rivers in May was disappointing. Bering reported that if an advance party of Chirikov's detachment had not arrived early in June with twenty-seven tons of flour for the voyage, "we certainly would have died of starvation."[18]

Despite hardships, little time was lost here. A single-masted vessel, built within a month, was launched on June 8. It was named *Fortuna* in hopes of better times for the expedition. With the *Vostok* fully repaired, Spangberg took the shipbuilder Kozlov and carpenters and blacksmiths, soldiers and sailors, forty-eight men altogether, 630 nautical miles across the sea to Kamchatka so that they could make an early start on building a ship the next spring. By the time the *Fortuna* and *Vostok* had returned to Okhotsk, Chirikov himself had arrived with another eighteen tons of flour and thirty-one head of cattle. He had traveled 685 miles from Yakutsk to Okhotsk in two months with no human fatalities and with the loss of only 17 of 140 horses.

On August 22 the expedition sailed for Kamchatka, where an overland struggle began again. It would have been easier to sail around the south end of the peninsula and follow the east coast up to the mouth of the Kamchatka River. But this way was as yet uncharted, and Bering was not inclined to take chances. After all, the goods they carried had now greatly increased in value and all were essential for the voyage.

At this time there were only three Russian forts on the 750-mile-long Kamchatka peninsula and no more than 150 Russians. Bolsheretsk, with fourteen dwellings on the shore of the Bolshaya River, was about twenty-five miles upriver from the southwest coast. Upstream from Bolsheretsk and over a portage to the headwaters of the Kamchatka River was the Upper Kamchatka Post, with seventeen dwellings. Down the river, about fifteen miles from its mouth, was the Lower Kamchatka Post, with forty households. The Russians were mostly military men and tax collectors. The "tax," called *yasak*, was an annual levy on adult native men—their tribute to the Russian state. Here sable and fox pelts were the coin of the realm.

The collectors faced the constant temptation to overtax. First, of course, came the government's share, one good pelt per year from each adult male. The collector's share was unauthorized. It was commonly more than people could bear. It took various forms: additional pelts, dried meat (especially salmon), and all too often women and children to work as servants. Consequently, native populations, despoiled and declining, were hostile. Here again Bering divided his command. The first party to leave Bolsheretsk—Spangberg, Kozlov, and their men— was able to use small boats and their own brute force to reach the Kamchatka River and to cut and haul timber for construction of a ship before freeze-up. Bering was not so fortunate. Because there were no horses, he needed dogs, sleds, and native drivers; but not enough were available for all the baggage. As a result, dogs died because sleds were overloaded. Even so, using eighty-five sleds, Bering reached the Upper Kamchatka Post in eleven days, and with sixty-seven sleds continued on to the Lower Kamchatka Post in a week, a total distance of 580 miles. Chirikov, left behind in Bolsheretsk, followed the next spring, carrying the remaining provisions and supplies on 170 sleds.

The Bering expedition had completed an amazing overland journey of 6,000 winding miles from St. Petersburg to the Lower Kamchatka Post, generally along the St. Petersburg parallel of 60° north latitude across 130° of longitude. It had covered more than a third of the distance around the northern hemisphere. Never on land had so many gone so far. It had taken Bering nearly three years to reach Kamchatka, but now at last he was poised for new discoveries and completion of his mission.

CHAPTER THREE

INTO THE ICY SEA

The ship itself was constructed near the small native settlement of Ushka, where the Ushki River runs into the Kamchatka, about 100 miles upstream from the Lower Kamchatka Post.[1] It was up the Ushki that Kozlov found larch trees suitable for shipbuilding. Most were cut before October 18, 1727, and the timber was hauled to the Kamchatka River by dogs and men. The winter was then passed chiefly fifty-five miles downriver at Klyucha, a large native village below 14,580-foot Klyuchevsk volcano (Klyuchevskaya) and close by the monastery of Our Saviour of Yakutsk.

The following spring shipbuilding was at first hampered by Kozlov's inability to obtain enough food for his workmen. Five men became ill, a carpenter deserted, and a caulker died. Once fresh salmon were available and provisions arrived with Bering and Chirikov, the decked ship took shape rapidly. It was 60 feet long, 20 feet wide, and 7 feet tall, the largest ship yet built on Russia's Pacific frontier. It had two masts and three cannon. Christened the *Archangel Gabriel*, it was launched June 9, 1728, fully rigged July 6, and loaded with provisions for forty-four men for one year July 9. It had 15 tons of flour, 3 tons of sea biscuit, and 20 barrels of fresh water. It also had provisions reflecting local culture— 12 tons of fish oil, 760 pounds of dried salmon, and a fermented drink made from "sweet grass" (*Heracleum lanatum,* or cow parsnip), which the Russians called *slatkaya trava.*

Carpenters, blacksmiths, other artisans, and native workmen were now released. Three soldiers were left at Klyucha to care for the sick and to assume responsibility for government funds, five tons of flour, and unused matériel. On July 13 the *Archangel Gabriel* departed from Ushka on a 125-mile slow sail down to the sea. It must have been an impressive sight—a big ship with its sloop towed behind. At the river's mouth Chirikov determined the latitude to be 56°3'N, quite close to modern readings of 56°13'N. The ship passed the bar and anchored at sea. The next day, the 14th, all sails were set. Chirikov and Chaplin took turns keeping the log. Once around Cape Kamchatka, the ship continued to follow the land. Instead of the generally north–south coastline indicated on existing maps (e.g., Strahlenberg's or Homann's), the ship's direction in hugging the shore became a surprise: *northeast.*

The ship handled well, averaging about fifty nautical miles per day during the first two weeks, with fog obscuring the land during the night. Landmarks were duly noted in the log, such as "point which juts into the sea" and "three-peaked mountain." On July 27 Chirikov notes, "On shore we sighted a waterfall and river that flows into the sea." The next day they sighted whales, sea lions, walrus, and porpoise. On July 30, with the ship but a mile or two from shore, Chaplin and four sailors took the sloop to land to look for fresh water. Finding none, Chaplin returned to the ship and they continued on, hugging the shore. Soon "an inlet appeared," the estuary of the Anadyr River.[2] On July 31 they passed a bay and, using the church calendar, bestowed on it the name Krest (Cross) Bay. On August 7 they came to another bay to which they gave the name Preobrazhenia (Transfiguration). Because they were now down to one barrel of water, Chaplin and his party again took the sloop ashore in the bay and found both streams and a lake, from which he filled all twenty barrels. They also found a dwelling and footpaths but no people.

The next day in the evening a *baidar* (open skin boat) bearing eight natives appeared, heading for the *Archangel Gabriel.* When they got close to the ship, one man got on an inflated seal bladder and splashed his way to the ship. Then he returned to the baidar and persuaded his companions to pull alongside the ship. Bering had two interpreters, both Koryak. The men in the baidar probably spoke Sirenikski Eskimo: they and the Koryaks had but few words in common.[3] As a result, Bering learned only that the Anadyr River was behind them to the west and that an island lay ahead to the east. It is doubtful that he could glean much other information about rivers, forests, or promontories extending into the sea, let alone anything these people might know about America. The meeting took place near Cape Chukotsk (Chirikov gave it that name). The next day they sighted an island with dwellings similar to those they were now seeing along the continental shore. They named the island St. Lawrence in honor of the saint of the day. They came within five miles, choosing not to land there. They were now in high latitudes, approaching 65° N with the sea still open to the north. Unknown to them, they were now entering the strait that Captain James Cook was to name for Bering fifty years later. Beyond was the Icy Sea.

Just as Columbus was not the first European to reach America (Vikings and possibly others having preceded him), so Bering was not the first European explorer to pass through the strait later named for him. In 1648, when ice conditions were exceptionally favorable, a Russian merchant named Semyon Dezhnev sailed from the mouth of the Kolyma River with ninety men in seven boats, each with a single mast and sail. Some of the boats were wrecked in the Icy Sea, two or three passed through the strait, and Dezhnev with fourteen men reached the lower Anadyr River. During the next year they built Anadyrsk, a winter post near today's Markovo village.

Little is known about Dezhnev's feat, verified by few contemporary sources. Dezhnev's own report was found in 1736 by Gerhard F. Müller in Yakutsk archives. Because this report was not forwarded from Yakutsk to Moscow, Dezhnev's achievement was all but forgotten, and the sea route he pioneered was never again used during his lifetime (he died in 1672). The hazards were too great: all seven boats were wrecked and most lives lost. Like Bering, Dezhnev was probably unaware that he had passed through a strait. In his report to the district governor he makes no mention of a "Big Land" (America) to the east, and he provides few details about the voyage. He writes that on October 1, 1648, he lost sight of Fyodot Alekseev's boat in a storm, that his own boat was wrecked "beyond the Onandyr [Anadyr] River," and that he and his men, "cold and hungry, naked and barefoot," struggled ten weeks on foot to get to the river. Here they wintered. In the spring they built a boat from driftwood and rowed upriver until they came to woodlands where sable could be hunted and timber used for a fort. The next year a party of hunters from the Lower Kolyma Post showed up. They too had heard tall tales about precious black sables so numerous they lived in herds along a river to the east. Dezhnev and his men joined forces with the newcomers and together they built boats in which to sail downriver to Anadyr Bay. In 1652 they made the trip. They found few sables anywhere, but in a sandbar they found another kind of wealth: nearly three tons of walrus ivory. Dezhnev wrote the report to the district governor in Yakutsk with the hope that he might receive recognition for his discovery of ivory and be salaried in service to the government.[4] He was evidently unaware that his voyage from the Icy Sea to the North Pacific Ocean might elicit interest.

Several years later in a Koryak camp Dezhnev met a Yakut woman who in 1648 made the voyage through the strait in that other boat with Fyodot Alekseev, the boat that had been separated from Dezhnev's in a storm. She said that they had reached the Kamchatka River and settled about 100 miles upstream at the confluence of Nikul Creek. According to Müller, the creek had another name, Fyodoticha (or Fyodotovka), evidence that Alekseev was the leader of the first Russian inhabitants of Kamchatka.[5]

Dezhnev asked her, "Do you want to return to your own people?"

She shook her head. "I have another master now. He gives me all the fish liver I want." She then opened her collar to reveal a silver medal on a chain, given her, she said, for her service.

Dezhnev apparently did not pursue the matter.[6] Was the medal a gift from Alekseev before he died of scurvy?

Some Soviet historians glorify Dezhnev as an explorer. One declares: "Dezhnev's name by right can stand next to the names of the great seafarers, Columbus and Magellan. If Columbus discovered a New World and Magellan sailed around the world on the southern side, then Dezhnev proved that the New World does not connect with Asia." The comparison has little merit. Dezhnev's voyage was virtually unknown for nearly a century. Also, as an American historian observes, "Dezhnev made his discovery in a part of the world from which few consequences of major or world importance could flow."[7]

Despite the dearth of information about Dezhnev's voyage of approximately 1,500 nautical miles, Soviet historians have identified "the great rocky point" he saw as Cape Dezhnev (James Cook named it East Cape) and the place where he was blown ashore as Dezhnev Bay, just west of today's Cape Navarin.[8]

On August 13 Bering called his two lieutenants to his cabin. He read Peter's instructions to them and then asked whether it was not clear, with the Asian shore turning westward, that Asia was separated from America by sea. From this question it is obvious that Bering mistakenly believed that Cape Chukotsk was the most easterly point of Asia and that little purpose would be served by proceeding much farther.

Chirikov, the first to reply in writing, proposed that they proceed at least until the 25th of the month, either as far as the mouth of the Kolyma River or up to the ice known to exist farther to the north. He suggested they search for an area where they could winter, "especially opposite Chukotsk Nos [Cape]," where, according to a secondhand report, "forested land" could be found. Spangberg, writing in German, proposed that the voyage continue northward until the 16th; then the *Archangel Gabriel* should return homeward to the Kamchatka River before winter for the safety of both men and ship. Spangberg noted that "on the Chukotsk land there is no harbor, firewood, or river course where we can take cover." Moreover, he believed that the Chukchi were hostile, and he noted that Peter's instructions did not indicate "how much we [are] to observe" in these northern waters.[9]

There is no question that Chirikov was very respectfully offering alternatives that Bering, as commander, could not accept. Go to the mouth of the Kolyma? Chirikov could not know that the distance involved, 30° of longitude, was far too great. It would have been impossible for the *Archangel Gabriel* to get there in twelve days, and once it passed Cape Shelagsky at 70° N, it would almost certainly become icebound. His second alternative, to follow the Asian shore to the west until they met the edge of the ice, was also risky, for in late summer at such high latitudes the ice might quickly lock in the ship. Finally, Chirikov's idea of wintering somewhere (America?) opposite Cape Chukotsk was hardly reassuring. If Asia did not offer safe haven, would any island or the American coast be any safer? Chirikov surely could not know that American natives would be any less hostile than the Chukchi or that there would be adequate shelter to protect the ship from winter storms and ice. And as for "forested land," would it really exist somewhere not too far east of Cape Chukotsk?

Many critics, Russian and American, accuse Bering of not searching diligently for America when indeed that continent was so close in the Bering Strait and even visible from Cape Dezhnev on a clear day. In defense of Bering, four arguments are paramount. First, because of ice, the sailing season at high latitudes was already coming to an end. (August 16, Spangberg's deadline for heading farther north, is actually August 27 according to our Gregorian calendar.) The small window for safe passage at sea north of Bering Strait varies unpredictably from year to year. The perennial ice, in the late twentieth century, extended from Cape Serdtse Kamen on the north coast of Chukotka at 67° N to a site at approximately 72° N some miles north of Point Barrow. In 1728, at 67°24'N, the *Archangel Gabriel*'s estimated northernmost latitude, Bering would have been getting close to this later perennial ice cover.

What in 1728 did Bering know? He was familiar with seasonal ice. In March it extends from the north shore of Hokkaido, Japan, to Kamchatka, covering nearly all of the Sea of Okhotsk and all of the Bering Sea north of approximately 60° N. In August, for the period 1979–96, seasonal ice has covered the sea from Cape Dezhnev at 66° N to Alaska at 70° N.[10] In 1728 Bering had penetrated the Arctic Ocean on the Asian side to the north of this later boundary. Whatever the yearly variation or whatever the trends over centuries because of global cooling or warming, it seems clear that Bering had good reason to be concerned about the proximity of ice and that he was wise to reject Chirikov's proposal to continue the voyage toward the mouth of the Kolyma River until August 25 (September 5). That westward route would almost certainly have become locked up in ice before the ship could retreat. An American historian who does not fault Bering for failing to see America, because "the whole time he was in the strait the weather was thick," nevertheless declares that Bering was in too "great a hurry to get away." After all, he says, "Captain Cook sailed on until he was blocked by ice. Bering could have done as much."[11]

Cook's experience *is* instructive—it exonerates Bering. In his attempts to find a northwest passage, Cook with two ships probed the icecap between America and Asia from August 16 to 29, 1778. On the 17th on the American side, out of sight of land, he reached 70°44'N. The ice was an impenetrable wall, ten to twelve feet high, and dangerously mobile in the fog. He had no choice but to retreat, moving eastward with prevailing west winds, one ship a mile behind the other. But he was moving into a trap. Just in time the fog lifted, the American coast became visible three or four miles away, the water started to shoal rapidly, and a wall of ice was coming down behind the ships.

It was a close call. Had visibility not improved, Cook's ships would have been grounded in the vicinity of a point he named Icy Cape. Immediately both ships tacked through a narrow opening to the southwest, escaping shallow seas and impenetrable ice.[12]

Cook found the ice to be "not quite continuous." There were openings like pools, but he judged it to be unsafe to enter them "at this advanced season of the year"; that is, on August 16. After tacking along the American coast for three days, August 17–19, Cook crossed to the Asian side. On August 29 he was still above 69° N, though the ice had advanced as much as twenty miles within forty-eight hours. As he approached land to the west and southwest, the sea once again rapidly shoaled. He was forced to turn again. In his journal entry for that date he admits defeat: "The season was now so very advanced that I did not think it consistant [sic] with prudence to make any farther attempts to find passage this year in any direction so little was the prospect of succeeding."[13] If it is assumed that the icecap in 1778 was roughly comparable to that in 1728, then indeed Bering came within 2° of latitude of that ice off Asia (about 69° N) only two days earlier (Cook's calendar was eleven days later than Bering's), though Bering, off Asia, was farther to the east than Cook. Given the movement of the icecap in 1778, Cook judged the season to be "very advanced." Cook had two ships to Bering's single smaller vessel, and Cook's two were more seaworthy than Bering's.

It is true that Bering did not sail far enough to the north to prove conclusively that there is no land bridge between Asia and America, but however far north he had gone, it could still be claimed that an isthmus might exist short of the North Pole. In other words, there was no way that Bering could satisfy all later critics. West to the Kolyma River, north to the Pole, or east to America, it was all the same—imprudent under the circumstances and arguably beyond his instructions.

The other three arguments in Bering's defense can be stated briefly:

First, Spangberg and Chirikov were in agreement with Bering about following the Asian coast *all the way*. This was the land they were charting. It is clear that charting was their primary responsibility. Second, if there were an isthmus in the north connecting the two continents, they would of course find it from the Asian side. Finally, because of weather conditions, Bering did not at any time see America. How, then, could he know where to head east to find it?

Because Bering had asked his lieutenants for written opinions, it was now incumbent upon him to express his decision in writing. He wrote as follows: "If we remain here any longer, in these northern regions, there will be the danger that on some dark night in the fog we will become beached on some shore from which we will not be able to extricate ourselves because of contrary winds. Considering the condition of the ship, the fact that leeboards and keel board are broken, it is difficult for us to search in these regions for suitable places to spend the winter. . . . In my judgment it is better to return and search for a harbor on Kamchatka where we will stay through the winter."[14] In this decision Bering did not choose to respond to Chirikov. He was essentially in agreement with Spangberg's recommendations, merely adding three additional reasons of his own, the nightmares of all seamen of his age: running aground in fog or at night, being trapped by contrary winds, and lacking the means to steer the ship safely through frigid seas.

Did Bering fail to take "reasonable risks"? For three weeks he had been taking such risks in uncharted waters. Now that the land had turned away to the west and the *Archangel Gabriel* was in imminent danger of meeting ice known to exist, what was the reason for continuing northward? Had they not reached a point where reasonable risks were becoming unacceptable risks?

Should Bering have tacked eastward in search of America? Should he not have taken a more easterly route homeward bound? Bering had good reasons for not doing so. He felt that the condition of the ship did not, in all prudence, allow such further exploration. Also, he most likely believed that his chart of the Chukotkan coast could be much improved, and indeed the *Archangel Gabriel*'s track homeward along the Chukotka peninsula is closer to the coast than its track northward. Finally, Bering did continue to sail several days northward, as Spangberg had recommended.

On August 14, at mid-afternoon during a moment of clear weather, they were startled to see land to the south, their first view of Big Diomede (Ratmanov) Island. As the ship continued to drift in a calm, Chirikov noted in his journal that "at a distance of fifteen miles, high mountains appeared, which we believe to be on Bolshaia Zemlia" (Big Land). But Chirikov was mistaken. The distance and the direction indicate that he saw high ground behind Cape Dezhnev. From the ninth hour of the evening, when the wind shifted to the northwest, Bering let the ship drift slowly to the northeast. By midnight the ship was at 67°18'N.[15]

August 15 was a day of fog, drizzle, light winds continuing from the northwest, and many whales. The next day was cloudy with moderate northwest winds. The ship continued to drift to the northeast as far as 167°50' west longitude. America remained out of sight, still 100 miles to the east. The ship had sighted no land for more than two days. At the third hour of the afternoon Bering gave orders for the ship to begin the return voyage. It had reached 67°24' north latitude and had gone slightly more than 30° of longitude east of the mouth of the Kamchatka River. At this point, he could still have reached the shore of Asia by going directly west about 100 miles.

It has been argued that the course of the *Archangel Gabriel* from August 14 to 16 indicates that Bering was looking for America.[16] There is no real evidence to support such a hypothesis. If indeed Bering were making a sustained effort to find America, why did he never report this intention in the ship's log? It seems more likely that Bering, in following Spangberg's recommendation and the three officers' understanding of Peter's instructions, was still looking for a land connection between the two continents, moving slowly to the north and largely letting the winds determine his course. When no land had become visible to the north after three days, Bering, still apprehensive about ice, finally called off the search and ordered a return to Kamchatka. It was a good decision.

By the end of August 16 the *Archangel Gabriel* was in sight of the island seen several days earlier. This time it was named: St. Diomede. The next day, the 17th, they sailed very close to shore along Chukotka south of Cape Dezhnev. They saw two Chukchi villages close together, and when their inhabitants saw the ship, "they ran up onto a high rocky hill." Farther south they recognized "a point of land with dwellings."[17]

On August 18 the *Archangel Gabriel* rounded Chukotsk Cape, then headed south away from the coast and again passed St. Lawrence Island, located twenty miles to the east. The 20th was a calm day with low cloudiness. Suddenly land appeared behind them and simultaneously four baidars with about forty natives. The man understood to be chief apparently knew some words of Koryak, in which Bering's two interpreters could converse, but evidently communication was very difficult. The interpreters understood that the Anadyr River was a "half day" to the south (and so it appears on the chart) when in fact it lay more nearly to the west. Also they understood that "across from here"—that is, on land across the sea opposite theirs—"people speak the same language as Chukchi used to speak."[18] What was this land? Did the natives mean an island (such as St. Lawrence or St. Diomede)? Or the Big Land (America)? If they meant St. Lawrence Island or the Big Land, the statement about language is puzzling, for the language of the Chukchi was not spoken by any people who had once lived in either place. One must conclude that little useful information was obtained from the interview. Bering did not have the interpreters he needed. He needed someone who knew the language of the natives, whether Sirenikski Eskimo or Chukchi.

Chirikov's journal makes it clear why the natives approached the ship. They knew about Russians and they came to trade. They had meat, fish, fox pelts, and walrus tusks. For these goods they got needles and fire starters.

On August 22 the ship came within sight of land about twenty-five miles away on the starboard side. Bering supposed that the Anadyr River was in this vicinity. On August 25 they encountered strong wind with heavy seas. The halyard on the foremast broke. They proceeded with the mainsail, continuing southwest. On August 30 they battled wind and wave close to a rocky shore. Sails came crashing down and rigging was in such disarray that they had to drop anchor to keep from drifting while the crew worked nonstop, in darkness and rain, to restore sails to some semblance of seaworthiness. Fortunately the storm passed.

On September 1 they reached Cape Kamchatka and the next day reentered the mouth of the Kamchatka River. After fifty days, the sea voyage had ended: thirty-three days out and seventeen days back. It was the culmination of Bering's mission.

The First Kamchatka Expedition was coming to an end. Through the winter at the Lower Kamchatka Post repairs were made on the ship. The river froze by the end of October, and early in May the ice broke up. The *Fortuna,* which had arrived the previous July 6 with more supplies than Chirikov had sledges to haul overland, again successfully rounded Cape Lopatka, at the southernmost extremity of the Kamchatka peninsula, during its return voyage to Bolsheretsk. The *Archangel Gabriel* followed but only after making a four-day probe to the east, away from the peninsula. Bering had learned at the Lower Kamchatka Post that on clear days land could be seen across the sea to the east. He supposed that such land could be North America, which of course had not made its appearance farther to the north. The third night, out in a storm, the ship's foresail ripped, and the following day, June 8, with no land in sight under overcast skies, Bering reversed course. Here he was at 55°32'N and 166°25'E, a short distance northeast of the island where he was to be shipwrecked and die a dozen years later. On July 1 Chirikov determined the latitude of Cape Lopatka at 51°10' (the modern reading is 50°53'). Two days later the *Archangel Gabriel* made a rendezvous with the *Fortuna* at Bolsheretsk. On July 24 the two vessels reached Okhotsk, where they were left with the *Vostok.*

Without the burden of heavy matériel and with fewer men, the expedition made good time returning overland to St. Petersburg. On January 11, 1730, it reached Tobolsk, where customs officials made a complete inventory of possessions and charged duty. On February 28 Bering arrived at St. Petersburg and within two weeks he submitted his final reports. In December 1731 he was promoted to captain-commander and awarded 1,000 rubles. Spangberg and Chirikov were promoted to the rank of captain.

The cost of the First Kamchatka Expedition was high: fifteen men died and many more deserted. Most of 660 horses died, leaving their Yakut owners destitute. The commandeering of dogs, sledges, and drivers so disrupted the well-being of Itelmens that the expedition almost certainly contributed to the unrest that led in 1731 to an uprising that resulted in the burning of the Lower Kamchatka Post and the further decimation of the Itelmen population when Russians put down the rebellion.

What did the expedition achieve? It concerned neither the discovery of nor the search for the strait later named for Bering, as later writers have claimed.[19] Though such a strait appears on Lvov's map, it is not mentioned in the instructions of Peter the Great, nor was it an objective for Bering and his two lieutenants. The search was simply for a land connection that did not exist. The search for land that joined or nearly joined two continents proved unsuccessful. In this search the Asian side of the Bering Sea and Bering Strait was first charted and two islands were incidentally sighted and named. The great gain for Russia was chiefly a new map of its Siberian territories based on fairly precise latitude and longitude observations, chiefly the work of Chirikov and Chaplin through their mastery of up-to-date Western European charting technology (Fig. 9). Captain Cook's praise is often quoted: "In justice to the memory of Bering I must say that he has delineated the coast [of northeast Asia] very well and fixed the latitude and longitude of points better than could be expected from the methods he had to go by."[20] The Bering map, shared with Western European governments, gave Russia new prestige.

This map clearly shows how much more extensive than previously imagined were Russia's claims to landholdings in northeast Asia. In following the land, the *Archangel Gabriel* sailed more than 1,000 miles to the east, not north or northwest, as the coast is shown on earlier maps. As an imperial power, Russia gained contiguous territories that became consolidated—not scattered global maritime colonial possessions that slipped away in the nineteenth and twentieth centuries as weakened Western European nations of necessity withdrew.

Although Bering was left with only the vaguest of notions about the position of North America vis-à-vis Asia, he did succeed in demonstrating convincingly that there was no isthmus between the two continents. True, in 1648 Dezhnev, in that long-forgotten voyage, had already sailed through Bering Strait from the north, but he did not leave, as Bering did, a reliable chart of his voyage.

If Dezhnev had charted the coast between the Kolyma River and the cape named for him, he might well have corrected the myth of a large cape appearing northwest of Cape Dezhnev: It is called "Nos Shalatskoi" on the Lvov map and similarly "Noss Tszalatskoi" on the Strahlenberg map. (Today it is Cape Shelagsky.) On the former, it is broad and open at the top, thus conceivably joined to the "Big Land." On the latter, it is drawn as a long, narrow point located just east of the mouth of the Kolyma River.

Figure 9. BERING MAP: ROUTE FROM TOBOLSK TO KAMCHATKA AND
THE ICY SEA, 1730 (COURTESY OF THE JAMES FORD BELL LIBRARY,
UNIVERSITY OF MINNESOTA).

Homann's map shows the west shore of the cape as an extension of
one side of the mouth of the Kolyma. Bering's map follows Lvov and
Homann in its depiction of a wide bay between Cape Dezhnev and the
large cape (unnamed on the Homann and Bering maps), and it follows
Homann's conception of the shape of the cape. Since Bering did not
see it (it did not, of course, exist), it is likely that the cape was included
only in deference to Lvov or Homann. The chief distortion of the
Bering map, it remained uncorrected until Captain Cook charted part
of the Arctic coast west of Cape Dezhnev in 1778. Also it is apparent
that the Bering map is in one respect inferior to Yevreinov-Luzhin's in
its portrayal of the contours of the Kamchatka peninsula, but superior
in showing correctly the peninsula's trend north-northeast. The Bering

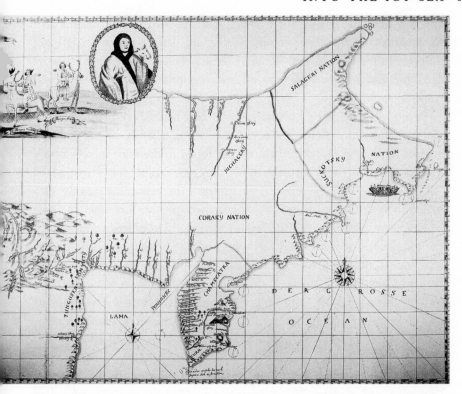

map was not per se Bering's creation. It is not known what the captain himself may have directly contributed to it. The map is a work of contemporary cartographic art, and Bering and the Senate were very proud of it: it shows the long, long way from Tobolsk to Kamchatka, and for the first time it shows the actual easternmost extremity of Siberia.

The expedition contributed little to an understanding of Siberian ethnology. In his report of March 12, 1730, Bering briefly describes various native peoples. That he has a poor opinion of them all is indicated by his use of the term "idolaters." Of the Tungus along the Upper Tungusta, Ilim, and Lena rivers, some, he says, have reindeer for food and transportation. Others without reindeer live on a river, eat fish, and use birchbark canoes. The Yakuts, he says, have horses and cattle for food and clothing. They "worship the sun, moon, and certain birds such as swans, eagles, and ravens." They have "sorcerers called shamans." Bering makes no real distinctions between "the Kuril people" (Ainu) and the Kamchadals, except to note that the former live in southern Kamchatka and the latter in the north, and that "some words[!]" are different in their languages. Some of these peoples, he says, are idolaters and "the rest have no faith at all and are quite devoid of any good habits."[21]

Bering proceeds to cite instances of "evil beliefs" and superstitions. He says that when twins are born, one is immediately killed, and that anyone near death is taken out into the forest to die with food for only a week. As for those already dead, they are left in the forest to be "devoured" by wild animals. The Koryaks, he reports, formerly cremated their dead until Russians obliged them to stop this practice. Such comments are made with little regard for the environment within which the indigenous peoples lived and with no appreciation and little understanding of subsistence and communal ways of life. As non-Christians, they were of little or no account. Although Bering paid some attention to indigenous peoples—and both used and abused them—his ethnological observations are insignificant compared to those of his contemporaries, especially Messerschmidt, Krasheninnikov, and Steller.[22]

Bering did not return to St. Petersburg at a propitious time. Empress Catherine had died in 1727. She was succeeded by Peter II, who died of smallpox at the age of 14 on January 19, 1730. He was succeeded by Anna Ivanovna, niece of Peter the Great and widow of the duke of Courland. Her ascent was initially subject to certain conditions: she agreed not to marry, not to designate an heir to the throne, and to keep in power the eight-member Supreme Privy Council, which had superseded the Senate as ruler of the country. However, when she took the oath of allegiance, rewritten by Archbishop Prokopovich, senior member of the Holy Synod, she was accorded absolute power without reference to "conditions." In fact, she publicly tore up the statement of conditions she had signed to show that she was no longer subject to them. On March 4, 1730, during Bering's first week back in St. Petersburg, she abolished the Supreme Privy Council and restored the Senate. The Supreme Privy Council had been dominated by several Russian aristocrats who intended to root out foreigners from positions of influence. Anna was more German than Russian herself. Married at 17 and widowed only two weeks after her wedding, she had spent all nineteen years of her adult life among Germans. She had a German lover who came with her to St. Petersburg. She formed a cabinet in which the German-born Ostermann was made first minister. Another German was appointed president of the War College and commander in chief.[23] Never before— not under Peter the Great, not under Catherine—had Russia been almost totally controlled by Western European immigrants, leaders who would be inclined to reward Vitus Bering. Because these changes in the reorganization of the imperial government took many months to complete, Bering did not soon gain a hearing for his new proposal; namely, that he return to Kamchatka and build larger oceangoing ships with which to find America.

Bering had been away from home for five years. He and Anna became parents twice again: A third son, Anton (called Tongin), was born late in 1730, and the very next year Anna (called Anuska), their only surviving daughter, was born.

In other respects the family had changed. In 1729 Anna's younger sister, Helena, became the second wife of Anton Johann von Saltza, a Swedish nobleman in the Russian service in St. Petersburg. Formerly a captain in the Swedish army, he was a financial administrator who in 1728 reorganized the city government of Viborg and through this connection met Anna's brother, Bendix, and her sister Helena. When the next year Helena accompanied her husband to their new home in St. Petersburg, Anna Bering also made the move back to St. Petersburg. She fully approved of Helena's marriage. She was frankly fond of Saltza, who willingly became a substitute father for her sons Jonas and Thomas, who in 1729 were respectively 8 and 6 years of age. It was no coincidence that her third son, Anton, was named for his uncle.

There were at this time two constellations of the family. In Viborg resided the merchant patriarch, Matthias Pülse, and his wife, née Margareta Hedvig Lund, and their only son, Bendix, also a merchant. In 1726–27 Bendix became chairman of the town's four elders, and in 1730 he was one of two representatives sent to Moscow to have the town's new charter certified. On this occasion Bendix's wife became godmother at Anton Bering's baptism. Unfortunately, Bendix and his wife lost seven of nine children as infants, only two daughters surviving.

In St. Petersburg, besides the Saltzas, resided Admiral Thomas Saunders and his wife, Eufemia. They had two children, a girl and a boy. It was here and in Moscow, where she spent a year, that Anna Bering made her mark. People like her were then becoming well integrated into the political and social life of the imperial court. Anna knew how to use her assets—and they were many. As a result of the First Kamchatka Expedition and her husband's trading in Siberia, she had new wealth with which to lease an upscale residence with servants to maintain and grace it. Her husband, as captain-commander, had at last a noble rank, enabling her to present herself as Anna *von* Bering. In her late 30s she was attractive in her exquisite dress of Siberian furs and Chinese silks and in her quick wit and charm, which barely concealed a steely resolve to improve her social standing. Toward this end she could present masterpieces on the clavichord, any of her four children, and a handsome husband who was then a rising star in Siberian exploration—and now looming New World exploration.

Anna's great conquest was the Austrian minister and his wife. He was Nikolai Sebastian von Hohenholz, most respectfully addressed as "Herr Resident" or "Herr Councilor." He represented Russia's closest European ally in the court of Empress Anna Ivanovna. But Anna Bering had for this most influential diplomat a pet name that she used in his presence with his obvious pleasure—Babska. As later personal letters also indicate, the Berings pleased this Austrian couple by declaring them to be their "very dearest friends and even closer than their own family." The Berings could afford to be generous. In a letter written to his maternal aunt in Horsens shortly before Anuska's birth, Bering mentions his desire to donate an inheritance from his parents for the benefit of the poor in Horsens. An arrangement for this purpose was formalized by a document dated March 28, 1733. He also asked his aunt (his mother's sister) about the Bering family coat of arms.[24]

By 1733, the prospects of the Berings were very promising.

CHAPTER FOUR

A DREAM OF EMPIRE

The Second Kamchatka Expedition, as it was finally organized, is also well named as the Great Northern Expedition. Its greatness lay in its size, the distance it was to go across the northern hemisphere, and the complexity of its various operations. Bering's primary interest was in finding America, but he understood the importance to Russia of finding a route to Japan from Kamchatka by way of the Kuril Islands. He was also cognizant of the desire of the Russian government to have an accurate map of its northern coast along the Icy Sea.

However, such large projects proved to be only a beginning. The second expedition was also to lead to the development of Siberia's resources by taking an inventory of peoples and the flora, fauna, and minerals; it was to initiate metallurgical industry and agriculture; it was to build new ports on the Pacific Ocean and find a new southern route from Irkutsk to that ocean; and it was to establish a dependable postal service east of the Ural Mountains.

Three key planners enlarged the scope of Bering's proposal for a second expedition. They were Count Nikolai F. Golovin, in 1733 appointed president of the Admiralty College; Ivan K. Kirilov, geographer and senior secretary of the Senate; and Count Andrei I. Ostermann, mastermind of intrigue and diplomacy at the ear of Empress Anna in her three-member cabinet of ministers. Although these men were prime movers in empire building, they relied on Bering to coordinate or carry out all these projects. Bering of course had connections of his own: in the Admiralty through his brother-in-law Thomas Saunders and indirectly with the empress through his friend the Austrian resident in St. Petersburg, who, as the representative of Russia's chief ally, at times met almost daily with Ostermann, Empress Anna's chief adviser. To these empire builders should be added the name of Vitus Bering himself. Though subordinate to Golovin, Bering had the experience both to initiate great plans and to carry them out. He of course submitted reports to the Admiralty, but he also addressed comprehensive reports of the expedition's progress directly to the empress; and on the eve of his departure from Kamchatka for North America he addressed a letter directly to Ostermann requesting reassignment to the Admiralty.[1]

Planning did not occur right away. At first, until Anna Ivanovna became secure on her throne by executing or banishing to Siberia several previously influential xenophobic Russian aristocrats, Bering had difficulty getting any more than a polite hearing. Times had changed. Cruys had died in 1727 and Apraksin the next year. The latter was succeeded by Golovin, whose father, Fyodor, like Apraksin, had been one of Peter the Great's most trusted leaders and companions. Not only did Peter's successors, including Anna, lack Peter's hands-on direction of government, but also during 1727–32 the Admiralty College remained in St. Petersburg when the seat of government was returned to Moscow. When on April 30, 1730, Bering presented certain proposals to strengthen the extension of empire eastward, Golovin, not knowing how those proposals might be received, sent Bering to Moscow to present his own case. There Bering found a champion in Kirilov, who recognized with no little enthusiasm what the commander had achieved for Russia through the First Kamchakta Expedition. In an undated memorandum, Kirilov wrote that Bering had "added the eastern side of Kamchatka to the map, and there were shown more than 30 degrees of longitude nearer America beyond previous information." Kirilov embraced Bering's proposal for a second Kamchatka expedition, foreseeing in it not only "expansion of the empire" but also "inexhaustible wealth."[2] But if Siberia were to accommodate a second, larger expedition, he agreed with Bering that a strong supportive administrator was needed at Okhotsk, that the route between Yakutsk and Okhotsk had to be improved, and that Yakuts and other native peoples should be proselytized and schooled to serve Russian interests.

But who would be the administrator? Once the Senate had responded favorably to Bering's proposal in December 1730, the administrator was soon identified. He was Grigory G. Skornyakov-Pisarev, an exile then living at Zhigansk, a village on the Lena River north of Yakutsk. He proved to be a disastrous choice, given to dissolute living, though once he had been a rising star in the reign of Peter the Great. Educated abroad, he had taught mechanics and artillery at the Naval Academy before becoming its director and advancing to the rank of major general. But in 1727, implicated in a conspiracy against Prince Aleksandr Menshikov, a favorite of Catherine I and the most powerful member of her Supreme Privy Council, he was knouted, branded, and exiled. (It was probably of little consolation to him that Menshikov himself fell from power a year later and died in exile in 1729.) In retrospect Kirilov noted that Skornyakov-Pisarev was selected because no one else available in Siberia "was adjudged more capable than he" for the position.[3] Unfortunately, it was an appointment made from afar without benefit of interview.

On May 10, 1731, Skornyakov-Pisarev was ordered not only to proceed to Okhotsk to assume command over the port and the Kamchatka region but also to develop Okhotsk as a major port with a wharf, to promote commerce with Kamchatka, and to recruit and induce a new merchant community to take advantage of trade without payment of duties. He was also directed to introduce cattle raising on the Pacific seaboard, to convert the natives to Christianity and provide schools to teach them basic subjects and navigation, to found new communities along the rivers between Yakutsk and Okhotsk, and to collect tribute from the people living in the Shantar Islands, located strategically near the mouth of the Amur River.

These orders, sent by the Senate, would have been difficult to carry out by even the most conscientious and competent commandant. Skornyakov-Pisarev could easily ignore them. Perhaps he knew the popular saying, "In Siberia, God is a long way up and the empress [or emperor] a long way off." In any event, he did not even go to Okhotsk until 1735, just ahead of Spangberg and his advance expeditionary unit. Of course there were no ships in Okhotsk, no wharf, no cattle, nothing much at all. Skornyakov-Pisarev proved to be a disagreeable liability, living two miles away in his own stockade, competing for workmen, building separate facilities, and accusing Bering of egregious self-interest.[4] Of all these woes Bering had as yet no inkling in 1731 in Moscow, where he was often kept waiting while his proposals were being considered. Unaccustomed to such enforced inactivity and weary of Moscow, on January 5, 1732, he requested and obtained from the Senate a leave of absence for his return to St. Petersburg.

Several months later, on April 17, Empress Anna ordered the Senate to carry out Bering's proposals. On May 2 Kirilov, in his capacity as presiding officer of the Senate, specified areas to be reached by the new expedition, not only North America and Japan but also virtually the entire Arctic coast, the Shantar Islands, and Spanish territories in America. Kirilov believed that further investigation would prove the existence of a navigable seaway along the Arctic coast to Kamchatka. He also unrealistically expected that Russia would eventually acquire, "through kindness" to embittered indigenous peoples, access to the gold and silver in Spanish colonies.[5] The small Shantar Islands, near the mouth of the Amur River, were part of Kirilov's plan to contain and isolate China through alliances with Korea and Japan.

If Bering were the catalyst, then Kirilov by virtue of his position became the primary driving force through his vision of Russia as an emerging world power. He persuaded Ostermann, who in turn persuaded the empress, that what Peter had accomplished for the glory of Russia through war could now be advanced in peace by support of Bering in his proposed second expedition.

On June 12 the Senate approved an academic contingent to travel with Bering as far as Kamchatka, "generally to learn everything that has scientific interest."[6] The Academy of Sciences appointed three professors: Johann Georg Gmelin to report on natural history; Louis Delisle de La Croyère, half brother of Joseph N. Delisle, to make astronomical observations; and Gerhard Friedrich Müller to describe native peoples. Of the three professors, Müller had been put forward by Bering himself and supported by Ostermann and Kirilov.

Bering could see that his original proposal had been so greatly augmented that the second expedition could become a logistical nightmare. Naval officers would now be accompanied by their wives and children. The professors would have sixteen assistants, including artists, surveyors, and students. A support staff of soldiers, boatmen, carpenters, and other laborers would amount to several thousand individuals. Was Bering to lead an expedition or a small migration? If transport, housing, and provisioning were at times almost insuperable problems during the First Kamchatka Expedition, how could they be solved during a truly massive new effort? Bering is reputed to have said many times: "There is no art in sending people off on a journey. . . . But to find them subsistence when they reach their destination calls for considerably more prudence and thought."[7]

With the return of the imperial government to St. Petersburg in 1732, Bering was much more effective in operating behind the scenes. For him a major question remained: How were adequate provisions to be delivered to the expedition at Okhotsk and at ports on Kamchatka? He remembered Okhotsk as a desolate place without trees or grasses; close in and around the settlement there was nothing but sand and gravel. Fish were seasonal. A Russian could not "go native" and live by the subsistence hunt or on the occasional beached whale. The peninsula of Kamchatka was a wild and dangerous place. Its potential for agriculture was virtually unknown.

There seemed but one good answer, one discussed at length with his brother-in-law Saunders and their commander, Golovin. Both had had experience at sea in the British navy, Saunders as recently as 1718, when he joined the Russian service. On October 1, 1732, Golovin proposed to the empress that two frigates and a transport vessel be sent to Kamchatka each year by way of Cape Horn, with Golovin himself in command. Such voyages were calculated to help fulfill Kirilov's vision of Russia as a dominant world power through the training of young seamen on the great oceans, Russian discovery and settlement of new lands, and consequent location of rich new mines. Golovin further observed that Dutch ships reached the Japanese port of Nagasaki every year, making the round trip within eighteen months. To Golovin's proposal Saunders added appealing details, such as the development of a suitable new Pacific port near the southern tip of Kamchatka, the presence there of ships with as many as fifty guns to protect Russia's interest in trade with Japan, the introduction of livestock and agriculture on Kamchatka, and the training and enlistment of natives for a Kamchatka Pacific fleet.[8] An unexpressed intent of these proposals was to beat the British into the Pacific Ocean.

Golovin, Saunders, and especially Bering must have been greatly disappointed that their projected expanded role for the imperial navy was not approved. There were, to be sure, obsessive concerns about secrecy: Russia's program of eastward expansion must not be visible to other seagoing nations. Kirilov had an overly optimistic idea about the ease of travel over Siberian river systems as well as strangely quixotic ideas about the dangers of Atlantic transport. In his view, Russia was especially "endowed by God . . . since all through Siberia there are natural canals: that is, the great rivers are close to one another, along which vessels with goods can readily go, and only in three places are there overland portages, and these are not lengthy." Kirilov supposed that these "natural canals" gave Russia a "great advantage over the Europeans who sail to the East and West Indies." Why? Because "it is not necessary to go to the equator and suffer intense heat" and "there will be no fear of the Algerians and other pirates."[9] Certainly Golovin would gladly have taken such risks.

With transoceanic transport forbidden, the Admiralty College gave Bering his instructions on October 16. After he had built two packets— two-masted decked ships—on the Kamchatka River, he was to take command of one and Chirikov the other and proceed as far north as 67° N to search within a single sailing season for the American coast. Each commander was ordered to keep a journal describing coasts, islands, channels, and other information for "a detailed and accurate map." Bering was to reach agreement with Chirikov "on all matters during the course of this voyage" and with senior and junior officers concerning problems of ice or other unforeseen problems that might extend the conclusion of the voyage.[10] These instructions are remarkable in that they envision little more than a repetition of Bering's earlier voyage: again he was to go to the northeast; only this time, with two larger ships, he was to persist (despite obstacles of ice) in finding America before returning to Kamchatka.

It is also curious that these instructions outline a voyage that had already been completed *that same year* by the surveyor Mikhail S. Gvozdev on the ship Bering had built, the *Archangel Gabriel*. This voyage was part of a military campaign, authorized by the Senate, to subdue the Chukchi and afterward to seek the "Big Land" (America) said to lie opposite Chukotka. In March 1730 the fight against the Chukchi failed utterly. The Russian commander was killed and his men were routed. Gvozdev now had the responsibility of finding that Big Land. On July

23, 1732, with thirty-nine men, he left the mouth of the Anadyr River; on August 20 he left Big Diomede for Little Diomede; the next day he anchored off the Big Land; and then he followed the American coast until two days later he met a native in a single-hatch *baidarka* off an island (King Island). On September 28 the Gvozdev expedition returned to the mouth of the Kamchatka River. News of this first known Russian sighting of America did not reach the Second Kamchatka Expedition until Spangberg reached Okhotsk in 1735. Gvozdev himself had been ordered to remain at the Lower Kamchatka Post until it had been rebuilt in 1735.

The Admiralty College's instructions to Bering are also remarkable in their foreshadowing of later challenges to his authority. Was Bering commander or was he co-commander with Chirikov? Was there already a plan that Bering, now aged 51, would be reassigned and his place taken by Chirikov?

On December 28, 1732, after hearing the "considered opinions" of the Admiralty College, the Senate submitted to Empress Anna its recommended instructions to Bering concerning the new Kamchatka expedition. These instructions give the impression that everything needful for the success of the expedition had been or soon would be done. Maps of the region had been examined. "All necessary supplies" would be sent. Siberian officials—the governor at Tobolsk, the vice governor at Irkutsk, and Skornyakov-Pisarev at Okhotsk—would all give assistance to Bering. Everything—provisions, equipment, boats, and ships—would consequently be ready or nearly ready at each stage of Bering's advance. In short, "the expedition [would] be fully manned and completely equipped."[11] Toward this end, at Bering's recommendation, 300 persons in the Yakutsk district had been ordered to Okhotsk and Kamchatka outposts, including peasants to work the land and natives to care for livestock.

Such instructions indicate that the lessons of the First Kamchatka Expedition had not been learned. One could not issue orders in St. Petersburg and expect locals scattered far and wide in another world to follow them. That other world, in its coldest regions, is primed for swift and joyful action during a few months of summer and for sleep and self-preservation the rest of the year. There it is a rule of survival to act according to local conditions, one's own instincts, and one's own devilish amusement. In Irkutsk, for instance, where state and church were in close proximity, it was widely known that a certain vice governor pleased himself by having cannons fired whenever he left his office. The bishop, not to be outdone, ordered that he be saluted by the ringing of church bells whenever he sallied forth. The merchants of Irkutsk, not far from emporiums of commerce at the Chinese border, were said to have served God and Mammon exceptionally well. Whether they paid a state levy or smuggled goods adroitly, they rolled in rubles.[12] Siberians generally did what they pleased with minimal circumspection, not caring at all about what was expected of them in Moscow or St. Petersburg. So long as the highest authorities there consulted only themselves, they acted with eyes more than half closed.

Nowhere was this folly more evident than in plans to build and send sloops downriver from Tobolsk and Yakutsk. The objective was threefold: to chart the Arctic coast, to find out if there were a navigable northern sea route, and to determine once and for all whether there existed a land bridge to America. The plan was to have a detachment of about fifty men commanded by a lieutenant go down the Ob River to its mouth and then proceed eastward along the Arctic coast to the mouth of the Yenesei, and have two similar detachments go down the Lena River, one going west to the Yenesei and the other east to whichever came first, the isthmus to America or the channel through which Bering had passed. To facilitate these voyages, the planners imagined that tribute collectors might be sent out early to alert fur traders and nomads on the coast that a sloop would be coming and that they should keep beacons lighted to facilitate its passage. As an incentive to beacon lighters, they should be informed that they would be rewarded by "trinkets up to one ruble in value" handed out by the lieutenant in charge of the sloop.[13]

It turned out that the sloop built at Tobolsk, commanded by Dmitry Ovtsyn, did eventually in 1737 succeed, after three tries, in beating the ice through the 45-mile-long Ob Gulf and, rounding a peninsula, entering the Yenesei. Apparently he accomplished this feat without benefit of beacons, but poor Ovtsyn had the misfortune to meet by chance the region's most infamous exile, Prince Ivan Alekseevich Dolgoruky, formerly a favorite of Peter II and now a state criminal. For this contact Ovtsyn was court-martialed, reduced in rank from lieutenant to ordinary seaman, and sent off to join Bering.[14]

Ovtsyn had the shortest exposure to the Arctic coast. Both of the boats built at Yakutsk were repeatedly stopped by ice. Saddest of all attempts was one made in 1736 by Peter Lassenius, a Swede who died of scurvy in makeshift winter quarters located well above the Arctic Circle. Only eight men in his detachment survived. West and east of the mouth of the Lena, exploration was eventually accomplished by overland parties only with stupendous effort and terrible hardship. No wonder Sven Waxell, another Swede who as lieutenant worked directly under Bering, could write years later with obvious sarcasm: "At the present time there are certain very learned persons who maintain that one ought to sail right out from the coast and cross the Icy Sea nearer the Pole; it being their opinion that by so doing open water would be reached. To me that [idea] seems so ambitious . . . that I am unable to understand it. . . . I have never heard or read of anyone being farther north than a latitude of 82 degrees; and what those had to endure in the way of effort and privations before they came back again is, indeed, a most harrowing tale."[15]

Bering could hardly object to risky projects for the glory of Russia. His orders to coordinate them elevated his role well above that indicated by his rank. But as an agent of the state, he could not in 1733 fully anticipate the burdens he was to carry two to eight years later.

CHAPTER FIVE

SET UP TO FAIL

Spangberg was the first to leave St. Petersburg. On February 21, 1733, with a small detachment, he set off for Okhotsk with some of the heaviest equipment needed for shipbuilding. The main expeditionary force, leaving the capital on April 18, consisted of Chirikov, eight lieutenants, and officers' wives and children—altogether about 500 persons, to whom were later added about 500 soldiers and about 2,000 workers to assist in the transport of freight.

Bering did not leave the capital until April 29. He left two sons, then 12 and almost 10 years of age, with a gymnasium professor and his wife in Reval, where he had been stationed briefly during the Great Northern War.[1] Then on May 14, with Anna and their two youngest children, a boy of 2 years and a girl only 1, he caught up with the expedition, which had traveled by horses to the Volga but was now continuing on boats on the Volga and Kama rivers and would use sledges in late autumn to get to Tobolsk. The last to leave St. Petersburg were the three professors at the head of their small itinerant academy. They left the capital on August 8 and drifted into Tobolsk separately between January 15 and 30, 1734.

The arrival of nearly 600 people requiring winter and spring housing in a small city with a population approximating 10,000 and 3,106 dwellings must have been a bit of a shock. Officers and their families expected separate lodgings. The professors were particularly sensitive about accommodations suitable to their status. Then there were demands for supplies and assistance. Spangberg, who had quickly passed through the city, had acquired there 3 riverboats, 7,200 pounds of iron, 1,499 pairs of saddlebags, and 74 workers. Now here were Bering and Chirikov needing more than 1,998 pairs of saddlebags as well as carpenters and other artisans to build a sloop to be christened the *Tobol*. They also claimed 200 of the 589 soldiers garrisoned in Tobolsk plus 1,500 workers, about one-sixth of the population. In normal times such an abrupt claim on workers would have been quite disruptive, but in the 1730s the entire Tobolsk region was under threat of attack. Villages were being sacked, cattle driven off, and captives taken. In a single year (1736) natives conducted three raids that resulted in the loss of 1,026 head of cattle.[2]

Why the raids? Native peoples could not compete with the influx of Russians claiming their lands. In all of Siberia there had been only 100,000 Russians in 1700. That number grew tenfold in only thirty years and pressures were greatest in the few agricultural districts between Tobolsk and Irkutsk. Demands for fur tribute severely interrupted indigenous tribal life. The hunting and trapping of sable, fox, and squirrels did not contribute to the welfare of native peoples, diverting men from essential subsistence pursuits.[3] Also, while fur-bearing animals were overhunted, native populations were kept in check. In Siberia in 1700, natives outnumbered Russians 2 to 1. In 1730, Russians outnumbered natives 4 to 1.

Who were the Russians? Some were exiles, some former serfs. A great many were cossacks. The word was derived from the Tatar *kazak*, denoting a free and bold spirit. Originating in regions north of the Black and Caspian seas, cossacks lived in their own settlements and elected their own chiefs. Subsequently many migrated eastward into Siberia to function as independent fur traders, fur-tribute collectors, military men, and government officials. Cossacks were the new Siberians, disdaining highly stratified Russian European society and living as opportunists by their wits and muskets. By and large, they were the ones who conquered Siberia.[4]

On February 27, 1734, Bering, his family, and a small party left Tobolsk for Irkutsk over a winter road. As he had recommended, he was authorized to acquire in Irkutsk gifts for native peoples to be met on forthcoming land and sea journeys. The gifts could include Chinese cottons "and other small goods . . . as well as Chinese *shar* [tobacco] . . . as much as 2,000 rubles worth."⁵ With his own funds Bering was also at liberty to purchase valuable items presumably for his own use, such as green tea, porcelains, and silk garments. With these goods Bering sailed down the Lena River, reaching Yakutsk in October 1734, only eighteen months out of St. Petersburg.

Meanwhile, on May 19 Chirikov—now in charge of the main contingent—left Tobolsk with a dozen riverboats only five days after the *Tobol* had departed. He followed the same river route he had taken eight years earlier. He exchanged boats for wagons and sleds on long portages as he proceeded laboriously during the winter on his way to Ust-Kut, on the Lena. On the first portage only half the wagons needed were available, so this long overland trip had to be repeated. Fortunately, there was still time at Ust-Kut for 100 boats, large and small, to be built for passage down to Yakutsk. By this time, however, laborers were deserting in such alarming numbers that severe measures were taken. Waxell writes, "We sought to prevent further losses by introducing harsh discipline; we set up a gallows every twenty versts [12 miles] along the river Lena," an action that had "an exceptionally good effect."⁶ At the end of June 1735, Chirikov with the main detachment rejoined Bering in Yakutsk and instantly increased the population of that isolated fur-trading center by 150 percent. Now there was a severe crisis in housing as the expedition continued to disrupt the normal activities of the town by its formidable demands.

Spangberg had already stopped here during the spring of 1734. For lack of sufficient boats ready for him, he was obliged to store in the town almost all the provisions (flour, groats, salt, and butter) he had brought. He left on June 27 with fifteen boats, on which he carried iron and shipbuilding matériel as well as only 43 of the 416 tons of provisions he was supposed to convey to Okhotsk. On September 15, when his progress was halted by river ice, he built storehouses to be guarded by most of his party while he and some other men skied overland to Okhotsk and others returned to Yakutsk to report to Bering.

Apart from sending continuous relief to Spangberg's men, Bering devoted his first year in Yakutsk chiefly to building and equipping two ships destined to go down the Lena River to its mouth. To one, the double sloop *Yakutsk*, he appointed Lieutenant V. M. Pronchishchev as commander. It left Yakutsk on June 29, 1735, reached open sea on August 13, and wintered west of the mouth of the Lena. It resumed its voyage on August 1, 1736, and despite heavy ice reached 77°29'N, just twenty miles south of the northernmost tip of Asia. By the end of the month his party was back in the same winter quarters as the year before, but here both Pronchishchev and his wife died of scurvy. Only in 1741–42 did Lieutenant Kharlam P. Laptev, Pronchishchev's successor, complete the coastline survey to the Yenesei River, largely on foot.

Bering assigned the other vessel, the *Irkutsk*, to Lassenius. It wintered about sixty miles east of the mouth of the Lena. When Bering received the tragic news of this lieutenant's death along with the deaths of thirty-nine of his crew, he appointed as commander Lieutenant Dmitry Laptev, the other Laptev's cousin, and ordered him and a new party to trek overland to the ship. Laptev set sail on August 11, 1736, and reached 73°16'N before meeting a sea of ice.

Upon receiving reports of repeated failure to penetrate the entire Arctic coastline, Bering invited both his officers and the academic members of the expedition to state their views about prospects for navigation on the northern coast. They were unanimous in asserting that a sea passage was impossible. These opinions did not, however, deter the Admiralty College. If the coast could not be charted from the sea, then it must be done by land. But Dmitry Laptev was allowed, if necessary, to leave the coast at the mouth of the Kolyma and go upriver toward Anadyrsk and all the way to the Kamchatka peninsula. In 1743 he finally completed an amazing survey over great distances in desolate and dangerous country.

In Yakutsk, Bering found himself mired in an administrative morass. Too little had been done. Much was needed. Nothing was going particularly well. Time was slipping by. He was not fulfilling his orders "to find the shortest route to the Sea of Kamchatka [Sea of Okhotsk] without going to Iakutsk."[7] He was expected to describe rivers flowing from the east into Lake Baikal and the Lena River and from the sources of these rivers to find a new route to the Ud (Uda) River, bypassing Yakutsk and shortening the distance to the Pacific Ocean and Kamchatka. The object of these orders was clear—to find a better way to the sea without disturbing the Chinese, who controlled the Amur River region.

Bering conscientiously attempted to carry out these orders. On August 10, 1734, before he left Irkutsk, he had sent off two surveyors with an interpreter, guides, soldiers, and carts full of provisions to follow the post road to Nerchinsk. From that military outpost near the edge of Chinese territory they were to continue eastward "to find the nearest possible route" to the Sea of Okhotsk. On June 3, 1736, both surveyors showed up in Yakutsk. They had not completed their assignment because the soldiers, guides, and interpreter had disobeyed their orders. When all but five members of the party had run off, the surveyors decided that, without an interpreter and a larger force, it was too risky to proceed.[8]

So once again, as with parties headed north to the Arctic Ocean, Bering made arrangements for the surveyors to return to Irkutsk and be reinforced again with an interpreter, guides, and soldiers, and this time with a corporal charged with preventing desertions. This time they nearly succeeded, having traveled 900 miles from Nerchinsk to the Zeya River, whose source is but a short distance over a divide to the sources of the Maya River, a tributary of the Ud. In other words, they came within a few hundred miles of their destination, Udskaya Bay of the Sea of Okhotsk. They were stopped because, they said, their guides did not know where to go beyond the Zeya River and, worse, they were running out of food.[9]

Two failures left Bering in a quandary. If he were to send out the surveyors a third time, they should have different guides, such as natives and cossacks who lived near the mouth of the Ud and were familiar with passes through the coastal mountains. But he was not convinced that the effort would be worth the added expense. The surveyors' report assured him that the post road to Nerchinsk was unfit for use. In places it was nearly impassable because of steep grades or boggy ground. Beyond the post road there were no habitations in which travelers could rest and insufficient forage for horses and oxen. Finally, although the distance from Irkutsk to Udskaya Bay was shorter than from Irkutsk to Okhotsk by way of Yakutsk, there was no substitute for the Lena River, especially with the Amur River off limits. It was not until January 22, 1739, when he was in Okhotsk, that Bering reported these findings to the Admiralty College and requested further instruction.

Another problem was the timely manufacture and transport of cannon and ball for ships to be built at Okhotsk, together with the construction of an ironworks in the vicinity of Yakutsk. From the beginning there had been bureaucratic slippage. It was not until the eve of departure from St. Petersburg, on January 5, 1733, that the Admiralty College even considered what artillery and artillery supplies would be needed for the Second Kamchatka Expedition. Bering was then asked to provide a list as well as a schedule of his anticipated arrival times in Siberian towns "where one could find what of ready-made items . . . have been made there in order to avoid superfluous expense and trouble in transporting them from here."[10] It was abundantly clear to Bering that Siberian towns could not immediately satisfy his needs. Evidently he persuaded the Admiralty College to act promptly because it issued orders for cannon to be produced at a private foundry in the Urals. But when the Admiralty increased the number of cannon, the decision was made to use government foundries instead. Then when in June the cannon produced by the first government foundry selected were found to be of poor quality, the Admiralty decided, on August 3, to use the Kamensky foundry, some 300 miles west of Tobolsk, and to send there a master caster and a bore driller. This foundry was a good choice; it was one of the oldest in Russia (established in 1700) and was reputed to be the very best for the casting of iron because of the excellent quality of its local ores. But delays continued to occur, first concerning the inscription to be cast on the cannon and then about getting certain apprentice furnace operators sent from Yekaterinburg, sixty miles away.

By the end of August production had finally begun and by the end of September, with Spangberg already in Tobolsk, came demands for delivery of cannon and ball. But they were not ready and Spangberg could not wait. On November 22 Bering stopped in Yekaterinburg to make inquiries about the status of cannon and to arrange for an ironworks to be built near Yakutsk. But only in February were cannon delivered in Tobolsk by means of a pack train of fifty-six carts.[11] All this artillery reached Yakutsk the following July and was expedited to Okhotsk by Chirikov and Waxell, arriving there on June 3, 1736.

The Yakutsk ironworks, built on the Lena River twenty miles upstream from the town, had a different outcome. It was not completed until September 24, 1735. To save expense, it had only a water-powered hammer and dam but no blast furnace. On December 8, 1735, Bering wrote Ostermann that this ironworks had produced little more than a ton of such articles as nails and bolts before October 2, when the "factory ceased operation because due to the great cold here the water in the river . . . froze and it was impossible to draw iron."[12] Ore for this factory, mined thirty-five miles farther upstream, was easily rafted to it. But in the end, it was no substitute at all for the Kamensky and other Ural foundries.

Like the governor at Tobolsk, the vice governor at Irkutsk, and the district governor at Yakutsk, Vitus and Anna brought Western European privilege, culture, and class into Siberia. Wherever they lodged, the Berings had household servants whom they brought with them. Anna had an early version of the piano, a clavichord, which she played to amuse herself, to teach her children, and perhaps even to entertain Siberian administrators, wealthy merchants, and officers of the expedition and their families who were welcomed into the captain-commander's home.

In dress the Berings were the exemplary lord and lady. From the lists of clothing sold at auction after his death it is possible to picture the commander from head to toe, adorned with a white wig, white collar, a shirt of Holland linen, a long satin vest trimmed with ermine, black satin trousers, black silk stockings, and laced-up shoes of Chinese velvet. Anna had a selection of dressing gowns of silk or velvet, Polish cloaks lined with Persian brocade, and a variety of furs.

Her table was also splendid. She had a silver service for everyday use and for company a fine porcelain service of thirty-six plates, cups, and saucers, six teapots, two vinegar pitchers, and two large silver tureens, each weighing more than eight pounds. Besides these treasures, she had large quantities of Chinese cottons and silks, six lacquer boxes, and nine dolls.

The Berings were newly and fashionably rich in a highly stratified Russian society. Their clothing and household possessions were considered appropriate even in Siberia. Such goods were a badge of who they were as responsible agents of an imperial state. The burden of transporting their belongings was wholly acceptable, as were the costs of a suitable residence in such frontier communities as Yakutsk and Okhotsk. Though they were exposed to inconveniences of travel on rivers and portages and even to the dangers of getting lost in the mountains, the Bering family on the Second Kamchatka Expedition had no occasion to become accustomed to what Samuel Clemens, in another place and time, called "roughing it."

By the time Müller, Gmelin, and Delisle de La Croyère, with their entourage, pulled up to the wharves at Yakutsk on September 11, 1736, aboard a dozen boats, the expedition faced a third winter in the town, still gearing up for the transport of freight over the coastal range sufficient for the voyages to Japan. Small flatboats were being built to convey about 1,000 tons of goods. Horses and workmen were being rounded up. Huts were being constructed at intervals along the 100-mile trail between Yudoma Cross and Okhotsk. Here guards would be posted to keep the huts warm to give relief to each man harnessed to a sledge with a 150-pound load or to men leading horses with 200-pound loads. Also storehouses were built along the treacherous Urak River, which debouched into the sea a dozen miles from Okhotsk. Waxell was to be in charge of this most difficult river transport.

With 800 of its people quartered in Yakutsk, a town with only 249 houses, the expedition was like an Egyptian plague of locusts. The arrival of the academicians caused an immediate housing crisis. But by the second night the professors had their own good houses, and as winter approached, their artists and students got better lodging.

The professors, however, were not satisfied. They were accustomed to commodious lodging, and they suspected that favoritism was being accorded to wealthy fur traders whose homes had not been requisitioned. Müller and Gmelin lodged complaints with Bering, to no avail. Then they attempted to go around the commander by appealing to the town's district governor, again without success. For the two professors the question of accommodations was critical. They were to continue on, with Bering's assistance, to Okhotsk and from Okhotsk across the sea to Kamchatka. (La Croyère knew that he would go farther, to America. As "extraordinary professor" he was outranked by his two younger colleagues and did not share their expectations.) If they were disappointed in their assigned quarters in Yakutsk, what would be their fate in Okhotsk and on Kamchatka? During the course of the fall and winter such questions became increasingly urgent. On November 10, while the two professors were being entertained by the captain-commander in his residence, Gmelin's house burned down. He lost almost everything, all his collections and notes of the past year and many of his books. He began to think that during the next summer he needed to repeat his travels between Yakutsk and Irkutsk to recover much of what he had lost. Müller became so concerned about his health that on December 16 he requested that, unless it improved, he be relieved of his responsibilities in Siberia. Undoubtedly he suffered from depression and poor circulation, for which frequent bloodlettings were no remedy.[13]

Both professors were also considering a five-year termination of their service to the expedition. If they proceeded on to Kamchatka, it seemed likely that there would be no speedy return to St. Petersburg within a year.

Indeed, for them the Siberian experience had been first a surprise and then a shock. They had had an auspicious beginning. Müller was highly gratified that the governor of Siberia had not only opened Tobolsk archives to him but also facilitated his copying of documents, and Gmelin appreciated courtesies extended to him when the governor accompanied him on an excursion outside Tobolsk. The professors could not then fully appreciate the governor's care for their safety by assigning extra soldiers to them and by insisting that cannon be mounted on each of their riverboats.

How different was Irkutsk! The vice governor there expected them to pay their own expenses, denying that their orders obligated him in any way. To continue on their way, the professors had to resort to having their men seize the horses they needed. Fortunately, when they later returned to Irkutsk, the new vice governor was more obliging, and they enjoyed a pleasant and productive winter.

Gmelin particularly had a hearty disdain for Siberians. He accused them of insubordination, laziness, and desertion. When they drifted down the Lena River with stops here and there, both professors learned the hard way that they dared not let any oarsman go ashore without a guard to ensure his return. "No kindness, no leniency, no friendly address is of any avail," writes Gmelin. "He must be treated with the utmost severity if he is to behave. The worst part, as far as we were concerned, is that we have had to learn all these things by experience, since we had nobody to advise us."[14]

Drunkenness was another matter. Gmelin enjoyed fine German wine and had several kegs with him, but he was appalled by the unrestrained drinking on holy days. Easter was celebrated at sunrise so that it would not interfere with the spree that started at mid-morning. "This ungodly drinking," he writes, "lasted four or five days without interruption, and there was no way of stopping the madness."[15]

Everything in Siberia was new to them—mice and mosquitoes and extremes of heat and cold. The wonder is that the two men were so disciplined, so well organized, and so endlessly curious that shocks to their systems did not deter them from compiling an encyclopedic inventory of the history and natural history of Siberia. Gmelin's signal achievement was his multivolume *Flora sibirica*. Müller, the collector of documents, made astonishing discoveries. Despite his ill health in Yakutsk, he conducted extensive interviews with Russians who had been on Kamchatka and the Kuril Islands, and of course he found in archives the long-forgotten report of Semyon Dezhnev. Bering was pleased to learn about this report.

But he was not pleased that Müller and Gmelin, as well as Skornyakov-Pisarev, were sending back to St. Petersburg alarming general criticisms about his leadership, that he and Spangberg "had little success in whatever they undertook," and that in Yakutsk "everything went on so slowly that one could not foresee when the trip to Kamchatka would begin." The professors even requested that "sterner orders" be issued to Bering concerning his responsibilities toward them.[16]

Perhaps Bering too was learning from experience that gentlemen of refinement and learning out of their element were not to be trusted. He had supported the appointment of Müller. He had been solicitous that they arrive in good time in Tobolsk. He had sought to advance all the objectives of the Second Kamchatka Expedition, to carry out all orders issued to him despite the handicaps under which he labored—the need to consult with local authorities, overcome their reluctance and inactivity, and endure the labors of Sisyphus—to repeatedly confront "local conditions," whether of Arctic ice, shallow rivers, uncooperative administrators, or rebellious temporary workers. It was time, Bering concluded, to put the needs of the projected voyages first. So on the eve of departure to Okhotsk, July 8, 1737, he would make no promises to Müller and Gmelin regarding their provisions, their lodgings, or their comforts aboard ship en route to Kamchatka. No doubt Bering was much relieved to learn that the two prickly professors decided to postpone their own trip to the peninsula, sending instead one of their students to prepare for their later projected arrival. This student was Stepan P. Krasheninnikov, who would accompany Professor Delisle de La Croyère as far as Okhotsk but act independently of him in carrying out instructions provided by Müller and Gmelin.

Even as late as the summer of 1737 the overland trail to Okhotsk was not well marked all the way. Also circumstances dictated the speed of travel. Once Anna Bering's horse ran off and left her and her small children at risk of hunger and cold. She wrote her brother-in-law Anton von Saltza: "My Bering himself did not know at that time where I lost my way." She implies that after they were rescued, she did not tell him everything about this mishap out of concern that he would blame himself.[17]

Fortunately, Krasheninnikov quotes from his journal in his later published work, *Explorations of Kamchatka*, wherein he describes the nature of the route. Generally, he says,

> it is not bad from Iakutsk to the Belaia [River] crossing, but from there to Okhotsk, it is as miserable and difficult as one could possibly imagine; one [must] continually follow the riverbanks or cross over wooded mountains. The banks of the rivers are filled with huge rocks and round stones; it is amazing that the horses were able to walk on them [at all]; a number of the horses were lamed. The higher the mountains are, the muddier they become. On the summits are huge marshes, and places filled with quicksand. If a packhorse becomes mired there is no way to pull it out; and when one is walking one is absolutely horrified to see how the earth quivers in waves for ten *sazhens* [seventy feet].[18]

The first part of the trek was relatively easy because the grade was gentle, fresh water was available from countless lakes and streams, and fresh horses were available at several stations built in 1735 and maintained by Yakuts or cossacks. It was possible to cover twenty miles during each of the first five days but only ten miles or fewer thereafter. Krasheninnikov reports that there was a post on the Kokora River where travelers could purchase beef on the hoof. Once bought, cattle were prodded in front of them along the trail. Then, as needed, an animal was butchered and the meat divided, roasted, and eaten all at once because it would not keep.

Difficulties began at the Belaya River because it had to be crossed three times. During heavy rains fording could be extremely dangerous because of the swift current and high water. Under these conditions parties had to wait rather than attempt to raft across. About forty miles beyond the Belaya the trail passed near a lake that remained frozen even during warm summer days. Further ascent, several days, and many stream crossings later led to several small glaciers lying across valleys.

Krasheninnikov reports that a crucifix still marked the ford of the Yudoma River en route to a small entrepôt consisting of two houses for naval officers, a tavern for soldiers, and five storehouses. A short distance away were several more buildings, including another storehouse for provisions and munitions destined for Okhotsk.[19]

The route twenty miles over a divide to the Urak River had two disadvantages: there was no place where horses could graze and the trail was so steep that carts or wagons could not be used. From the Urak River landing the trail crossed the river five times during a steep descent. Fortunately heated huts had been built for the expedition's use at approximately ten-mile intervals. The final segment of the trail followed the Okhota River down to the old village, about four miles from the new port of Okhotsk.[20]

Until 1735 Okhotsk had remained, in Bering's words, "new and empty," with "no construction of any sort." There were still only the same houses he had known during the First Kamchatka Expedition. It had not become the thriving commercial port envisioned in 1731, when Skorniakov-Pisarev was appointed commandant. Spangberg's first project was to build sleds to haul logs with which to build a new expedition town. The new port was situated off a spit of the Okhota River where newly constructed ships could be sheltered. By 1742 Okhotsk had 102 buildings, of which 73 were houses. Even so, the new site was far from ideal. Fresh water had to be hauled two miles, wood for stoves four or five miles, and timber for ships twenty miles. The river current was so strong that it was difficult to keep ships in their berths. The water depth in the harbor was only ten to twelve feet. Also, just beyond the mouth of the river was a sandbank only seven feet underwater, ready to snare an unwary vessel. The port itself was subject to flooding when the highest tides rolled in. Okhotsk, with all its drawbacks, was ill suited to be a permanent port.[21]

Spangberg's decision to build ships here was dictated both by the availability of timber nearby for shipbuilding and by the likely danger of attack by Itelmens on Kamchatka. From Yakutsk Bering and Chirikov were able to maintain a steady supply of provisions on the trail to Okhotsk to keep Spangberg's carpenters fed and busy. In 1737 he had not only refitted the *Archangel Gabriel* from the First Kamchatka Expedition but also constructed two new ships, the brig *Archangel Michael* and the double sloop *Nadezhda*. Provisions arriving with Bering in the summer of 1737 were sufficient to supply all three ships for their first voyage toward Japan the next year.

Meanwhile, Skornyakov-Pisarev, operating from the old village, assumed responsibility for the *Fortuna*. It had returned from Bolsheretsk on August 23, 1737, just a few days after Bering had arrived to set up his headquarters in new Okhotsk. After being loaded, the *Fortuna* left the port with Krasheninnikov on board for the shuttle to Kamchatka. At this time the little ship was a supply link between the commandant in Okhotsk and the military and government men on Kamchatka for whom he was responsible. The tenuous nature of this link is evident in Krasheninnikov's account of his passage.

Only nine hours out of Okhotsk the ship had taken on an alarming amount of seawater. "Men down in the hold," says Krasheninnikov, "were standing in water up to their knees." The water did not recede even with two pumps operating and with every man on board bailing water constantly with pots and pans and anything else that was handy. When seawater began to flood the ship through portholes, Krasheninnikov says, "We threw overboard everything on deck or fastened around the ship; but this had no effect and so we jettisoned about four hundred puds [7.2 tons] of cargo in addition, taken at random." With such desperate measures, the water subsided and remained controllable as long as the pumps were manned continuously. After ten days of exposure to snow mixed with rain, passengers and crew were much relieved to see the estuary of the Bolshaya River. But their situation was now life-threatening. The sea was at ebb tide, sending out high, foaming waves from the mouth of the river. In Krasheninnikov's words: "These waves were so wild that they swept right over the ship, which was very badly split in many places. There was no hope of entering the mouth of the river, because of the unfavorable wind and the swiftness of the outgoing tide. . . . We were cast up on shore. . . . Our ship was soon completely out of the water, for the tide continued to go out." After flood tide the next morning, the survivors on the shore found only planks from the wreck of the ship. They were black, "so rotten," says Krasheninnikov, "that one could easily break them by hand."[22] The rest of the ship had been swept out to sea. A week later boats from Bolsheretsk rescued the beleaguered men. Thus did Krasheninnikov begin the academy's work on Kamchatka, almost literally with only the shirt on his back.

It was just as well that Müller and Gmelin had not accompanied him. Somehow he managed on his own with whatever he could beg or borrow in Bolsheretsk. Two miserable, complaining professors might have been too great a burden for their student. More to the point, the loss of the *Fortuna*, built in 1727 and by its very name auguring well for the First Kamchatka Expedition, now seemed to signal the foundering of the much larger Second Kamchatka Expedition.

Bering in Okhotsk was set up for failure. On the one hand, the government in St. Petersburg had promised to facilitate transport in Siberia. Nothing would be lacking. Authorities would have riverboats, horses, munitions, provisions, and workers ready. On the other hand, it is clear from the last instructions issued Bering in March 1733 that the Russian government had wholly unrealistic expectations about what the captain-commander would be confronted with in mounting multiple voyages along the Arctic coastline, along the Kuril Islands toward Japan, and from Kamchatka to North America. "Find a way to buy and transport provisions without [great] effort and expense," his instructions say.[23] How was Bering to accomplish economies? His instructions direct him to consult with local authorities and with his own officers. They direct him to find a less arduous, shorter route to Kamchatka. When others (such as Skornyakov-Pisarev) did not carry out their instructions, Bering was expected to assume their responsibilities so as not to delay the whole grand enterprise. In fact, the imperial government expected that no more than four years would be needed to complete all objectives of the Second Kamchatka Expedition, and that its cost, apart from salaries and freight, would amount to no more than 12,000 rubles. After four years Bering was still in Yakutsk, and after five years, with the captain-commander at last in Okhotsk, expenses were exceeding 300,000 rubles. What had been accomplished?

Nothing and everything. Nothing had been wholly and satisfactorily completed, but practically everything was diligently being carried out— at a cost not just in rubles.

For Bering's instructions distributed pain all around. First, there was pain for the Siberians, who were understandably reluctant to deplete their own resources. Rural areas of the Irkutsk district especially fell into "extreme ruin." Its peasants were obliged to haul expedition provisions to distant places. Some men were away for years, unable to plow their own land, harvest their crops, or repair their homes. Bering's own men suffered privation, especially in Okhotsk in 1738 and 1739. Bering's report of July 11, 1738, to Golovin is grim: "There are no clothes or shoes for the servitors of my command . . . because no salaries have been sent from Irkutsk by the provincial administration. . . . While transporting provisions, they became very emaciated, and in wintertime some hands and feet were frozen by the severe cold, and because of such difficulty and the lack of other victuals many can barely walk, and throughout the month of June, 22 men were sick, and all became emaciated."[24] Spangberg's three ships, with a total of 151 men aboard, took nearly all the provisions in Okhotsk when they departed for the Kuril Islands on June 29, 1738. Consequently, Bering had to retrieve the provisions warehoused in Yudoma Cross.

There were two routes from the Urak River landing, the trail used throughout the year and the river itself, but only in the spring when its water level was highest. At that time, with a little luck, a riverboat loaded with three tons of freight could travel 138 miles downstream in seventeen hours without using oars or sail. But according to Waxell, risks were extreme: "The moment a little rain falls [the river] overflows its banks and submerges a large, low-lying part of the country. . . . Our boats were often swept [two miles] or more into the forest."[25]

Getting those boats back into the river channel as quickly as possible before the rain stopped was agonizing toil. Under these circumstances Waxell was notorious for the tongue-lashings he gave his workmen.[26]

Lack of food and timber affected construction of two ships for the American voyage. One keel was completed on August 27, 1738, but work stopped for lack of timber. A total of 665 logs was needed for building two packets. These had to be cut and hauled down the Okhota River.[27]

But Waxell says that during 1739 it was the shortage of provisions that interrupted shipbuilding. "We were forced to send most of [twenty carpenters] to the storehouses on the Urak [River] and to Iudoma Cross to assist in transporting our supplies from those two places."[28] Only in late 1739 and early 1740 could shipbuilding be resumed. It was finally completed on July 2, 1740, with the arrival of sailcloth from St. Petersburg and adequate provisions from Yudoma Cross.

Bering himself was severely criticized as the time of the expedition was prolonged from four to eight years, from 1737 to 1741. Spangberg thought that his commander was too considerate in his dealings with the "foul-tongued" Skornyakov-Pisarev, to whose written complaints Bering attempted to respond. "For a correspondence with him alone . . . I might use three good secretaries," the captain-commander writes. Spangberg's way was to ignore Skornyakov-Pisarev altogether and to force native inhabitants to work under threat of being attacked by the huge dog he often held by a leash. Chirikov, who in Okhotsk regarded Spangberg as his "archenemy," was also a critic of his commander. In a letter of June 28, 1738, he writes Golovin: "I am reduced to virtual uselessness since my proposals to [Bering] are not accepted. . . . He bears only malice toward me for them."[29]

Chirikov, however, was not deterred from proposing that in 1740 he be sent to survey the coast of America opposite the Chukotka peninsula. Bering would not give permission because such a trip was not in his instructions. Of course, by this time he knew that the *Archangel Gabriel* had already been there under Gvozdev in 1732. Given the tensions of sustaining an expedition of such magnitude for so long, Spangberg and Chirikov might well be exasperated by their commander's insistence on working with local authorities and adhering to instructions. Bering was well aware that he was now under close scrutiny in St. Petersburg. As an expression of dissatisfaction with the slow progress of the expedition, the Admiralty College in 1737 had cut his salary in half. On September 13 of the next year Anna's cabinet consulted with the Senate and Admiralty about abruptly terminating the expedition. Bering no longer had outspoken defenders. Saunders, Bering's brother-in-law, had died in 1733 and Kirilov in 1737. Kirilov's successor proposed that Spangberg, who moved quickly and decisively, should replace Bering.[30]

Golovin, who argued effectively for the continuation of the expedition, was more inclined to trust Chirikov than Bering. When Lieutenant Mikhail G. Plautin accused him of arbitrariness and extravagance (and, more seriously, of embezzlement during the First Kamchatka Expedition), Bering put him under arrest. Golovin ordered Chirikov to investigate and to make his report to Bering as well as to the Admiralty.[31] In this case, Chirikov was authorized to free Plautin if he concluded that the arrest was not justified. Plautin in fact was released and sailed to America under Chirikov. This incident was obviously humiliating to the commander and no doubt disconcerting to the subordinate who was obliged to pass judgment. Perhaps the imminent launching of the two packets, with a divided command at sea, preserved a naval relationship that might otherwise have become unbearable.

Meanwhile, Spangberg's first sea expedition had limited success. The three ships became separated in the foggy, stormy Kuril Islands. About thirty islands were seen, and all three ships returned to Bolsheretsk by September 4, 1738, without making landings or seeing Hokkaido or Honshu.

A second sea expedition the following year had spectacular results. Leaving Okhotsk on June 1, 1739, a flotilla of four ships again became separated. Spangberg commanded the newest vessel, the sloop *Bolsheretsk*, constructed on Kamchatka the previous winter. He came within sight of the northeast coast of Honshu on June 27, traded goods with two junks, and broke off exchanges when seventy-nine Japanese boats appeared around him. Spangberg was able to describe the Japanese boats and the stature and physiognomy of the Japanese. He reported also the visit of four men to his cabin. They wore cloaks embroidered at the shoulder and waist. Upon entering the cabin they knelt and bowed down to the floor. They seemed to relish the food and drink Spangberg served them. When he showed them a chart and a globe, they informed him that they called their nation Nippon, not Japan.[32]

Spangberg was confident that he had found Japan. He had sailed between 38° and 40° north latitude, where Europeans already knew Japan was located. He had received, he was sure, Japanese coins. After stopping at one of the Kuril Islands, where eight Ainu came aboard (their entire bodies were covered with quite long hair), Spangberg was back at Okhotsk on September 9.

Lieutenant William Walton, commander of the *Archangel Gabriel*, reached the southeast coast of Honshu at 37°42'N on June 27. He sent his longboat ashore with eight men to obtain fresh water. The men were able to land and get the water. Two stayed with their boat while the others were treated to wine, rice, and fruit in town. They were the first Russians in Japan. Upon their return to the ship, Walton continued to sail to the south along the coast before reversing direction northward on July 5. A month later he too was back in Okhotsk.[33]

The other two ships had indifferent success, one wintering at Bolsheretsk and, because of ice, not returning to Okhotsk until the spring of 1740.

Upon his return from Japan, Spangberg submitted a report and log-books to Bering, who in turn shared them with Skornyakov-Pisarev. The latter insisted that Spangberg and Walton had reached Korea, not Japan, and that their charts of Japan and the Kurils were erroneous, because they were at odds with earlier maps showing larger islands extending toward America. Skornyakov-Pisarev's views were respected in St. Petersburg, since he had once been director of the Naval Academy. But obviously he was getting his revenge against Spangberg, who rushed off to St. Petersburg to defend himself but was stopped in Ust-Kut by an Admiralty order to repeat his voyage.

In the foulest of moods, Spangberg returned to Okhotsk.

Twin ships were anchored in the harbor. They were well built. Each was 90 feet long from stem to stern, 23 feet wide, and 9½ feet high (the height of the stern post). Each had a displacement of 211 tons. Each had fourteen mounted cannon. Each had a fairly commodious captain's cabin where a dozen officers could meet, an officers' cabin for six men, stern quarters with bunks and hammocks for eighteen men, mid-quarters with double bunks for twenty-four men, a bow storeroom bunking six junior officers, bow quarters with bunks for twenty-two men—alto-gether spaces for seventy-six men, not including the captain.

There were to be provisions for each man for six months. With ballast, firewood, 100 barrels of water, and artillery, the cargo weighed 106 tons. There were eighteen barrels of salted beef; other foodstuffs for the sea voyage would go as far as Kamchatka on a separate vessel. Supplies included seventeen barrels of gunpowder. In the hold were two large anchors and two small spares. Two pumps were located in front of the larger of the two masts for getting any seawater out of the hold. Behind the same mast was a capstan to be used with heavy rigging. A windlass at the bow was for raising anchors and taking down foresails. The deck itself had three hatches and one cargo opening. The two shore boats were a ten-oared longboat, nineteen feet long, and a six-oared yawl. The longboat could accommodate ten barrels with twenty-five buckets. Each shore boat had a mast with rigging.[34]

On August 19, everything in the port was nearly ready for departure.

The two ships destined for America were about to be loaded. Anna Bering and her two children, now 10 and 9 years of age, were packed. They said their good-byes. Now accompanied by the many expedition personnel who were not leaving on the two packets, they started up the trail, Anna and her two children carried in a sedan chair. They were beginning the long journey back home to St. Petersburg.

Vitus Bering would never see his wife and their children again.

LETTERS HOME

Anna Bering in Command

About a dozen personal letters for Vitus and Anna Bering arrived in Okhotsk on December 4, 1739, delivered by a lieutenant who was a special courier from the Admiralty College in St. Petersburg. Letters the couple wrote in reply, and several others as well, are dated February 2, 4, and 5, 1740. Some of them, particularly the longer ones, were probably written over days, if not weeks, the date indicating their completion. The wonder is that the letters sent from Okhotsk—six from Bering, eight from his wife, and two from 9-year-old Anton—have survived. They were found in February 1996, 256 years later, in archives of the Russian foreign ministry and published the following year in Denmark.[1]

The letters are a revelation. They show the anguish of a family riven by time and distance. They disclose the identity of two of their highly placed and potentially influential correspondents. They reveal Anna as a mother who is smart, outspoken, and persistent. She is also imperious in relationships with her siblings and amazingly frank in writing to a powerful friend. As for her husband, the captain-commander, it is clear that they were almost always of one mind on family matters. It is also clear, by inference, that she was influencing the course of his career. They were a most ambitious couple.

It was a critical time. They were soon to part, he to go to sea and she, with two young children, to begin her return journey. But the letters do not show particular concern about the approaching separation. From their perspective, the voyage to America and the return to St. Petersburg were entirely in God's care.

It is also remarkable that the letters say little about Okhotsk. It is in "a wilderness." Native peoples of the area, the Tungus, are only occasionally mentioned. Anna remarks that they are better-looking than the Yakuts. She seems amazed that native women as well as men ride reindeer. Both Anna and her husband note that a few dozen Tungus were baptized that winter. Bering himself, however, does not seek more missionaries. Instead he wants schoolmasters for both the Okhotsk seaboard and the Kamchatka peninsula.

Virtually nothing at all is written about members of the expedition, including the few officers' wives. Chirikov had his wife and daughter with him. Spangberg was also accompanied by his wife, but according to Chirikov, they were busy with their own gain, Spangberg distilling vodka and exchanging it for furs and his wife selling tobacco to native women for "unheard-of high prices."[2] However critically Chirikov regarded the Spangbergs, Vitus and Anna Bering outwardly remained above such feelings in their hospitality to the officers and in Bering's responsibility for the entire expedition.

In her letters Anna is singularly obsessed with her two older boys, whom she has not seen in nearly seven years. She knows that the future of the family depends on them. The elder has left the Reval gymnasium and the professor's family with whom he was boarded. Anna worries that, having obtained their permission to go into the army at St. Petersburg, he might be throwing his life away by consorting with wastrels in the military. By all reports, the second son is excelling in his studies and may be destined for a university. They are 19 and 16 (17 in May), but one suspects that Anna still sees them as they were when she left them, not yet teenagers and certainly too young to be making their way in the world without her guidance. She concentrates her anxieties on these two boys, particularly on the older one.

Her mother having died, Anna is the matriarch. Even though she is 5,000 miles by river and trail from St. Petersburg, though she has been away from her father, brother, two sisters, and two sons for nearly seven years, she attempts to continue her beneficent, firm rule through correspondence. In this rule her husband is wholly supportive. He often prepares the way by introducing a topic. Then she follows up, usually with strong feeling, making specific points. He suggests; she calls for action. He initiates; she concludes. He writes man to man, whether brother-in-law, son, or influential friend. In this way he gives legitimacy to her explicit follow-up. This team approach takes advantage of the particular skills each brings to a subject of concern. She writes not only woman to woman but woman to man. If he seems distant and at times obtuse, she moves in swiftly with art and grace. Above all, she makes her meaning very clear.

They operate, it is true, in overlapping realms, he over the expedition and she over their family. While he is a kindly paternal figure in the family, she is outspoken in decrying their nomadic life with the expedition. They are a commanding couple, but the letters suggest that she has influence far beyond his; therefore, she is invaluable to him. Moreover, however imposing his physical appearance, she truly commands the commander intellectually in her articulation and emotionally in her expression.

Three letters to Anton and Helena von Saltza serve to illustrate the Bering husband-and-wife team approach. Bering and Saltza have much in common. They are close in age (Bering is two years older). They both have Scandinavian roots, Saltza having served under Charles XII of Sweden in the Great Northern War. Both have noble rank, Bering by virtue of his promotion to captain-commander and his brother-in-law through his hereditary prefix *von*. Both enjoy distinction in service to Russia. As assessor in St. Petersburg, Saltza is a financial manager in civil government, if not also by this time a member of the city council.

Through their marriage to sisters, Bering and Saltza are bound together in substantial family responsibilities, especially Saltza, who represents the family in St. Petersburg in decisions affecting Jonas and Thomas Bering. He is not, however, alone in these decisions. He is expected to confer on major questions with Nikolai Sebastian von Hohenholz, the Austrian resident in St. Petersburg, whom Bering addresses as "dearest friend" and "your highness." Although the captain-commander may be an absent father, he retains primary responsibility for his two older sons. Yet the letters indicate that this is not simply a responsibility he shares with his wife; she is the driving force for whom he is the obliging, concurring partner. In short, he heralds her extended solo act.

Following wishes for health and a future reunion and thanks for acting on his behalf in receiving funds from the Admiralty College, Bering introduces his primary concern to Saltza, the welfare of his two sons. It makes sense, he says, that the younger (Thomas) advance to prime— that is, to the pre-university course with instruction in Latin—in the gymnasium he has been attending in Reval. As for the older (Jonas), he acknowledges that "last year I and my dear wife granted him his wish to join the army as a private in an ordinary regiment."[3] But now there are concerns: He might forget what he has learned at school. He might not use his free time to good advantage by learning Russian and horsemanship. Bering does not make any specific requests but expresses two wishes: that Jonas keep learning despite "weak eyes and a poor memory" and that he not leave St. Petersburg with his regiment before his mother's return to that city.

Bering's letter is cordial and thoughtful while maintaining a respectful distance. The two men are acquaintances, having met only at intervals when Bering was in St. Petersburg in 1732–33, when Saltza was newly married to Helena.

Anna knows Saltza better, writing him confidentially as "my brother" in answer to two of his letters, including his questions about her well-being and specifically about her getting lost on the trail between Yakutsk and Okhotsk. "What I cannot tell *him*," she says, "I will tell you."[4] She supplies a justification. It would make her husband sick to know what might have happened to her and the two children. But the fact remains: there is a trust, a secret, a line of communication that she is suggesting is established between them.

Moreover, what he has she wants. It is not said outright; it is implied. She pities, she says, two of their female relatives who must cope with the paralysis of their mates. "With officers," she says, "it is the same. *It is an unsettled life*."[5] The message she intends to convey is that she pities herself. This message is an invitation for him to commiserate with her. He has a settled life.

As for Jonas's situation, she confesses that "for the life of me, *this* I cannot deal with." Does it take longer to get into the horse guards? What's the rush? After all, she writes, "he's just turned 19." She does not want him sent off with the army. He still has a lot to learn: Russian and horsemanship, of course, and, above all good judgment. She dwells on money. Money is what she and her husband have to provide for their children's future.[6]

What she really wants is for Jonas to change his mind and obtain a position in civil service. But if the military is his preference, then she'd have him become a sublieutenant, even his father's adjutant, or join the horse guards. Though her mind is quite made up about alternatives for Jonas's future, she pretends to invite Saltza's counsel: "I leave to you whether Jonas should be a musketeer or spend a year or more to be a sublieutenant." She adds: "I hope that my brother does not think ill of me for not concealing my thoughts. Jonas's situation has cost me many tears. I cannot have peace until I get better news."[7]

Saltza is "brother," not brother-in-law. As brother, he is privy to her insights into her husband's possible feelings if he were to know that she and the children had been lost on the trail. He is privy to her yearning for a settled life, and he knows what she desperately wants for Jonas. Obviously she confides in this man who has been a father figure to her two older children, who, from her perspective, are very definitely still children in need of parental guidance.

Whereas Bering's letter to Saltza expresses gratitude for Hohenholz's trouble and care on behalf of both Jonas and Thomas, Anna's letter to Saltza does not mention the Austrian minister, nor indeed does it mention Thomas. She makes herself vulnerable with tears, appeals for guidance, and flattering confidences. It seems clear that these two have become very close.

Anna's tone is predictably different with her sister Helena, who has told her that both sons came to St. Petersburg and stopped at the Saltza home. Whereas Thomas was returning to Reval, Jonas stayed in the capital. But who could take him in? Her sister writes that she wanted to, but she had no vacant room. Anna responds: "Thank you for your kind inclination. He should not be presumptuous. I know well that you have a house full of small children." She adds that there was no problem: "The most honorable wife of the Resident put in another bed for him." The inference here is that her sister might have done the same. Perhaps Helena is tired of responsibility without reciprocal benefit? Next Anna informs her sister that her husband has recommended that Jonas go to a certain Colonel Uxquil, a riding master in the horse guards, who has other young men like Jonas under his supervision. Anna seems to assume that this information would be news to her sister because it would not necessarily be relayed to her by her much older husband. Such an assumption by an older, all-knowing sister could be hurtful. Finally Anna makes a pledge to Helena: "Anything done for my children in my absence, if God permit me to live, I will do for yours."[8] Anna knows that she has been gone too long. She is indebted, but how deeply she does not know exactly. She must suspect that her sister is weary of obliging her and weary of her worry.

The letter from Anna to Eufemia (now called Elfa) is brief. She knows that this sister is expecting her first child in her second marriage. She tells her that upon her return she will ask for two rooms in her sister's residence and stay "until I see how things turn out."[9] There has been no letter from Eufemia in the last mail; Anna suggests that a letter could be delivered to Frau von Hohenholz for forwarding.

There is also no letter to Anna from her brother, Bendix, but she does not write him. She is concerned about their father, who also lives in Viborg, but strangely she thinks about making inquiries about her father only through Hohenholz. Her letter to her father is affectionate. She is relieved that his house in Viborg was spared in a great fire. She asks if he needs money. (Her father passed away within two months of her letter to him.)

There remain the letters the Berings write their sons. Here the tone is very different. Bering's brief letters to his sons are sobering. He seems to know that these letters could be his last. He faces a voyage. He has not seen his two older sons for seven years. His words of advice seem valedictory.

He addresses Jonas not as a child but as a man. He wishes only what is best for his son's future, and he offers pointed fatherly advice: Listen to your mama. Continue your studies. Learn Russian. Be a good Christian. His benediction is a prayer and a promise: "The Almighty will protect and preserve you."[10] He seems to be saying that Jonas will always have a heavenly Father.

He also expresses positive feelings to Thomas: satisfaction in reports about his studies. His advice to his second son seems to reflect Bering's own prescription for a good life: Fear God. Pray that the Almighty lead you and grant you success. Be at peace with all men. Seek to improve your companions. Despise no one. Be neat and clean in your clothing. Do not think yourself wiser than others. Obey your professor. He concludes by referring Thomas to the admonitions of his mother and by commending him to God's protection.

Anna's advice to her sons is similar: Fear God, show your good upbringing, make us proud of you, and God will pour out his blessings. But while she has warm feelings for Thomas, she, unlike her husband, expresses disappointment and anguish in writing her eldest child. She recommends that Thomas take up Russian to "find fortune in this land." She proposes that he ask Professor Sigismundi, in whose home he is living, to employ a tutor for lessons in playing the bass viol "so you can play a masterpiece for me upon my return." She approves of her son's devotion to his "beautiful fräulein," a daughter in the Sigismundi family.[11]

Anna's letter to Jonas shows her distress. It begins with a rebuke: "With all my heart I rejoice over your good health, but I have very much wondered that my son has no spare time to write a separate letter to his dear mama. His pursuits have not yet become so great that they prevent him from it." She exposes him to a mother's lament—her tears upon learning that he is a musketeer in an ordinary regiment. What a fate, to give up his studies to become a private in the army! "We cannot disguise ourselves, God forbid." She reasons that the person who has learned nothing but what concerns soldiers must stay in a regiment and be subjected to a wandering life. She adjures him to improve his qualifications. She informs him that she has asked Hohenholz to take him out of his regiment. If he wants to stay in the military service, she thinks the horse guards would better promote his welfare. Finally, reflecting no doubt upon what she has written and his reaction to it, she adds a final admonition: Don't be cross.[12]

Anna Bering was a most devoted mother who earnestly and constantly made every effort to give her children advantages. She valued learning and the finer things: music, dress, tea, and conversation. Like her husband, she does not express a developed theology. Their faith is simple and sure: God will help. In her larger family, she claimed precedence over her siblings by virtue of her seniority and her status through her husband's position and their ready cash. Her cultural center was St. Petersburg. She dreamed of having a home there once again, with of course a country estate in the vicinity of Viborg, combining the locales of her birth (Nyen) and upbringing (Viborg) with the splendor of cosmopolitan St. Petersburg.

The letters show that Anna Bering remains focused on her family while also indirectly serving her husband's career. She can do what her husband cannot—pierce through a man's thin shield, engage him, please him, and then stunningly come right to the point. With Hohenholz she is properly grateful and respectful for all he has done, but she also flatters and dazzles him in asking more, much more, for the benefit of her eldest son, Jonas, and indirectly for her husband and herself. Her success with such a man is obvious. She begins by making him the exclusive center of her attention. Her words flow as she opens up and envelops him with confidences, appeals for advice, and sudden turns of language. She shifts from familiar, even intimate address to sharp criticism, then quickly backs off to deflect her sudden thrust yet leaves her concern plainly before him.

This kind of adroit attack is demonstrated in her letter to Hohenholz. She never tells him outright that she blames him for obliging them to give Jonas their parental approval of his desire for a military life. But she is not reconciled with this decision. It gives her bad dreams. She imagines that at his tender age of 19 he will be drawn into sordid living, staggering into pubs and ruining his life in all manner of wretchedness.

She knows she cannot usually pour out her misgivings on men (Jonas excepted), but she can come quickly to the point, win Hohenholz's sympathy, and enlist his aid. Her letter, then, shows her modus operandi for captivating men of influence in any social situation. Her letter to Hohenholz is an introduction to her larger world, her character, her resolve, and her social success.

She begins her letter with expressions of "everlasting debt" and "indelible remembrances" for his benefactions. "It is enough," she says, "that I indicate my feelings." She has the "greatest gratitude" for letting her sons come to him, but she must be frank. "My dearest Badska," she says, "why have you employed [Jonas] so poorly?"[13] Anna is not merely writing a polite, respectful letter. She is confident of her own charm in addressing him in a teasing, familiar way and then bringing him up short with a bluntly critical "so poorly." She has warned him about her feelings, first effusively grateful but now, without warning, sharply critical. Anna evidently knows how to excite and amuse the esteemed diplomat by sudden shifts in her tone. She is conveying to him a conception of who she wants to be to him, a captivating lady friend unpredictably serious and yet playful.

She now instantly drops her bluntness by a disingenuous observation: "*This* is without doubt my brother von Saltza's counsel." Then in her next sentence she bares her deepest feeling: "I have been heartsick over it"—over Jonas's going into a field regiment, of course.[14]

And she is not now asking her distinguished friend what should be done. She is boldly saying that "what is done can be changed."[15] Not by her friends getting Jonas a promotion in his regiment (as he had offered to do). Her husband, in writing Hohenholz, *suggests* such a change as a parental preference, but she wants him to go ahead to get Jonas a transfer.

Anna is pointed. She requests, respectfully of course, that the minister *act* on their behalf. If Jonas could become a noncommissioned officer in the guards, in recognition of time he has already served in his ordinary regiment, such promotion would be "most welcome." Anna also asks her "dear Badska" to arrange for both Russian and riding lessons for Jonas, and she promises to pay the costs. Anna next informs Hohenholz that she has written to Count Ostermann. In writing to him, Anna has truly gone to the top, to Empress Anna's closest adviser and a minister renowned for his cleverness and shrewdness as well as for his ability. What does she ask Ostermann? All that she tells Hohenholz—and it is very little—is that she has asked Ostermann to recommend Jonas and Thomas for any opportunity that may be available. She adds that she hopes that Ostermann is not "against" them.[16]

This bit of information has design. She does not need to be explicit. She knows that the two ministers represent two nations that are closely allied. Hohenholz at various times has volunteered to use his influence in various ways to benefit the Berings. Anna knows that he could (if he would) continue to show proofs of friendship through very private words with Ostermann.

Anna Bering has a pleasing woman's touch in acknowledging and promoting friendship. At the end of her letter she promises Hohenholz a gift of green tea and a beautiful little box for playing cards. With this happy prospect she signs off "with all imaginable gratitude and esteem."[17]

Bering's letter to Nikolai Sebastian von Hohenholz, dated February 2, is in reply to his letter of February 10, 1739. The salutation is lengthy: "Resident and Councilor of His Imperial and Catholic Majesty in the Imperial Court of Russia at St. Petersburg" and "Highly honored, noble Herr Resident, my dearest friend."[18] It is the first of six personal letters that Bering is writing. It is the longest, and it is crucial not only for the future of his sons but also for his own career. It is possible that Bering and Hohenholz genuinely liked each other, but the basis of their unusual friendship appears to have been the calculated tangible benefit each man could derive from it. Their differences in profession, nationality, and social rank were considerable. Hohenholz was foremost among foreign diplomats in St. Petersburg. On August 6, 1726, he concluded for Austria a treaty with Russia that endured for a century. He became minister a few years later. Finally in 1727 he was named councilor to the emperor of Austria.

How did they first meet? It is possible that Anna first befriended the Austrian minister's wife, perhaps interesting her in the Bering children. It is more likely that Bering took the initiative sometime during 1732 or early 1733. It is known that early in 1733 Bering called upon the Dutch ambassador, who reported on May 5, 1733, that he had received from the commander a copy of a Russian map of northeast Asia.[19] Bering of course had once served under the Dutch. But if he made a call to the Dutch, perhaps he similarly called upon other Western European ministers sometime during the period 1730–33 to cultivate an interest in serving another government if he found Russian recognition of his service unsatisfactory. Alternately he could have feared that in Russia foreign-born leaders like him might at any time be summarily dismissed.

In any case, Bering's long letter to Hohenholz does settle one issue. There was in fact a quid quo pro, and much was promised. On one side, the immediate beneficiaries of the friendship are the two older sons. Profusely deferential and flattering, Bering declares at the outset, "I trust your highness's very kind friendship for my children [and care for their upbringing] even more than I trust the care of my closest relatives." He then expresses gratitude that Jonas and Thomas have been welcomed in the Hohenholz home and that the minister has informally tested the sons' ability in subjects they studied at the Reval gymnasium. Bering suggests that, with the Austrian minister's influence, further assistance would be welcome. If Jonas were to pursue a career in the military service, perhaps he could be stationed permanently in the imperial court if he were transferred to the cavalry. If, on the other hand, he were inclined to leave military service, perhaps, "if it pleases you, you might employ him." In either case, Jonas should learn Russian and at his impressionable age develop an upright character. As for Thomas, "whatever your benevolent decision," he can remain at the Reval gymnasium.[20]

But the chief potential beneficiary was Bering himself. Evidently in his last letter Hohenholz had expressed "with pleasure" his intent to intercede to get Bering promoted to the rank of admiral. How might such graciousness be repaid? It would be well rewarded, for Bering promises, "When our sea voyage is completed, anything noteworthy met upon it I will not fail to communicate to your highness as soon as possible."[21] Such a promise *in writing* is breathtaking. It flies in the face of the Russian government's efforts to preserve secrecy by having expeditions traversing Siberia instead of great oceans and by putting all principal persons on expeditions under oath. If it became widely known, Bering's promise would certainly have inflamed Russian paranoia about foreign-born leaders in government service and led to punishment for his intention to break his oath. If Hohenholz also received a Russian map of the discoveries of the First Kamchatka Expedition and if he too were made aware of likely additional findings of a second, longer and larger expedition, Hohenholz's personal assistance to the Bering family was certainly not disinterested.

That the Berings wrote to Ostermann is astonishing. Both were aware of displeasure in St. Petersburg concerning the expense and delays of the expedition. Moreover, how could they expect that Ostermann would even know enough about the two sons to recommend them? The Berings were obviously asking a favor, and they could not know the political circumstances and Ostermann's disposition toward them at the time he received Anna's letter, paired with Bering's own respectfully deferential letter as an introduction to Anna's request. Perhaps, too, Anna wrote simultaneously to Ostermann's Russian wife.

Nowadays, with the publication of the Berings' personal letters, it is possible to speculate concerning the reception of their personal request. Chances are that Ostermann would not have agreed to any request to assist the two Bering sons. Time and circumstance militated against such action. The letters to Ostermann were almost certainly included with the other sixteen letters written by the Berings. The fact that these letters have been written is announced not only in Anna's letter to the Austrian minister but also in three of the other letters, to Thomas and to the professor and his wife with whose family in Reval Thomas was being boarded. All these letters, written early in February 1740, would reach St. Petersburg toward the end of the year. But on October 16, 1740, Empress Anna died. She had named as her successor the newborn Ivan VI, whose mother was an indifferent regent guided by none other than Count Ostermann.

Since the death of Peter the Great, successions to the crown gave rise to uncertain times under two women empresses, Catherine and Anna; one boy, Peter II; and now, late in 1740, an infant. Ostermann, who had served under five Romanovs while unobtrusively accumulating offices, titles, and estates, surely had apprehensions about his own future in the very presence in Russia of the mature, hitherto deliberately excluded Elizabeth, Peter the Great's daughter by Catherine.

Even if Ostermann were inclined to please Anna Bering (assuming they had met socially in earlier days), all his proverbially cautious political instincts would instantly negate such inclinations.

So what happened? The very existence of the Bering personal letters is testimony that they were never delivered. Why? A good guess is that Ostermann regarded them as political liabilities. If he read one or more of the letters addressed to him, it follows that he ordered that all sixteen remaining letters be retained, perhaps secretly, under his control in files of the Foreign Office. If Anna's letter to him made any reference to Hohenholz, Ostermann would almost certainly have reacted with alarm, even if he did not read any of the other letters.

There remains a question about the letters' having gone directly to Ostermann. Normally they would have been distributed by the Admiralty College registrar. But apparently Ostermann had reason in advance to prevent distribution. Had he become aware of the correspondence between the Berings and Hohenholz? Had he been moved to intercept the correspondence because of warnings from Skornyakov-Pisarev in a report to Empress Anna's cabinet, dated July 25, 1738, including the statement, "One can say that the expedition has come to Siberia only for the purpose of stuffing its own pocket, and Bering has already procured enormous quantities of goods in Yakutsk"?[22] Was Ostermann surprised to find letters addressed to *him* (of all people), letters he removed from the others?

It would appear that, for all their cultivation of eminent persons in positions of influence, the Berings, the commanding couple, badly miscalculated. What they clearly desired, and did not achieve after the First Kamchatka Expedition, was the reward of an enserfed estate from new lands acquired from Sweden after the Peace of Nystad. Such an estate, though held provisionally at the pleasure of the monarch, was in Russia the surest claim to prominence and stability from generation to generation, far better than title or rank and much more to be desired than cash. Bering made an application to the Senate on December 15, 1731, asking specifically about an appointment, an award, and an estate in recognition of his management of the First Kamchatka Expedition. He asked in particular about an estate in the Viborg district, noting that in 1715 there were fifty-nine estates not yet awarded at that time.[23] In response to this application there exists a rough draft report of the Senate, dated December 24, which indicates that Vitus Bering is to receive a promotion to captain-commander, an award of 500 rubles, and an estate. But "estate" is deleted and the cash award increased to 1,000 rubles. Bering was disappointed and soon thereafter began to reflect upon alternative service that might be open to him in Western Europe.

One Soviet historian thinks him dishonest because of his dealings with the Dutch embassy. But like many other Western Europeans in Russian service, Bering was in Russia to take advantage of opportunities. If personal rewards and satisfactions were not forthcoming, he was prepared to go where they were greatest. His first loyalty was to his family. His second loyalty was to Russia. In 1740 he had served Russia for thirty-six years. During that time he had learned Russian, fought in a war in which Russia triumphed over Sweden, and led an expedition that expanded and consolidated its empire. Under the most trying conditions in Siberia, he had reached the Pacific seaboard and built two ships for a transoceanic voyage. He had done his best, and he was humble enough to confess to Steller a year later that perhaps the leadership of this second expedition should have been "entrusted to a young, energetic, and determined man of the Russian nation."[24]

The sacrifices that Vitus and Anna Bering made were awesome. They included years apart—his absences in the Great Northern War and in the First Kamchatka Expedition. Now again they are about to separate, he to sea and she returning to gather her children and await his expected triumphant homecoming and the fulfillment of their dreams.

It is not in the least surprising that she reacted so vehemently against her first son's going into the Russian army. He was, after all, following his father by entering a military profession. Her diatribes against such a career reflected her feelings of being in the wilderness, unsettled, and separated from her loved ones. It was enough, this sacrifice that she and her husband had already made. It was then no wonder that Bering, in the very next year when he was about to set sail farther to the unknown east, used her thinking, if not also her language, in his request to Ostermann to be relieved of his command upon his return and to be assigned to the Admiralty College in St. Petersburg. "I have been in the service for 37 years," he writes, "and have not reached the point where I can have a home in one place for myself and my family. I live like a nomad."[25]

PART TWO

VOYAGE TO AMERICA

STELLER SIGNS ON
WITH BERING

In the journal of his travels from Irkutsk to Okhotsk and Kamchatka (March 4 to September 16, 1740), Georg Wilhelm Steller describes his first meeting with Bering.

Steller was new to the academic contingent of the expedition. Born near Nuremberg, he was a student of theology and medicine who had attended two German universities, Wittenberg and Halle, for five years before leaving without a degree to seek his fortune in St. Petersburg. Appointed an adjunct in natural history in the Academy of Sciences, he was assigned to the expedition and joined Müller and Gmelin in Yeniseisk. When the two professors learned that the newcomer was eager to go to Kamchatka, they agreed to send him there with detailed instructions. On the way he met Spangberg.

Now on August 13, in the late afternoon, riding on horseback along the Okhota River, he and Spangberg approached the new port near the river's mouth. Steller notes that they were riding over sand banks covered with small clean stones. It was as if the horses were "clattering over hazelnuts." Upon their arrival in the port, expedition leaders who saw them were curious to know why Captain Spangberg was back. They had thought he would be in St. Petersburg by now.

Steller says that they dismounted at the captain-commander's residence, where his "beloved wife" was seen by the window. Under it was a sedan chair, prepared for a journey. After they greeted her and entered the house, young Anton Bering mistook Steller, dressed in a smock frock, for Spangberg's servant and ordered him to go through the door leading out to the family dog.

Just then Bering, Captain Aleksei Chirikov, and Lieutenant Ivan Chichachev came in, and Spangberg told them who Steller was and what Anton had said.

For their amusement Steller started toward the door, saying, "I sincerely hope this dog will be the last one I'll go to." Everyone had a good laugh. Then Bering embraced Steller and the other men embraced him as well.

After this auspicious and memorable welcome in the Bering residence, Steller writes, Spangberg took him to another residence, where he was greeted by Lieutenants Waxell, Walton, and Plautin and Midshipman Alexander Shelting, who had just returned from a voyage toward Japan. Later, after eating, Steller was taken to share quarters with Professor Delisle de La Croyère.[1]

These were very busy but upsetting days for the expedition. Spangberg, on his way to St. Petersburg, had been stopped at Ust-Kut by a courier, who gave him an Admiralty order to return to Okhotsk to make a third voyage to Japan. Spangberg had indeed wanted to make another voyage—but not to Japan. He had proposed going back to the Kurils to collect tribute and thus extend Russian control along a Kurilian trade route to Japan. Instead the Admiralty wanted him to repeat the destination of his first two voyages to acquire exact geographical information. Spangberg had already had two summer sailing seasons, in 1738 and 1739, to explore a route to Japan. His new proposal, not specifically authorized by Admiralty instructions, was a part of his own report, sent by courier to St. Petersburg from Okhotsk on September 6, 1739. Through a council meeting of expedition officers called by Bering, Spangberg was given permission to travel to the Admiralty to make his case.

Meanwhile, preparations had been made for the voyage to America, and on the very day Spangberg unexpectedly returned, traveling with Steller, the *Nadezhda*, one of the ships Spangberg had used, was already loaded with provisions to be delivered to Kamchatka. Also, within two days, with ships already launched and rigged, Bering and Chirikov expected to leave Okhotsk on the *St. Peter* and *St. Paul* en route to a new port within Avacha Bay, on the southeast side of the Kamchatka peninsula.

There could be no change of plans. The voyage to America had priority. Spangberg would have to await availability and provisioning of ships.

Bering did not have time to get acquainted with Steller, but later he did learn that the newcomer had an "insatiable desire to visit foreign lands" and that he would like to go to North America.[2] They would learn about each other—only too well—the next spring, on Kamchatka, when Steller joined the expedition.

For Bering this last summer in Okhotsk was turning out poorly. It had started out very well. There was plenty of fish in the rivers. The ships were nearly ready. Best of all, a new commander of the port of Okhotsk, Anton Emanuel Devier, had arrived toward the end of July to replace Skornyakov-Pisarev, and hostility gave way to mutual respect and cooperation. Born in Portugal, Devier was another protégé of Peter the Great, who made him both count and lieutenant general. Like Skornyakov-Pisarev, Devier was convicted of conspiring against Prince Menshikov during the reign of Catherine I, lost rank and position, and was knouted and exiled to Siberia.

The first bit of unwelcome news came on July 19. A courier arrived with an order from the Admiralty, dated January 8, ordering Bering to send a member of his household, Johann (Jagan) Lund, Anna's nephew, home to his mother in St. Petersburg. The mother, Anna Erla Lund, had written a complaint to the Admiralty. After admitting that she had consented to her son's leaving home in 1733 for the experience of the trip, she made three assertions: that "my nephew, captain-commander of the navy Bering," had not replied to her letters; that her son was being treated like a servant; and that in her old age she wished to see the boy again and provide for his education.

The order was irritating because Bering felt obliged to explain a family matter in complying with it. "It was my wife," he writes, "who in 1733, during her visit in Viborg, took the boy solely because of his mother's request." Since his father, Jacob Lund, was dead, the boy would benefit from a family relationship and from training in seamanship and artillery. "For this reason I have intended also to take him along to sea from here, for which I hoped all kinds of gratitude from his mother, since I am fully as concerned for him as if he were my own son." Moreover, the boy has "never been grouped with the house servants," nor has "even a single letter come from the mother."[3]

Bering's reply, dated July 23, went with the courier, who now found himself in charge of the boy. It must have been a wrenching parting. Jagan had been a member of the family for seven years. On the voyage he would have been a companion to Laurentz Waxell, the only boy to go on Bering's ship.

On August 19, expedition personnel not on ships' rosters—ship-wrights, carpenters, and soldiers—left Okhotsk for the long journey home. Included in this numerous company were officers' families, among them the commander's beloved Anna and their two children and servants.

No sooner were they gone than there appeared an official sent from the cabinet of her majesty, the empress. He was Avram Drukort, quartermaster sergeant of the Imperial Household Troops. By decree of the empress, he was to obtain a detailed report on the status of the expedition, including the extent to which written instructions given Bering had been carried out. Such a report was to be prepared by expedition members and signed by all officers.

The decree could not have come at a worse time. Bering called his officers to a council and together, on August 29, they responded "that it was absolutely impossible to prepare such a report."[4] Time was critical. It was in her majesty's interest that the voyage not be further delayed. Autumn was at hand. It was already late for a sea voyage to reach Avacha Bay. With further delay, ice conditions could hold up departure from Okhotsk until the following June. Never before had Bering refused a direct order from the Russian government, nor had he ever had the audacity to inform the empress what was in her best interest. He attempted to mitigate his refusal to follow the decree immediately by directing Spangberg to respond on matters related to voyages to Japan, so that Drukort would not return empty-handed, and of course Bering promised to complete a comprehensive report upon his arrival on Kamchatka.

Such a report was daunting under the best of circumstances because certain instructions had not been carried out satisfactorily, nor could they be carried out even if the expedition were to remain in Siberia indefinitely. The Senate, in its orders of March 1733, directed that post offices be established to replace the need for expensive special messengers. "You, Bering, must require information from the governor of Siberia about how to establish postal routes."[5] To what end? So that mail between Moscow and Tobolsk would be sent twice a month, between Tobolsk and Yakutsk once a month, and between Yakutsk and Kamchatka once every two months. Not only were post offices to be set up and staffed intermediately but the time required for delivery and costs of service were to be determined.

Obviously an effective postal service, mandated in 1733, had not yet been realized in 1740. Bering was in no mood in late August 1740 to take the time to explain the failure. To begin with, how was he to supervise a Siberian postal service when he himself was moving from place to place across Siberia? How could he coordinate responsibilities through district bureaucracies? He had consulted the governor of Siberia and his governing council about locations for offices and the people and horses needed. He had made reports to the governor, who issued an edict to authorize locations, but always the burden of implementation fell back on Bering. What could he say? It was always "You, Bering, must arrange everything."[6] Yet he and his officers discovered that post offices in remote locations had to be managed by native people who often had no inclination to remain on duty and abandoned their new offices at will. Other areas, especially on Kamchatka, were dangerous. The Chukchi, for example, were besieging Anadyrsk in 1738. Kamchatka had not been wholly pacified since the 1731 rebellion. There was no way, by sea covered with ice or by land with hostile natives, that Kamchatka could have mail service once each alternate month.

With everything nearly in readiness, it was maddening to be confronted by messengers coming into Okhotsk almost at the last minute with extraneous demands. But the worst blow was yet to come.

Two days of contrary winds prevented the departure of the *Nadezhda*, bound for Avacha Bay, and the *Okhotsk*, headed for Bolsheretsk, on the southwest coast of Kamchatka. On August 30 both ships were boarded in the evening. Early the next day the *Nadezhda* was in the lead. Steller's journal entry for August 31 tells what happened: "On Sunday morning we saw Mr. Khitrovo's double shallop [the *Nadezhda*] sitting on a sand bar at the mouth of the river."[7] The bar was concealed seven feet below the surface of the water. It was a double setback. All the sea biscuit for two ships bound for America was lost in the Okhota River. Not all of it could be replaced.

Almost as unfortunate was the further delay of eight days needed to offload the *Nadezhda* so that it could float free from the sand bar and be repaired and reloaded. Finally on September 8, three weeks behind schedule and fearing a difficult passage, Bering boarded the *St. Peter* (Fig. 10) and Captain Chirikov the *St. Paul,* and at ten o'clock in the morning the two ships departed from the Okhotsk harbor on their maiden voyage across the Sea of Okhotsk. The *Nadezhda,* still skippered by Khitrovo, followed the two packets.

The *Okhotsk,* a small, single-masted cargo vessel called a *galiot,* carried Steller, Delisle de La Croyère, and their assistants to Bolsheretsk. After leaving Okhotsk the evening of September 8, it was accompanied on its first day at sea by two whales that entertained the passengers by diving and spouting water. The next night the brightest star of the Pleiades was reflected like phosphorus glowing on the sea. On the 15th, in good weather, the coast of Kamchatka came into view, a mountain range in the background. To Steller it was "a paradise gently wafted by wind." He had the panorama sketched by one of his assistants, the artist Johann Christian Berckhan.[8] Five days later, at noon on September 20, the *Okhotsk,* having entered the mouth of the Bolshaya River, reached Bolsheretsk, administrative center of Kamchatka. The passengers were greeted by the student Krasheninnikov, whose own passage three years earlier on the *Vostok* had ended in shipwreck near the mouth of the river.

Krasheninnikov had housing for the newcomers. The cargo offloaded from the *Okhotsk* provisioned the stockade for the winter. The ship was Devier's responsibility, and the military contingent at Bolsheretsk was under his care.

Meanwhile, on September 26 the three expedition ships approached the channel between Cape Lopatka and the northernmost Kuril island (Shumshu). Here the channel is about four miles wide, but near the center is a great rock reef over which waves constantly crash. The two packets, followed by the double shallop, ran into heavy seas as they entered the outer half of the channel. A stiff west wind behind them was countered by tidal waves running up against them. As the *Nadezhda* and the *St. Paul* hung back, the *St. Peter* slipped downward into the

Figure 10. MODEL OF BERING'S *ST. PETER* ON A SCALE OF 1:48 BY
GENNADI A. ATAVIN (COURTESY OF THE ANCHORAGE MUSEUM OF
HISTORY AND ART).

raging waters, waves breaking over the deck on both sides. A ship's
boat, towed behind, was flung up against the stern of the ship, nearly
sweeping the deck of seamen. At every moment they feared that in the
deep trough of a wave the ship would hit bottom in shallow seas, or
that as a violent wind came up, the mainmast or rudder would break
and all would be lost. As it was, with foresails and main–topsails catching the wind, it was a perilous struggle to keep the *St. Peter* pointed
downwind. When the contrary tide began to ease, the ship began to
make progress. When the ship named for the chief of the Apostles had

cleared the channel, the *St. Paul* made its run from the Sea of Okhotsk to the Pacific Ocean. The passage was surprisingly easy. In an hour and a half, both wind and tide had abated.[9]

Khitrovo's *Nadezhda* was nowhere to be seen. It had retreated to the mouth of the Bolshaya River, and on October 8 it anchored in the roadstead at Bolsheretsk.

The two packets followed the shore from Cape Lopatka at 50°53'N to the narrow entrance of Avacha Bay at 53° N. Then, because of fog and storm, the ships put out to sea. The shore boat, already damaged and still towed by the *St. Peter*, suddenly sank. After ten days the storm broke, and on October 6 the *St. Peter* and *St. Paul* became the first seagoing vessels to enter the huge circular bay, eleven miles in diameter, with spectacular volcanic mountains to the north and south.

On the north side of the bay lies a small inlet shielded by a long spit that nearly closes it off and leaves inside the snuggest possible harbor, deep and long enough to accommodate twenty sailing ships. Bering called it the Harbor of the Apostles Peter and Paul, after his ships. In the summer of 1739 he had sent one of his officers, Ivan Yelagin, to investigate the bay and build a lighthouse (called Vaua) at its entrance and lodges and storehouses in a suitable harbor in the bay. Yelagin and his men had carried out their assignment. Shelter was available for the entire command in the first year of the port, later to become known as Petropavlovsk-Kamchatka and for more than a century the Pacific home of Russia's fleet.

Khitrovo's failure to get provisions to Avacha Bay necessitated the winter transport of those provisions across Kamchatka from Bolsheretsk to Avacha Bay, a distance of 140 miles. There were still no horses and no roads, so dogs, sledges, and their native owners were compelled to bear the hardships of freighting. To get enough dogs and drivers, Russian militia and expedition seamen went as far as 350 miles north on the west coast south of the Tigil River, where, in the village of Utkolotsk, they tried to impress Koryaks into service. Waxell was sympathetic. Some of these people "had no previous experience of the work of driving with dogs; they had never heard of such a means of transport. Nor had most of them ever been farther than [20–25 miles] away from where they were born, and now here they were having to go off with us, as they understood it, to the end of the world, and that, into the bargain, with their dogs, which they loved above all things. In the main they did not care about money, having no means of using it; in fact most of them had no idea what money was." In their fear one of the Koryaks persuaded some of his fellows to join him in getting rid of their oppressors. During the night, while the Russians slept in the *bara-bara* they had commandeered, the plotters stealthily pulled out the ladder from the opening that served as both a smoke hole and an entry to the underground dwelling. Then they threw in wood, set it ablaze, and closed the opening. The Russians, trapped, died of suffocation. There were seven of them. Six were soldiers and one an expedition sailor.[10]

News of the murders reached Avacha Bay in January and February 1741. Bering and his officers feared the worst—another native rebellion. Utkolotsk was along the overland route to Anadyrsk. It was not far from the new Tigil River stockade, in which it was learned some Russian merchants had taken refuge. Also, the expedition had several hundred reindeer browsing in the vicinity of the Tigil stockade. Those reindeer were an investment in fresh meat for the Russian diet on Kamchatka that winter, so that flour and other staples might be conserved for the voyage to America.[11]

There was no time to request instructions from St. Petersburg. In a council Bering and his officers decided to send about a hundred soldiers to Utkolotsk to get the murderers. From the port on Avacha Bay would go Ensign Legashev with his twenty men garrisoned at the port. This force would recruit fifty others from stockades at the Upper Kamchatka Post and the Tigil stockade. From the Lower Kamchatka Post were sent its commander and his militia. Bering directed that this small army should not make an immediate attack but attempt to use friendly natives to persuade the Koryak villagers to identify the culprits and turn them over.[12]

This stratagem was apparently unsuccessful, for Utkolotsk was subjected to swift and terrible vengeance. The attackers tossed grenades into *barbaras*, killing countless women and children. Those who escaped the massacre fled to a steep, rocky islet at the mouth of the Okola-vaem River. Though just a stone's throw from land, the islet was like a fort and the intervening seawater a barrier, so the Russians ruled out a direct charge. They set up a line along the beach, intending to starve the Koryaks into submission. But they did not have long to wait. A grenade thrown on the islet was picked up, exploded, and killed several Koryaks and wounded others. Everyone on the islet quickly waded ashore and surrendered.[13]

Before the militia with Koryak prisoners arrived at the Harbor of the Apostles Peter and Paul in the early spring, Bering wrote Steller, inviting him to come to the harbor to discuss "certain matters." The ship's roster lacked a mineralogist.

Steller got the letter in Bolsheretsk on February 17. He wasted no time. He made the trip by dogsled in ten days, arriving at the harbor on March 3. As he expected, Bering wanted him to go on the voyage to America. In a report to the Senate dated November 16, 1742, Steller explains why Bering wanted him. He needed someone qualified to make observations related to natural history and the physical sciences, including identification of objects in the sea and the direction to land; someone also to identify soils and minerals and plants and animals on land, including detailed descriptions; and finally, someone to observe and describe peoples, especially Americans, who might be found. Bering said such a person was needed because the officers would not have time to undertake such work.[14]

Steller expressed concern about his request to the Senate, made earlier, for permission to go to Japan. What if permission were granted after he had departed for America?

Bering assured him that this matter was not a problem, promising that he would inform the empress's cabinet and take full responsibility. After all, the voyage would be simply an "extension" of his assignment.

Steller signed on. Back in Bolsheretsk, he made assignments for his assistants in his absence and took one young man, Thomas Lepekhin, a good hunter, with him. On March 10 they arrived on Avacha Bay. Steller writes, "Those individuals who were to make preparations for my arrival were incredulous that I had come so quickly."[15]

Bering kept his promise. In his comprehensive report about the status of the expedition, dated April 18, 1741, he writes: "Steller, the adjunct in natural history sent from St. Petersburg, is now here, and he has stated in writing that he has the necessary skill in searching for and assaying metals and minerals. For this reason the captain-commander and the expedition's officers decided to take Steller with them on the voyage. In this matter Steller stated that besides this he would, in accordance with his responsibility, make various observations on the voyage concerning the natural history, peoples, conditions of the land, etc. If any ores should be found, adjunct Steller will assay them."[16]

No sooner had Steller arrived than male Koryak survivors of the attack on Utkolotsk, having been brought about 400 miles down and across the peninsula, showed up with their captors at the new port in Avacha Bay. They were forthwith interrogated and tortured by what Waxell calls "a good dose of the knout."[17] No Koryak would betray guilty comrades. Several, long under arrest away from their home, committed suicide.

Steller was horrified. There can be little doubt that he confronted Bering directly for cruel treatment of the Koryaks. Otherwise there is no explanation for Steller's statement in his report of November 16, 1742: "Scarcely had I arrived in the port of the Holy Apostles Peter and Paul than I found myself treated in an obnoxious manner. I found myself despised and blamed. And all things considered, I was not received as I should have been, according to my character, but was treated like a common soldier and underling to Bering by those close to him. Bering did not call upon me for any advice." In his journal of the voyage from Kamchatka to North America, Steller does not directly blame Bering for driving the Koryaks from their village and treating them "in a totally unchristian and cruel manner." Rather he blames "cossacks of the sea command."[18] In this same journal, revised in 1743, long after Bering's death, Steller avoids accusing Bering, even though the commander was responsible for any cossacks under his command, and even though he was present and directly responsible for the torture administered by use of the knout.

The rift between Steller and Bering was painful. Chirikov had endured a similar rift in Okhotsk, where he had persisted in making recommendations that Bering judged irrelevant because they did not serve to fulfill imperial instructions. In a letter to Golovin dated June 28, 1738, Chirikov's complaint of "being reduced to virtual uselessness" is comparable to Steller's being "despised and blamed."[19] Happily, it was Bering's way to restore men like Chirikov and Steller to his good graces as if all were forgiven.

Using his authority as commander to put down and, for a time, keep down an outspoken critic is a serious flaw in Bering's leadership. On the other hand, Bering, as commander, needed some way to offset the constant and most serious threat to his authority, the Russian naval institution of the sea council, where subordinates could outvote him. Steller, of course, was outside the naval hierarchy, and as an outsider he was particularly difficult to control. He could speak as if he were the voice of God, and he could not tolerate abuse, particularly of native peoples.

This man who wore the smock of the common peasant had a power that contrasted with that of the commander, who dressed in costly attire like a lord and ruled by virtue of his rank and position. Bering looked for direction from the Admiralty, the Senate, and the empress. Steller from his youth felt called and directed by God because of the way he interpreted the circumstances of his birth. In his valedictory address at his gymnasium in Windsheim, Franconia, he had recited an original poem that laid bare his sense of destiny. In the first stanza he reflected on his being apparently stillborn, intended for a coffin. In the second stanza he declared that "through love" a "woman friend" of the family saved him from "Ion's cup"; that is, from a cup of deadly poison (an allusion to a midwife's desire to confirm his death by use of sulfur). In the final stanza, Steller presented himself as one prepared to do something special when God showed him the way. God led him as a naturalist to an end of the world, to terra incognita in America. Like his smock, his academic rank was modest. But the person Bering had to cope with was a prodigy who viewed his work in natural history as supremely important to the expedition, not of lesser value than Bering's work as commander—and God would judge between them.

As it turned out during the voyage to America, Bering found a weakness in Steller that he exploited mercilessly, but no matter how many times he put Steller down, he rose again because of his indestructible self-assurance. Steller did not hesitate to communicate directly with the Holy Synod and the Senate in St. Petersburg. In April he ordered the student Krasheninnikov to join him at the harbor to translate into Russian two petitions he had prepared. To the Synod he reported the deplorable state of the clergy, who exacted payment from the natives for weddings, baptisms, and funerals, and he urged that new missionaries be sent out to attend to the spiritual needs of Itelmens and Koryaks as well as Russians. To the Senate he wrote about injustices imposed upon native inhabitants and about ways to improve Russian administration on Kamchatka. He predicted accurately that the new Tigil stockade would have to be abandoned for lack of a ready supply of fish and timber. He pledged Krasheninnikov to secrecy concerning the contents of these unsolicited petitions.[20]

Steller did not expect that much attention would be given to his appeal to the Senate, but because of his service to the late archbishop Feofan Prokopovich, and because of ties between the Russian Orthodox Church and the theology faculty of the University of Halle, he had good reason to expect his appeal to the Holy Synod to be welcomed. Certainly, before he left on the voyage to America, he wanted to make a positive contribution to advance social justice on Kamchatka.

It is curious that Steller, son of a large family, never returned home but moved farther and farther away during his illustrious career. In St. Petersburg, late in 1737, he married Brigitta Elena, widow of Dr. Daniel G. Messerschmidt. They started out together en route to Kamchatka. When they reached Moscow, she elected to stay behind with her young daughter. Deeply disappointed, Steller continued without her. He never informed his parents or any of his siblings in Germany that he was married.

As a Pietist, he followed in the reformed Lutheran tradition of August Hermann Francke, famed as a pastor to the poor and the tireless founder of a famous boarding school whose buildings for 2,000 students dwarfed those of the city itself during Steller's years at Halle, 1731–34. Just as Francke turned no orphan away, he also accepted all deserving theology students, no matter how poor. He boarded these students first in his own home and then as part-time teachers in the orphanage. In 1731, several years after Francke's death, Steller became one of those teachers with board provided in the orphanage. Francke had established a Latin school, where Steller also taught. Steller's patron at Halle was another Pietist, Friedrich Hoffmann, professor of medicine, royal physician in Berlin, honorary member of the St. Petersburg Academy of Sciences, and one of Europe's most prestigious medical scholars. Hoffmann sponsored Steller as a lecturer in botany at the University of Halle, called him to Berlin to become certified in botany, very likely introduced him by letter to Prokopovich when Steller decided to go to St. Petersburg, and, like the archbishop, recommended him for appointment to the St. Petersburg Academy of Sciences.

On Kamchatka, much as Francke as pastor was led to succor the poor, Steller as ethnologist was drawn to Itelmen villages. He quickly befriended these people, partly because of his interest in learning their language and customs but also, like Pietists before him, because he was sympathetic to non-Christians. Whereas to Bering such folk were "idolaters," to Steller they were masters of their own environment and not bereft of redeeming characteristics. Indeed, he found that the farther the Itelmens were separated from Russians, as doves from serpents, the more they showed their own uncorrupted selves, living carefree in their poverty, imaginative, cheerful, generous, and without care for the morrow. The men adored their women and cooked, hunted, and fished for them. They were all musically gifted, and had innumerable songs and dances. But they were not, nor had they ever been, "noble savages"; lacking Christianity and European refinement, they were too much given to pleasures of the flesh—to eating and copulating. Still, Steller found them intelligent and eager for instruction, though many lived embittered, without hope. He reported that of the 800 people living in Kamchadal villages on the Bolshaya River at the time of Russian contact a century earlier, only 28 remained in 1740. He did not equivocate: the greedy cossack was the "originator" of rebellions, collecting excessive tribute in fox and sable pelts, making servants of women and children, and forcing men into menial, unwelcome labor.[21]

It is not surprising, given his Pietist convictions, that Steller became godfather to an Itelmen boy, christened Aleksei Steller, in the village nearest Bolsheretsk. It is also not surprising that he participated, in the fall of 1740, in organizing a school in Bolsheretsk to teach reading and writing to both cossack and baptized Itelmen children. Bering had recommended the school. Devier had authorized it.[22]

Even as Bering ignored his mineralogist and physician, feelings of gratitude lingered in Steller. The commander was the last of a series of famous men who had provided him with advantages and opportunities: Francke, Hoffmann, and Prokopovich. Bering had eagerly invited him to participate in the voyage and assured him he would have assistants— and Steller just as eagerly accepted.

As a scientist, Steller knew how to make himself useful. En route to Okhotsk he had heard about the scurvy epidemic that had decimated the Bering expedition party wintered in 1735–36 on the Icy Sea. Why did Europeans get scurvy and Siberian natives did not? Even before

Steller left Okhotsk for Kamchatka, he was sure he had the answer from the natives: it was a question of diet. They knew what to eat.

On Kamchatka, Steller sought answers to a second question: Where is America nearest to Asia? From Gmelin and Müller he already had the news that in 1732 Mikhail Gvozdev had sighted a foreign coast opposite the land of the Chukchi, without, however, making a landing.

Also from Müller he received a manuscript titled "Geography and Condition of Kamchatka," a compilation of information that Müller had drawn up in 1737, using Yakutsk archives and interviews with Yakutsk residents. In this work Müller concluded that America could not be far from Kamchatka, for several reasons. First, some twenty years earlier a foreigner from the east who lived among the Itelmens reported that in his country there were very large cedars with large cedar nuts (in contrast to the small ones on Kamchatka), large rivers flowing westward into the ocean, and large skin boats, or baidaras, like those that had carried this foreigner and his companions across the sea to Karaginski Island, where his companions were killed and from which he alone escaped to Kamchatka. Second (as Bering noted in his proposal for the Second Kamchatka Expedition), large beams of fir or spruce were washed ashore on Karaginski Island and used for support in yurts built there. Third, in the fall, strong easterly winds drove ice floes upon the Kamchatka shore, and people who traveled on that sea (today's Bering Sea) maintained that it was not wide. Finally, the Chukchi said that the land they occupied was opposite a large continent to the east. From such information, Müller speculated, the American continent stretched from California to the northwest just as Asia stretched to the northeast, and the two continents came closest in the north; and therefore the map that Joseph Delisle prepared to show the relation of Asia to America was faulty in showing the two continents to be more than 2,000 miles apart.[23]

When Steller arrived at Bolsheretsk, he interviewed traders and cossacks from the north who had information about America. On the basis of these interviews—reluctant informants having been lubricated by brandy—he learned that trading had taken place between Asians and Americans and that knives and axes had been part of this trade.

Steller says in his journal that at Avacha Bay, during preparations for the voyage, he was greatly discouraged when Bering dismissed the information out of hand: "People talk a lot," and "Who believes cossacks?"[24]

Bering chose not to include Steller in the sea council called on May 4 to decide the direction to go to reach America. Steller's views would have opposed those that prevailed because of a misleading map that Delisle de La Croyère brought to the meeting. Steller was convinced that the ships should go northeast to "begin exploration across from Cape Chukchi [the Chukotsk peninsula], where everyone assumed land [America] was closest." Should Steller have been present? Bering's instructions, dated December 28, 1732, from Empress Anna, prepared by the Admiralty College and the Senate, are somewhat ambiguous. He was "to take counsel concerning various routes to America with the professors sent by the Academy of Sciences."[25] He chose to interpret these instructions strictly. He could claim that Delisle de La Croyère represented the academy and that Steller, after all, was a mere adjunct.

Waxell reports the decision of the sea council: Delisle de La Croyère "brought with him to the consultation a map [showing] the so-called Juan de Gama's land as lying to the SE by E of Avacha on latitude 47, 46, and 45 degrees north. . . . On the basis of the new information given by this map we agreed that we ought to touch at that Juan de Gama's land. So we all approved a course of SE by E as far as latitude 46 degrees north and longitude 13 degrees east. To this we all put our signature." The "new information" showed Juan de Gama's land farther east "about 13 degrees," suggesting that Delisle de La Croyère must have had a different map from the Joseph N. Delisle map given Bering with his instructions (Fig. 11). The identity of such a map and the circumstances of Delisle de La Croyère's acquisition of it remain a mystery.[26]

Chirikov reports that the decision was made in the belief that Juan de Gama's land was "a part of America because, on the general charts, land is indicated all the way from California to Juan de Gama land."[27] But even if it were an island, as suggested by a broken line on the Joseph N. Delisle map, they assured themselves that the course southeast by east was justified because Admiralty instructions called for exploration of islands between Asia and America.

The chosen course was directed toward Juan de Gama's land. If reliable information about Kamchatka, first pieced together by Müller, was as yet virtually unknown in Europe, then it is not surprising that the North Pacific Ocean—its size and its configuration—was generally a deeper mystery still.[28] It had been penetrated around the edges by

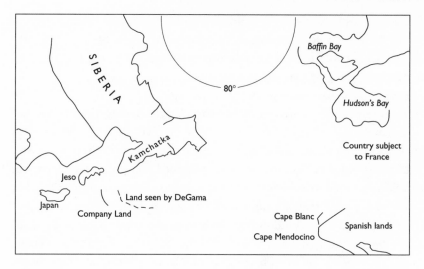

Figure 11. J. N. DELISLE MAP: ASIA AND NORTH AMERICA, WITH JUAN DE GAMA'S LAND AND COMPANY LAND INDICATED BY BROKEN LINES.

Dutch and Portuguese ships in the vicinity of Japan, by a few Spanish ships venturing off the northwest coast of North America, and by solitary Spanish galleons traversing the great ocean between Manila and Acapulco. Despite such voyages, including Sir Francis Drake's from California (New Albion) to Java in 1579, many European mapmakers speculated that North America was a big island and that the North Pacific Ocean was a small sea. Joseph N. Delisle's map was misleading, but it did leave blank a vast area between Spanish America and the Kamchatka peninsula. As for Juan de Gama, he subsequently proved to be as fictitious as the land named for him and the voyage from China to Spanish America attributed to him.

The decision of the May 4 sea council changed the entire plan of the voyage. Instead of going east or northeast to America, the expedition now was to find America to the southeast in the direction of Spanish America, to follow the North American coast back to 65°30'N, where Gvozdev had found it, and to return to Avacha Bay from there. Such a huge circuit would have meant wintering in America (as Steller hoped), but Bering was authorized to find America in only a single sailing season; that is, from the end of May to the end of September. Given the unknown vast expanse of the North Pacific Ocean and the direction in which he was to go, he was once again almost certainly set up to fail.

On Kamchatka he had already accomplished a lot. He had founded a nearly ideal port. He had completed a long report concerning the expedition. He had restored order in the region of the Tigil River. Now he transferred the interrogation of Koryak prisoners to the commander at Bolsheretsk. He completed rosters for his two ships, but just before they were to sail his physician wanted to be dropped from the roster because of illness. Fortunately Steller agreed to serve as replacement physician as well as mineralogist. The addition of this duty gave Steller a bed in the commander's cabin and a bucket of vodka in appreciation.[29]

It was time for countdown to departure. As early as April 23, Khitrovo began the first of two logs for the *St. Peter*, "with the help of God." The other, titled "The Journal of Captain Bering and Lieutenant Waxell," was begun on May 24 by the assistant navigator, Kharlam Yushin. (Chirikov kept both a ship's log and a daily journal.) Day by day, excepting Sundays and holidays, Khitrovo's log is a record of many tasks: loading, rigging, caulking, pitching, cleaning, securing, carpentering, stowing, hauling, hoisting, fitting, repairing, scraping, polishing, and greasing.

On May 25 Bering inspected the crews on both ships. When he left the *St. Paul*, its crew gave him five hurrahs, to which the *St. Peter*'s crew gave five hurrahs in return. This day also he moved his quarters to his flagship, the *St. Peter*, and gave Chirikov a copy of the signal code to be used at sea. During the next few days, extra anchors were hauled aboard and stowed in the hold and fresh drinking water was replaced.

On May 29, following a short religious service, a shot was fired to get both ships under way. It was anchors aweigh at the sixth hour of the morning.

CHAPTER EIGHT

FROM KAMCHATKA TO NORTH AMERICA

For Bering the sea voyage was a welcome break from the setbacks of a multifaceted trek through Siberia, where he was dogged by long winters, downcast by loss of life downriver to the Icy Sea, delayed repeatedly by shortages of provisions, and bedeviled by difficult instructions and uncooperative Siberian administrators. He expected his search for a direct passage to North America to take perhaps a week. He expected a quick circuit of the ocean's northern rim on his way back to home port, the Harbor of the Apostles Peter and Paul. He would chart the coasts en route, taking on fresh water as needed, noting harbors, and befriending Native Americans by giving them useful items for daily use. The circuit might take a month, maybe two, to lay claim to a rich new world for imperial Russia. It would be virtually free for the taking. It would crown his career. It would also bring him home—to stay at home, with Anna and the children.

To all appearances, Steller was extraneous. At sea he was out of his element, a greenhorn with a bucket of vodka granted him by order of the commander and delivered to him by an intermediary, Ensign Lagunov. Steller shared the commander's cabin as his personal physician, but these quarters with two beds in them, however spatially tight, were yet deceptive. For the two men in the cabin were as distant from each other as planet and sun. It was a matter of rank—of the commander's inclination to remain properly aloof. He was a Nordic sun, typically emitting a chill and radiating a smirk instead of a smile. As landsman, Steller awaited landfalls and disembarkation. His science was grounded; he flourished on terra firma. The ship was confinement, the sea poverty, and his commander a continuing enigma.

The *St. Peter* and *St. Paul*, out of the harbor and into the bay, primed for action, were yet stalled, helpless, before the gate, the narrow opening separating bay from ocean. For two days there was no wind to power sail. For four days headwinds barred passage through the entrance between the lighthouse on one side and native dwellings on the other. At anchor in the roadstead of the bay, the twin ships played a waiting game, taking soundings, issuing signals, practicing tows, and warping about. The longboat was sent ashore again for more fresh water. The anchor was raised, cleaned and checked, and lowered again.

On June 3, to everyone's surprise, the double sloop *Nadezhda*, coming from the south, blew into the bay. It fired a five-gun salute and was greeted by three guns. When it came alongside the *St. Peter*, its men gave three cheers for the captain-commander. The men on the flagship returned the compliment with three cheers, only to be saluted again with three cheers more.

There was something to celebrate. The double sloop had successfully rounded Cape Lopatka, and it brought the remainder of provisions not transported by dogsled over a long winter's snows. Now each ship took on in turn all the additional ninety-pound sacks of rye flour and groats it could hold while the remainder was unloaded at the port for use by Ensign Legashev and his men.

Each ship was now supplied with 4½ tons of rye flour, 4 tons of groats, 3 tons of dried beef, 1¼ tons of pork, 3 tons of butter, and 650 pounds of salt. Fresh water in 102 barrels weighed 26 tons. The provisions were adequate for its complement of men for four months. The water would last normally about two months.

On June 4, at four o'clock in the afternoon with a gentle northwest wind, both ships, with sail set, steered for the mouth of the bay, met a strong tide head on, and slipped silently into night and a boundless sea (Fig. 12).

It proved to be a boundless or open-ocean voyage once the lighthouse was behind them and the land faded from sight, and even the two ships played hide-and-seek in fog and night. Now began a new regimen, very familiar to experienced seamen but at times puzzling to soldiers, artisans, interpreters, and other specialists (such as Steller) recruited for the voyage. The setting at sea had drastically changed. Instead of an expedition village with residences, barracks, warehouses, blacksmith shop, guardhouse, clinic, and chapel, the ship offered crowded quarters on two decks for seventy-seven men and one boy. Under these circumstances a daily ritual of prescribed duties promoted safety, security, and morale.

As packets, the *St. Peter* and *St. Paul* were eighteenth-century sailing ships of moderate size originally designed by the Dutch to carry passengers, mail, and cargo from port to port along the North and Baltic seas. Bering's twin ships, however, were modified to serve as warships, each having fourteen cannon and three falconets. The *St. Peter* stowed 679 cannonballs and seventeen barrels of gunpowder. Steller found that the medicine chest had plentiful supplies to treat wounds that might be incurred in skirmishes with Native Americans or in a naval battle but nothing at all for asthma, a common complaint at sea. Obviously it was expected that the expedition might meet ships from other European nations, particularly from Spain. It was also presumed that landings could be dangerous, and for this reason the *St. Peter* had a complement of one midshipman guard-marine (Ivan Sindt), four marine grenadiers, and fourteen soldiers as well as four cannoneers.

The sea command was made up of four senior officers with an impressive appearance of authority: first Bering in splendid attire with accouterments to match: gold watch, short silver sword with silver inlined sword belt, gold cuff links, and silver shoe buckles. His immediate staff consisted of an adjutant, personal physician, two trumpeters, one drummer, and two personal servants. His lieutenant Sven Waxell, directly under Bering's authority, was gaining experience to qualify as a captain by routinely managing the ship and charting the coasts. The fleet master, Safron Khitrovo, supported and substituted for Waxell and was capable of making sketch maps. Each of these two senior officers had a single personal servant. The fourth senior officer was the septuagenarian navigator Andreas Hesselberg; under him served an assistant navigator, Kharlam Yushin.

The four senior officers made up the sea council, to which on occasion Yushin and five other junior or petty officers might be invited to par-

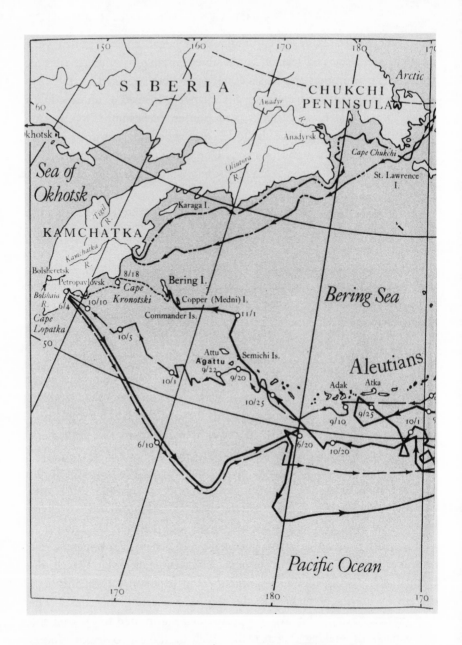

Figure 12. BERING'S VOYAGES, 1728 AND 1741–42 (FROM GEORG
WILHELM STELLER, *JOURNAL OF A VOYAGE WITH BERING, 1741–1742*,
ED. O. FROST, COPYRIGHT © 1992, BOARD OF TRUSTEES OF LELAND
STANFORD JR. UNIVERSITY, WITH PERMISSION OF STANFORD
UNIVERSITY PRESS).

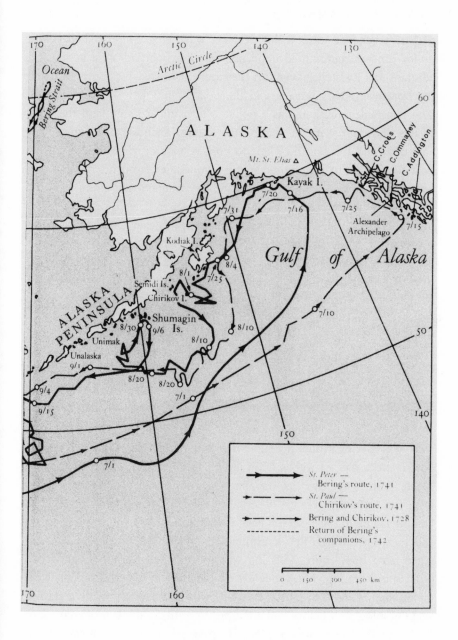

ticipate whenever some major decision was being contemplated. These junior officers represented important functions aboard ship: besides the adjutant and assistant navigator, they were the constable, Boris Roselius; the boatswain, Nils Jansen; and the boatswain's mate, Aleksei Ivanov. The constable functioned as a police officer aboard ship, and the boatswains (bosuns) were in charge of rigging, anchors, and rope. They also provided the bosun's chair to convey visiting dignitaries up from boat to ship or to lower the captain-commander from his flagship to a boat, often a ceremonial event marked by trumpets and drum.

Outside the command structure but subject to it were personnel having specialized roles, such as the purser, physician (Steller), assistant surgeon (Matthias Betge), artist (Friedrich Plenisner, friend of Steller), blacksmith, sailmaker, two coopers, caulker, four carpenters, and three natives of Kamchatka to serve as interpreters. Of these people, Steller, Waxell, Khitrovo, Yushin, Roselius, Ivanov, Betge, Plenisner, the sailor Dmitry Ovtsin, and the carpenter Sava Starodubtsov especially distinguished themselves during the sea voyage or the shipwreck that ended it.

No task was more important for navigation than the keeping of the log or daily journal. It was not only a measure of a mariner's reputation but also an assurance of a ship's preservation and of everything and everyone in it, to say nothing of the success of sponsoring organizations and the welfare of dependent families left behind.

It was Bering's duty to supervise and review the punctual writing down, every day, of information in five columns about hour of the day, speed of the ship, wind, course, and such occurrences as weather, sightings, sea council meetings, observations, health of seamen, repairs, and landings. The log also served each day as a record of the ship's progress and location through the determination of latitude, longitude, and distance from home port. This log was so vital that Bering assigned two officers to keep logs independently of each other. The assignments were given, significantly, to native Russians who had already made a start at keeping a log well before embarkation. Very likely the veteran navigator Andreas Hesselberg was available to give advice to his assistant navigator, Kharlam Yushin; and Waxell could similarly serve Khitrovo. The master instructor was the captain-commander, who could compare the two logbooks and confer regularly with their keepers. The exercise had the objective of achieving accuracy so far as conditions and instruments (such as compass and sextant) allowed. Logs as well as charts were the basis for the production of maps undertaken after a voyage, in Russia usually at the Admiralty College, near St. Petersburg.

A person not a seaman (such as Steller) could not appreciate the deliberate process of preparations for a voyage. First, there were imperial instructions to Bering, prepared by the Admiralty College and Senate, dated December 28, 1732. They cite a report that the Big Land lies east of Cape Chukotsk. Therefore, Bering is to proceed to America from there and "explore islands and lands" and specifically "look for harbors and places where one could take refuge during storms or ice at sea . . . forested areas that have lumber suitable for shipbuilding . . . [and] rich mineral deposits."[1] He is ordered to promote friendship with native peoples at all times by presenting gifts and to avoid hostilities.

Second, there are decisions recorded in the sea council of May 4, 1741, prescribing the perimeters of the voyage of a single season with return to the harbor by the end of September 1741. These decisions, once made and recorded, could be altered only by subsequent decisions of a sea council held by officers aboard ship. Decisions were deliberative and ironclad, not instantaneous or arbitrary.

Besides the two logbooks on the *St. Peter* and one on the *St. Paul*, the sea voyage of the second expedition had final reports by Captain Chirikov and Lieutenant Waxell, dated respectively December 9, 1741, and November 15, 1742. Years later (by 1756) Waxell prepared a journal. Independently Steller wrote both a report, November 16, 1742, and a journal of the voyage (1743) compiled from his diaries. Missing from this documentary record is a final report by Vitus Bering, who died before the conclusion of the voyage of the *St. Peter*. Partly as a consequence, from the start of the voyage he appears not only aloof but remote. Waxell mentions him infrequently. The logbooks note his leadership only briefly. Bering is known during the voyage chiefly through Steller, who is at first a highly biased and opinionated antagonist.

Almost from the start, Steller's journal becomes a jeremiad. He is isolated. He is spurned. He will not be silent. Journal writing is his therapy. He complains about "the unreasonable behavior" of "the officers," who "mocked whatever was said by anyone not a seaman as if with the rules of navigation all science and powers of reasoning were spontaneously acquired." "Anyone not a seaman" is of course Steller. "Officers" is a generalized allusion to Bering, Waxell, and Khitrovo, but it is Bering who is the chief source of his grief and disappointment. Bering, Steller says, "thought it ridiculous to accept advice from me since I was no seaman."[2]

Steller rightly understood that he was to make observations "related to natural history and the physical sciences about various objects occurring in the sea" and to give advice about whether land was near or far. But on the voyage from Kamchatka to North America, Steller found that his recommendations about the direction to land were not welcomed. He made them anyway. Repeatedly ignored, he claims in his journal that on at least three occasions Bering and his two senior officers failed to act upon signs that land was near and that consequently the voyage was needlessly prolonged.

These are serious charges. Can they be substantiated?

On June 13, nine days and nearly 700 nautical miles southeast by east from Avacha Bay, the two ships "sounded in 90 fathoms found no bottom" as they reached 46° north latitude. Here Bering and Chirikov conferred by speaking trumpet (a megaphone then in use at sea) and agreed to change course from southeast by east to east by north as originally planned if land were not sighted. At this time Steller apparently intervened. On the basis of "many different sea plants" floating around the ships and "gulls, terns, and ducks" flying overhead, which Steller identified as "all land birds," he "supposed" that land would "soon" be reached if the ships continued on their initial southeast-by-east course.[3]

Steller was mistaken. The two ships were sailing over what today are called the Emperor Seamounts. The nearest land, the westernmost Aleutians (Near and Rat islands) were about 400 nautical miles away in an arc from north to northeast. Had the ships continued indefinitely southeast by east, they might eventually—with luck—have come upon Midway Island or the Hawaiian Islands after traversing more than 1,000 nautical miles of open sea.

It was on this new course, generally east by north, that a week later, in a gale, near midnight on June 20, the two ships, little more than ten nautical miles apart, lost each other. About this time Steller reports in his journal, "When various men said they had seen land in the north—a not infallible yet very probable claim—the officers neither accepted nor even gave a thought to it."[4]

This time land was indeed to the north—Amchitka of the Rat Islands.

But it was at least 100 nautical miles away, well outside the *St. Peter's* range of visibility. Should some attempt have been made to investigate this supposed sighting? Under the circumstances, with each ship, as agreed beforehand, obliged to find the other at the point where it was last seen, it would have been ill advised to seek an island instead of a sister ship, each potentially a lifeboat for the other.

The two vessels, hampered by unfavorable winds, consumed a few precious days in a vain search for each other, after which the *St. Paul* resumed the east-by-north course. The *St. Peter*, however, made a four-day run farther to the south, to 45° north latitude, presumably to find out if Steller were right. Again no land was found, and the *St. Peter* resumed a general east-by-north course. At this point Bering almost certainly felt justified in his opinion about the value of Steller's advice. If necessary, he could defend himself if the Senate or Admiralty later criticized him for not following it.

Two to three weeks later, Steller was sure that land would be found to the north. He noted that several species of seaweed were drifting from that direction. Though the *St. Peter's* log does not note this sighting of seaweed, Chirikov and his crew several days earlier saw masses of vegetation "resembling a sea nettle" in what was probably the same general area.[5] Until July 13, the *St. Peter* was three to five days behind the *St. Paul* as both ships entered the Gulf of Alaska, neither having actually seen land since their departure from Kamchatka.

This time Steller was right. Since June 25 the *St. Peter* had been sailing along the Aleutian Trench, out of sight of land, several hundred nautical miles south of the Aleutian Islands and later, along the same arc, the same distance south of the Alaska Peninsula and Kodiak Island.

As early as July 1, when a two-fathom length of driftwood was seen (and noted in the ship's log), land was expected to appear at any time. Bering did not change course. Soundings were taken at 90 and 180 fathoms without touching bottom. More "good-sized" driftwood appeared on July 8, but lead dropped 90 or 180 fathoms still did not touch bottom. On three successive days, July 11–13, as the *St. Peter* averaged each day a distance of about 100 nautical miles with favorable winds, other signs of land were recorded in the ship's log. Waxell writes of one of them: "Straight ahead of us, and at some considerable distance, we caught sight of something black on the water. It was thickly covered with an incredible mass of seabirds of all kinds. We could not conceive what it was and took a sounding, but without reaching bottom; then we altered course slightly. . . . In the end we realized that it must be a dead whale, and so we sailed right close in towards it."⁶ The whale appeared at the sixth hour of the morning (that is, between five and six o'clock) on the 11th. More driftwood passed by during the next two days.

Why did Bering hold persistently to the same course? He had already deviated once from the plan each ship was committed to follow. On that occasion, he turned the ship south for nearly four full days, covering about 275 nautical miles without sighting land. Had he and his officers agreed to alter course by turning north and sailing 300–400 miles at any time between July 1 and 10, they would have sighted the Shumagin Islands of the eastern Aleutians, the Alaska Peninsula of the American continent, or Kodiak Island.

Very likely Bering did not at first consider going north for two reasons: first, because given the known location of Spanish America, the American continent was sooner or later bound to show up if the ship continued on an easterly course; second, he now had further reason to be wary of Steller's recommendations. Not only had the academician already been badly mistaken but he was now claiming to see signs of land that were invisible to everyone else. These new signs were "the frequent appearance of sea animals,"⁷ which Steller identified in his journal as seals and sea otters, mammals that he knew could not feed beyond certain depths and hence certain distances from land. Until July 12, fog and rain were nearly daily occurrences. Perhaps excited by the appearance of driftwood, seaweed, and the whale, Steller actually believed he saw the two sea mammals.

How could he delude himself? The voyage had been long and largely uneventful. It had offered little of biological interest. He was becoming haunted by the prospect that, once back in St. Petersburg, he might not be able to justify his accompanying Bering. He felt compelled to find and to present ever more convincing signs of land to show that he had a contribution to make and that he gave good advice in pleading that the *St. Peter* go north. The fact remains that, although it is remotely possible that he saw migrating fur seals (which he would have called "sea bears"), Steller almost certainly did not see sea otters before July 16, when Mount St. Elias and North America suddenly became visible about 100 nautical miles away.

The evidence is twofold. In the twentieth century, no trained biologist has reported seeing a sea otter more than about fifty nautical miles from land, and there is no record of otters diving more than fifty fathoms for food.[8] At no time between June 6 and July 16, from departure from Kamchatka to arrival off North America, was the *St. Peter* within 100 nautical miles of land. Even *after* America had been sighted, the ship's log indicates that, at both the 10th and 11th hours of the evening of July 16, no bottom had been reached at 180 fathoms.

There is compelling evidence in his journal that Steller himself was aware that others aboard ship were skeptical about his sightings. He declared that he was the first to see land, that he saw it on July 15, but he says, "because I had announced it and it was not so visible that it could be clearly delineated, it was, as usual, dismissed as something peculiar to me."[9] The irony here is that Steller may indeed have dimly seen Mount St. Elias, since the mountain was within the *St. Peter's* range of visibility on the 15th.

It may be true, as Steller says in his journal, that Bering was inclined to agree with him in the privacy of their cabin that land would be found to the north. So why did the commander not show his "character and authority"?[10] His response seemed weak to Steller, but it reflected the reality of the Russian imperial navy that Bering had known for thirty-seven years: a commander could be overruled by his own officers in a sea council, and he probably would have been if he had proposed to go north. After all, Steller had first made a mistake about the direction to land which had cost Bering four days or more.

Waxell, in an account of the Second Kamchatka Expedition written some fifteen years later, confesses: "My blood still boils whenever I think of the scandalous deception of which we were victims," a reference to what he describes as the "false" map showing a "pretended" land that initially led the sea expedition astray.[11] Waxell does not criticize in writing either Steller or his commander, but he might well have had strong feelings about Steller's advising them to go farther south than the sea council of May 4 had agreed to go and about Bering's persuading the command to take the *St. Peter* farther south later—and still in vain. If Khitrovo shared Waxell's feelings (and the two were often of the same mind), their commander could foresee substantial difficulties in persuading them to agree to go north, deviating again from the original plan.

Thus three circumstances—a misleading map, a poor recommendation, and going off course to make a double check—very likely combined to fix the *St. Peter*'s course and to overextend its voyage. Only an alarming new circumstance finally altered its course: a shortage of fresh water. As early as July 1 the ration per man was reduced, and thick rather than "watery" mush was served in the evening. On July 14 at least half the fresh water was gone. That fact could not be ignored. On its easterly course the ship was sailing farther and farther from Kamchatka. By turning north, it might approach land supposed to exist there, "judging by various reports," as stated in the ship's log.[12]

The one person making these reports was of course Steller, who was not given the satisfaction of knowing that just one hour after the sea council met on the morning of July 14, the *St. Peter* finally changed course. Steller's report states that after the failure to find land by going southeast, the ship was kept on the same generally easterly course until America was sighted.[13]

On July 14 the sea council of senior officers could not know that America was just as close to the east as to the north and that the ship was but two days' sail behind the *St. Paul*.

With generally favorable winds, the *St. Paul* proceeded east by north as agreed upon from the day (June 23) its officers gave up looking for its sister ship until America was sighted between one and three o'clock in the early morning of July 15 (Fig. 13). The land had come upon them quickly: on July 12 they saw a duck; on the 13th a duck, gull, and "two old floating trees"; and on the 14th "a large number of shore ducks, gulls, a whale, porpoises, and three medium-sized pieces of driftwood that had been in the water for some time."[14] The land then showed up. It was mountainous.

Coming in closer to shore at 55°30'N, Chirikov took compass bearings of a point to the southeast (Cape Bartolomé, Baker Island, southeast Alaska, west of Ketchikan) and of a point to the northeast (Cape Addington, Noyes Island). On the nearest shore were "three projections" (Cape Chirikov, Granite Point, and Outer Point, all on Baker Island). On the basis of maps he had, Chirikov supposed that the *St. Paul* was "not far from parts of America that are well known"; that is, Spanish America.[15]

But these maps reflect Spanish claims rather than a Spanish presence north of San Francisco Bay. Acapulco, Spain's northernmost port on the

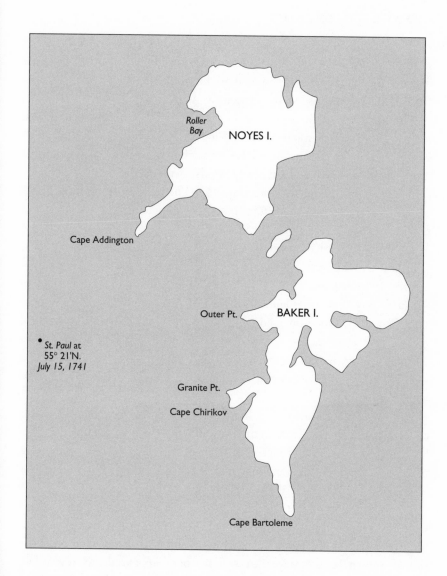

Figure 13. CHIRIKOV'S AMERICAN LANDFALL (WEST OF TODAY'S KETCHIKAN, ALASKA).

Pacific Ocean, at 16°49'N, was roughly 3,000 nautical miles from his position at 55°30'N, off North America, considerably farther than the distance he had come—estimated to be about 2,150 nautical miles—from Vaua Lighthouse at the mouth of Avacha Bay.[16]

The next day, at three o'clock in the afternoon, Chirikov sent a boat toward shore to investigate a bay (Windy Bay, Coronation Island). The bay proved to be unsatisfactory for an anchorage because it was unprotected from westerly and southerly winds. Seen on the beach were large spruce trees and many sea lions on rocks. The next morning huge flocks of murres and cormorants flew over the ship. Chirikov's course was now north-northwest along the coast.

On July 18, at half past three o'clock in the afternoon, at 57°55'N, Chirikov and his officers agreed to send the fleet master, Avram Dementiev, with ten armed men to board the longboat and head into a bay (Takanis Bay, Yakobi Island, northwest of Sitka) and go ashore if possible (Fig. 14). Once on land, they were to signal the ship by firing a rocket, give gifts to any Native Americans who might be found, make a sketch of the harbor, identify trees and any precious minerals in the soil (silver ore was sent with Dementiev), and fill two empty barrels with fresh water.

The *St. Paul* followed the longboat toward the bay, but the water about a nautical mile from shore was still too deep to anchor the ship. So Chirikov hove to and tacked in front of the bay. No one on the ship could see whether the longboat had made a landing. No rocket was heard, and for five days there was no sign of the longboat.

On July 23, when the fog lifted, a fire was seen on the beach where Chirikov supposed his men had landed. Toward evening in fair weather, he fired a gun seven times at intervals to signal that any men on shore should return to the ship. But still no boat appeared. As night fell, Chirikov had a lantern hung out in hopes of guiding the boat back to the ship.

The next day Chirikov and his officers decided to send the yawl ashore with a carpenter, a caulker, and tools to repair the longboat in case it had been damaged. A boatswain and sailor volunteered to go along, with orders to leave the repairmen ashore and to return immediately in the yawl with Dementiev and three or four others (the yawl had a capacity for six or seven men). When the four men departed shortly before noon, the weather was fair with little wind. The distance

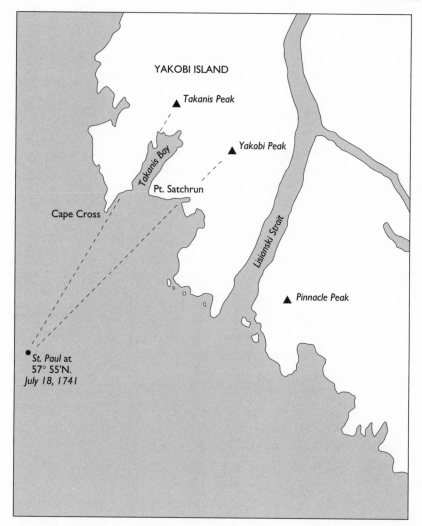

Figure 14. CHIRIKOV'S FIFTEEN MEN WERE LOST IN TAKANIS BAY
(NORTHWEST OF SITKA).

to be rowed was nine nautical miles, and the ship followed it in. At five
o'clock the yawl was close to shore. It was seen to be making an approach. But just at that time the ship, now close to land, encountered a
heavy-running sea and had to pull away.

The yawl made no signal, and it too did not return to the ship. Now a nautical mile or two from shore, the ship was over a bottom of big rocks at a depth of sixty to seventy fathoms. Toward shore "many rocks were seen both under and above water on which the surf was playing." Unable to anchor, the *St. Paul* moved out from shore, but at eight o'clock again moved in "so close to shore that we could see the rocks and the surf playing on them."[17] Because night was falling, the ship moved out again to a distance of three nautical miles from shore. A cannon was fired to summon the men to the ship.

The weather seemed ideal for a boat to leave the shore, but no boat appeared. But now a fire was seen intermittently on the beach.

The next morning the *St. Paul* again tacked close to the beach where the boats had headed. The ship's position at noon was 57°51'N. At last, shortly after noon, two boats were seen coming from the bay, one small, the other large. "When the small boat drew close to us," writes Chirikov, "we became aware that it was not our boat, for it had a sharp bow" and "those in it did not row with oars but paddled."[18]

The small boat did not come close enough so that Chirikov could see faces, but he saw four persons, one standing in the stern while the others paddled. Then suddenly all four stood up in their canoe, shouted "*Agai! Agai!*" twice, waved their hands, and turned back to shore.

Chirikov had his men wave white kerchiefs to make a gesture to these strangers to come closer, but these gestures had no effect. There was no wind to follow the small canoe, which traveled very fast back to the large one, which had remained farther away.

The two canoes continued to pull away until they disappeared in the bay where they had first been seen.

Chirikov and his officers were now convinced that "some misfortune" had overtaken the fifteen men in the two boats. The weather had been fair. There had been plenty of opportunity for them to return to the ship. The Americans who came out in their canoes seemed to be culprits who "had killed or detained our men."[19]

Not yet giving up all hope, Chirikov directed that the *St. Paul* continue to hover near the opening to the bay. When he steered for shore again, at three o'clock in the afternoon, he again saw a fire in the same place but also, this time, the two canoes they had seen earlier. But now the canoes pulled out from shore and, following the shore away from the ship, again disappeared. Where the fire had been there was now only smoke. As night again fell, lanterns were hung out.

Another day passed. The ship had no more boats to put ashore to investigate what had happened. On July 27 a sea council was called and a fateful decision made: the ship was to leave and return as directly as possible to the Harbor of the Apostles Peter and Paul. Only forty-five barrels of fresh water remained. There was no way to collect more other than by catching rain from sails.[20] That day, with strong wind and rain, the *St. Paul* covered ninety-two nautical miles as it started across the Gulf of Alaska.

Two questions remain: Where did Chirikov lose his men? What happened to them?

It has been asserted, on the basis of Chirikov's log, that all evidence points "with certainty to Lisianski Strait as the place where the boats of the *St. Paul* met with disaster."[21] There are several problems with this assertion. It assumes that Chirikov's noon sightings are "very good" and that there is no reason to question the accuracy of 57°50'N, which would put the *St. Paul* off the opening of the strait. It ignores the fact that during fair weather Chirikov consistently writes of "a bay" rather than a strait. Finally, it does not consider Chirikov's description of the shore from the bay, his indication of direction from the ship to the bay, or his bearings to mountains (Takanis and Yakobi peaks) in the vicinity.

These bearings alone may be determinative. A French hydrographer finds that Chirikov's logbook latitudes differ an average of five minutes from those of modern charts for Capes Addington, Ommaney, and Cross. He thinks it was in Takanis Bay, just south of Cape Cross, that Chirikov lost his men.[22]

This particular bay fits details given in the ship's log: "the bay into which the [longboat] was ordered bears NNE 3/4E, distant 5 [nautical miles]." If this bay were Lisianski Strait at 57°50'N, the direction to it would be easterly, not north-northeasterly. Another telling detail concerns "the low shore" that "stretched to SE and SE by E." Presumably this shore, seen to the northeast seven nautical miles from the ship about seven o'clock in the evening of July 18, runs from the mouth of the bay entered by the ship's boats. If so, it accurately describes the shore extending from Point Satchrun at the entrance to Takanis Bay. It in no way describes the broken shoreline south of Lisianski Strait. Indeed, the land running south-southeast from the opening to this strait has two offshore islets nowhere mentioned in Chirikov's log. The evidence seems conclusive. The bay with "details relating to it" can be "easily identified," as Chirikov claimed.[23] It is Takanis Bay.

The mystery of what happened to the men in the boats is most persuasively explained by an ethnologist who lived among the Tlingit in the early twentieth century. He believes the two boats were swamped in the riptides that commonly occur at narrow mouths of bays and straits along the American coast that Chirikov followed. In other words, the men in both boats drowned without ever reaching shore. Such misfortune fits the circumstances. No rocket or gun was fired from shore to signal a landing. "*Agai,*" or Tlingit *agou,* means "Come!" or "Come here!"[24] It was very likely a friendly invitation for seamen aboard the *St. Paul* to follow the canoes ashore to see any flotsam that might have washed up. Chirikov, fearing the worst, supposed that the Americans did not come any closer to his ship because they had killed or captured his men. Actually it appears that the smaller of the two canoes did get close enough to convey a message, which of course could not be understood.

In any case, the decision to return posthaste to Kamchatka, sad as it was, was eminently sensible.

At one o'clock in the afternoon on July 16, 1741, Captain-Commander Vitus Bering and his seventy-seven men aboard the *St. Peter* saw North America unveiled to the north all across the horizon as a curtain of clouds and drizzle lifted. First they saw a shoreline broken up with islands, capes, and bays. Next they saw a band of thick, dark forest on a narrow plain along the littoral. And finally, in very clear weather and with the sun shining, they saw a huge mountain range of perpetual snow topped by a single volcanic peak rising almost from sea level to a point higher than any mountain they had seen in Siberia. It was the top of the world.

It was today's St. Elias Mountain Range.

According to Steller, shouts of joy instantly rang out. They had come so far and waited so long, and here it was at last—America! It raised their spirits. Their hopes soared upon it. They congratulated themselves. Some wanted to congratulate the commander, but Steller says that after Bering gazed steadily upon the new land, he shrugged his shoulders and abruptly left the deck.

In his cabin, with the din of happy cries pressing in, the old man said to Steller and his surveyor, Friedrich Plenisner: "They are like pregnant windbags, puffed up with expectations. They don't consider where we are, how far we are from home, and what trouble we may yet have to get home. Who knows but what the winds will blow up and keep us from getting back. We don't know this country, and we don't have provisions to keep us here through the winter."[25]

At that moment Steller felt gratified. Bering had rarely confided in him. And "pregnant windbags." That bit of sarcasm Steller knew was intended for his ears. He could appreciate it. All the wild talk, conceit, and back-slapping he had witnessed on deck—it was ridiculous.

The ship sailed on to meet the high-rimmed continent. Passing high clouds thickened. Easterly winds became variable and then died down almost completely in the night. For six long hours the ship rocked in the swells. They weren't going anywhere. With the wind knocked out of their sails, rapture finally gave way to reality.

Bering did not head for the mainland. A landing there could be dangerous. There might be reefs or hostile savages. It was time to begin the homeward voyage and reconnoiter the coast at a safe distance in search for a drainage having a source of fresh water. Two-thirds of their supply was gone.

Steller could not resist a bright remark: "So we have come only to carry American water to Asia!"[26]

When easterlies resumed the next morning, the ship kept heading north till noon (as if to land) and then turned northwest (as if to reconnoiter and record landforms on a chart). As they slowly came up along the coast on the starboard side, they could see beautiful conifers close to a flat, smooth, sandy beach. They had not seen trees growing close by the sea anywhere they had traveled along the Asian Pacific seaboard.

By eight o'clock in the evening on July 18, a decision had to be made. They had come within fifteen nautical miles of a narrow channel between a cape and a long, high, wooded island extending twenty statute miles to the southwest into the sea. Would they enter this channel to look for a safe anchorage within it, or would they beat a retreat from the land in case a storm came up in the night?

Bering gave the order. The ship tacked, backed off, retreated.

Steller was beside himself. He tried to explain to Bering the nature of the opportunity they were losing. He pointed out that, from the channel, currents carried flotsam visible along the coast ten miles out to sea and flowing toward them. He said that he had tested the seawater and found that it had low salinity. He was sure that the current was of a river that emptied into the channel and that its mouth was probably large and deep enough to provide a harbor for the ship.[27]

Bering's retort was cutting and quick. "Have you already been there and made sure?"[28]

That devastating sarcasm referred to an earlier incident. In the presence of officers, Steller had sought to enlighten the commander. Currents in the ocean had brought clumps of seaweed in the vicinity of the ship. Patiently and with all the modesty he could muster Steller suggested that if the ship's course were adjusted northward, they would soon see land.

According to Steller, Bering challenged him by saying that the whole sea is overgrown with plants near Cape Verde and Bermuda and in many parts of the ocean.[29]

Steller assured him that he was familiar with plants that grew in the ocean around Cape Verde and Bermuda, but conditions differed in northern regions and plants growing here in seawater he knew quite well, and anyone could understand how they were transported.

But it was no use. No one would admit to such an understanding. Everyone had a good laugh, some saying it was ludicrous to claim that currents existed in the sea at all. They laughed all the more when Steller said that they could see the movement of the current by objects floating in a definite direction, even opposite to that of the wind.[30] No one would believe him, even with the evidence before their very eyes.

During the first three months of the sea voyage, Steller was often humiliated. Bering took a leading role in taunting him, and other seamen took their cue from the commander. Once a seaman, pointing to a map, declared that their course was in the Atlantic Ocean off Canada. Another argued that the Maldive Islands were in the Mediterranean Sea, not in the Indian Ocean. Steller was so gullible that he thought they did not know any better. Of course, they "argued vociferously" when he attempted to correct their errors in geography.[31] Making sport of Steller was a way to relieve the monotony of the long voyage.

He was painfully aware of his isolation and impotence. His advice was rudely rejected and his learning discounted for lack of a mariner's experience. He was tired of being put down as "no seaman," as if, ipso facto, with the study of navigation the officers had mastered all science. Steller recorded his own sarcastic rejoinder in his journal: "They, of course, have been in God's council chamber!"[32] It had become a question of honor with him that, in the midst of the playful seamen, he had to be right.

Privately in their cabin, Bering sometimes agreed with him, but out on the deck he was not inclined to do so. So when Steller attempted to offer advice to advance the objectives of the voyage, he found himself the butt of ill-natured humor and the laughingstock of coarse and arrogant "gentleman" officers. More than once he promised himself that he would keep his mouth shut and speak not one word more. But such restraint was out of character—a little joke Steller played on himself.

Now along the coast of America, Bering could see how eager Steller was to begin exploration. For all their pretensions, his officers were not a problem. They knew how to take orders. But Steller, this academician, did not know his place. He would have to be kept on a short leash. And as for entering the channel, it was out of the question. The current sweeping through it was ominous. Besides, it was too late in the day to consider dispatching a boat to have a look.

Bering made a wise decision. If he had investigated the channel, he would have found it shallow, without the mouth of a river flowing through it. What Steller observed was a hazardous sea current sweeping by the cape (Cape Suckling) northeast of the channel.

Away from land, the ship tacked back and forth through the night, marking time until daylight. Then it headed on a straight course westward past the south end of the island (Kayak Island) to get on its lee side to seek there an anchorage sheltered from brisk east winds and to find fresh water. From the south the island has the aspect of a slithering snake with its fang an inverted eyetooth or pinnacle rock that is only several hundred yards away from the precipitous pyramid peak with which the island abruptly terminates. What's more, the island on its southwest side is guarded by rock reefs, partially submerged, threatening to wreck a ship.

Giving the west side of the island a wide berth, Bering had the ship

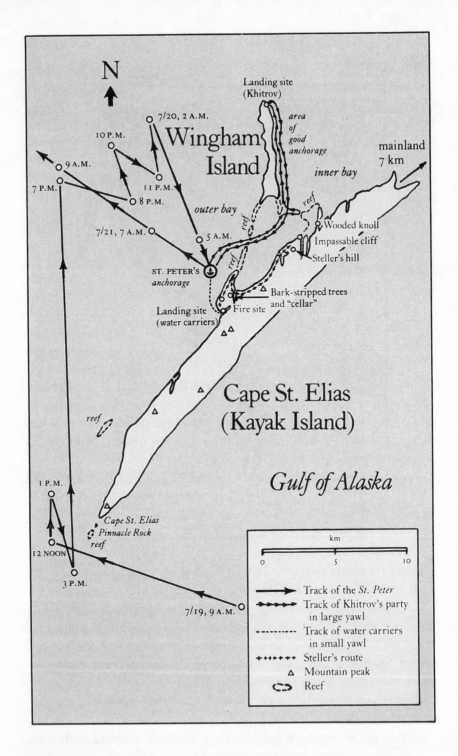

Figure 15. FIRST LANDING, KAYAK ISLAND (FROM GEORG WILHELM STELLER, *JOURNAL OF A VOYAGE WITH BERING, 1741–1742,* ED. O. FROST, COPYRIGHT © 1992, BOARD OF TRUSTEES OF LELAND STANFORD JR. UNIVERSITY, WITH PERMISSION OF STANFORD UNIVERSITY PRESS).

tack through another night, this time edging northward fully five to ten nautical miles away from the island. Near dawn it slipped in cautiously to the southeast toward an outer bay formed by the near juncture of the snakelike island and a shorter one only four miles long, a broad tower of rock capped with conifers (Wingham Island). Between these two islands the ship brushed perilously close to another reef but turned away southward in the nick of time, inching its way for an hour till it came to a spot about a mile off a hilly wooded cape midpoint on the west side of the longer island (Fig. 15). Here at six o'clock in the morning of July 20 it dropped anchor over a muddy blue bottom.[33]

On this day would occur the first documented European landing on the northwest coast of North America. Within a vast region of terra incognita, it was the first known intrusion on aboriginal societies by representatives of a rapidly expanding foreign power. It was the beginning of a new era of exploration and colonization, the beginning of the history of a huge territory to be called, however presumptuously, Russian America.

CHAPTER NINE

FIRST LANDING

Kayak Island

At the side of the *St. Peter* two shore boats, lowered into the water, stood ready at daybreak. It was July 20. Where were they?

Today about three miles directly north of the ship's position lies the high point of a rock cliff at the southern end of the smaller of the two islands (today's Wingham Island). To the northeast, five miles away, is a low, narrow point off the larger island (Kayak Island, called St. Elias Island by the Bering expedition).[1] Beyond this point farther to the northeast is the end of the island and beyond it, about fifteen miles away from the ship and four miles from the island, is the nearest part of the American continent.

Between the two islands is a strait (Kayak Entrance) about two miles wide but partially closed off by a visible reef running north-northwest from the larger island toward the smaller. Beyond the strait to the north appears a large, sheltered inner bay (Controller Bay).

Bering was where he wanted to be. To the north on the mainland was potential danger. Native Americans would be there. He would send the larger shore boat (longboat) under Khitrovo's command, with his assistant navigator and fourteen armed soldiers, to find safe passage through the strait and try to locate a sheltered anchorage in a harbor or roadstead somewhere within the large inner bay. The assistant navigator, Kharlam Yushin, would take soundings. Also, this party would be on the lookout for timber large enough for ship repairs. Such information would be useful if they, or some other Russian ship, were to return to complete the charting of the coast. It would also be a beginning toward fulfilling imperial instructions.

The smaller shore boat (yawl) would look for creek water around the point only about a mile to the southeast.[2]

By seven o'clock in the morning, with almost everyone on deck, Bering had already organized activities for the day. He had not spoken to Steller.

In both his journal and his report of November 16, 1742, Steller gives a memorable account of the confrontation he had with his commander. The account appears nowhere else in records of the voyage, but there is no reason to doubt its veracity. It underscores the differing characters and attitudes of the two men. It also marks an abrupt deepening of the rift between them.

Because Bering had said nothing to him that morning when the two boats were being readied for departure, Steller approached him and asked permission to go with Khitrovo. According to Steller, both Khitrovo and Waxell supported his request.

It was denied. What Bering might have said is this: If Khitrovo went ashore, savages might ambush his party and men might be killed.

Steller was affronted. He thought Bering was trying to "scare" him "with some gruesome murder stories." In his reply, his words show that his anger mounted the more he said. In dangerous situations, he declared, he had "never acted like a woman," and he "did not know any reason why [he] should not be permitted to go ashore," where he could do his "chief work, profession, and duty." Moreover, he had served her majesty faithfully according to his ability and he wanted "to maintain the honor" of that service "for a long time yet." Then Steller concluded with a threat: "If for reasons contrary to the purpose of the voyage" he were not allowed to go, he "would report such conduct in terms it deserved."[3]

Steller carried out his threat by including it in the two documents sent off to St. Petersburg. His threat was useless, as he admitted, because Bering had nothing to fear off Kayak Island, halfway around the northern hemisphere. The threat is noteworthy because it shows Steller's pent-up fervor for his work and for representing that work as meeting substantially "the purpose of the voyage."

He could not see that Bering's priorities were justified. There could be no argument about the need to find fresh water. Exploring the area for a good anchorage and for timber suitable for shipbuilding was in his instructions. He had but two shore boats, and they could not accommodate Steller with the assistants he wanted. Finally, Bering knew that he should remain on board to monitor the winds. If the easterlies of that morning veered around toward the west, the ship would be endangered in its open roadstead. Then on short notice he would call both boat parties back to the ship. He could not have Steller off with assistants in the woods somewhere.

Bering's response to Steller's threat was to defuse it. At the moment he was treating the men to drinks of chocolate, a delicacy from his private stores. He called Steller a "wild man" who wouldn't be kept from his work even by a treat.

Steller would not be put off. He would not, he said, be forced against his will "to inexcusable neglect of duty." He writes, "I put aside all respect and uttered a particular prayer."

This statement is usually interpreted to mean that Steller cursed the commander. It makes better sense to take "a particular prayer" literally. As a Pietist, he inveighed against the cursing he heard aboard ship. Surely he could not admit to cursing himself. Also, Steller says that his prayer "immediately mollified" the captain-commander. Surely Bering could not have had this reaction if he were cursed among all the chocolate-drinking celebrants around him. In such a case, his recourse would probably be to have Steller restrained and carried off. While the "particular prayer" itself is open to speculation, one like "God forgive us" or "God have mercy upon us," uttered in a despairing loud voice, would likely elicit pity and cause Bering to relent.[4] Whatever happened, there were two conditions that Bering stipulated: Steller could go ashore with the water carriers, not with Khitrovo, and he must be satisfied with the assistance of his only servant, the cossack Thomas Lepekhin. These conditions were imposed to keep Steller away from possible danger and to avoid overcrowding the yawl.

It was nine o'clock in the morning when Steller got in the boat. As the boat pulled away for the shore and trumpets blared from the ship, Steller had these thoughts: As his last gesture, Bering was having a mocking farewell salute. He would ignore it. He would not have cared for such an honor even if it had been given sincerely. But he couldn't help wondering if Bering, in sending him off as an object of derision without any additional help and so exposing him and his servant to possible grave misfortune, hoped never to see him again. It now occurred to him that Bering had invited him to join the expedition not to undertake a responsibility as mineralogist but to meet a requirement to fill a roster. After all, for eight years no mineralogist had been sent out from Yekaterinburg and Bering had let the only one around—Simon Hartepol—go off to Yakutsk to join Captain Spangberg, who would be sailing back toward Japan. It also occurred to him that while most of the officers remained aboard ship to monitor the winds and thus make "windy" observations, he was headed ashore to make "watery" ones. He thought of the proverb "In water is poverty." For the past four maddening weeks, the ship had followed land—but just out of sight of it. Signs of land had been in the air—shore birds—and in the sea— mammals and seaweed. Nobody had believed that land was near, and on and on they had sailed. Now here he was, headed south, away from the mainland, away from Americans, on a quest—for water. At least he had this comfort: Getting to terra firma, in the service of this commander, was in itself an authentic achievement.

These fleeting thoughts were now interrupted.

This is Steller's remarkable story on the island. He landed at the mouth of a stream that ran down the beach. Ahead to the left was the solitary wooded hill of the cape. Between hill and a long high cliff of the island's mountainous spine was the densely forested watershed of the stream. Today the cape is known as Cape St. Peter, the hill as Steller's Hill, and the stream as Steller's Creek.

Steller had four objectives—to find and describe Americans, to gather native American plants, to seek signs of mineral wealth, and to look for an anchorage for the *St. Peter* along the channel separating the island from the continent. He needed at least a year for all this exploration. He knew he had but part of a day.

It was already about ten o'clock in the morning.

On the beach he moved quickly, followed by Thomas carrying musket and ax. They headed west toward the southwest point of the cape. Occasionally Steller stopped to dig up an unfamiliar plant, using a long knife he carried. If the plant were one he thought he had seen before in Europe or Asia, he just pulled it up by the roots.[5]

He had gone nearly a half mile when he reached the point. Here he was startled to find footprints in the sand and signs of a camp—a log hewn as a trough, meat left on some bones scattered about, and dried fish. It seemed as if a meal had been interrupted, as if those who were eating had quickly retreated into the forest above the beach. Next to the fish were mussels eight inches in diameter and various shells shaped like bowls. Sweet grass (*Heracleum lanatum*) over which hot water had been poured was still in them.

Near the trough had been a fire, its embers still warm. Here too were a fire drill and tinder made of algae bleached in the sun.

Just then the boat came up offshore. Having filled empty barrels with fresh water, the men were returning to the ship. Steller called them ashore to see the campsite. He wanted them to be forewarned that Americans were out of sight but close at hand. Also, he decided that Thomas should go back to the ship with them. He could take a few plant specimens already collected, including a sample of the tinder.[6]

The boatmen were startled by the sight of footprints in the sand and warm embers in the fireplace. They had already seen five red foxes running on the beach. Steller had already seen excrement of sea otters "everywhere" on the shore. The island seemed alive with men and beasts, seen or unseen.

Then the boatmen, with Thomas, were off. Alone at the campsite, Steller considered the significance of what he was seeing. The dried fish was the same as what he had found in native villages on Kamchatka. The sweet grass, called *slatkaya trava* by the Russians and *kattik* by the Itelmens, seemed to be prepared and consumed in the same way in America. Only the tinder was different.

He wondered if Itelmens had ever engaged in trade with Americans, if they had ever emigrated to America, if Itelmens and Americans were one and the same people. He observed that fallen trees on the ground had been cut by a blunt instrument, presumably by a bone or stone ax.

He took some notes and then continued on his way.

The ship was now in sight, and, as prearranged, the boatmen were already approaching to drop Thomas off on shore. Then, reunited, the two men proceeded north along the cape to its northwest point. Rounding it, they were once again out of sight of the ship. They followed the shoreline of a small, shallow bay, going generally eastward.

Steller estimated that they were two miles from the campsite when they came upon a path to the south leading into deep, dark woods. It had been made all the more noticeable by someone's attempt to conceal it by covering it with leafy branches. Perhaps this was the work of some unseen sentry guarding entrance into the woods.

From the landing site Steller had elected to follow the shore around the cape. Though twice the distance, this route was known. It had been visible from the ship earlier in the day. Before going into the woods, Steller writes, he came to an understanding with Thomas. There would be no shooting unless Steller gave the command, no matter how many people they might meet.

No sooner had they made their way on the path through the thick understory than they came into the rain forest itself, open all around like an amphitheater but darkened by high branches of Sitka spruce and hemlock forming a canopy over all. Steller was amazed at the girth of these trees, shielded from wind and storm by the hill of the cape. He noticed that many had been stripped of oval sheets of bark, front and back, no higher than a tall man's reach.[7] Soon he would discover one use made of this bark.

He marveled at these trees. Steller later wrote in his journal that they could furnish wood for shipbuilding "for centuries."[8]

He had a habit of exaggerating whenever something that might be useful astonished him. The trees were indeed "immense," more than 100 feet tall, but the forest in which they appeared was not itself "immense," as he claimed. It was limited by a valley roughly two miles long and a half mile wide between the 350-foot hill (Steller Hill) on the cape (Cape St. Peter) and the abrupt 500-foot cliff of the island spine.

Trees, many bark-stripped, remain today in the same location where Steller entered the woods. Core samples indicate that some are 250, even 350 years old.[9]

Once in the rain forest, Steller could no longer see the north shore of the cape only a few hundred feet away. He decided not to follow various small paths leading deeper into the woods but explored instead the northern perimeter of the valley to the east.

After half an hour he and his man found a rectangular plot at ground level covered with cut grass. Removing the grass, Steller discovered a covering of rocks over sheets of Sitka spruce bark supported by poles. Such was the roof of what he called "a dug-out cellar," whose dimensions he recorded as 14 feet wide, 21 feet long, and 14 feet deep. It was a large subterranean cache of smoked red salmon stored in containers made of bark.

Though he wrote that he was fearful of being caught in the cellar, he had Thomas help lower him into the deep storage area so that he could make a quick inventory. First he sampled the salmon. It was delicious, better than any he had tasted on Kamchatka. A winter's supply was already stored here in North America at a time when on Kamchatka the salmon were just entering the rivers from the sea. Next, while Thomas continued to stand guard above him, Steller recorded other items: sweet grass; grasses like hemp, perhaps used to make fish nets; the innermost bark of Sitka spruce rolled up and dried and (he supposed) consumed as food;[10] bundles of strong seaweed straps; and large arrows, very smooth and painted black.

What Steller had stumbled upon was a store of food and household items that had been gathered on the island and along rivers of the mainland. They were hidden here near island camps from which the Eskimos would return with their goods in the fall to islands in Prince William Sound. Steller of course had already investigated one such camp at the southwest point of the cape, a strategic spot from which lookouts have a panoramic view to the southernmost point of the large island nine miles away, all the way around, open to the sea, to the south point of the smaller island four miles to the north. That camp had evidently been vacated that morning when the *St. Peter* sent the boat ashore.

Along the coast of the Gulf of Alaska during the early eighteenth century there was conflict between the Chugach Eskimos and various Indian tribes, Tlingits moving westward from Yakutat Bay, Athabascans coming eastward from Cook Inlet, and a smaller group, the Eyaks, who had migrated down the Copper River.[11]

Another bit of history: On July 29, 1790, forty-nine years later, an old Eskimo man, described as "very good-natured and intelligent," came aboard a ship of the Russian-sponsored Joseph Billings expedition when it was anchored off Hinchinbrook Island in eastern Prince William Sound. Through an interpreter this Eskimo conversed with Captain Gavril Sarychev, who asked, "How long has it been since the first ships made their appearance among you?" "I was a boy," he said, "when a ship came close into the bay on the west side of Kayak Island." He explained that his people frequented the island during summers of fishing and hunting in the region. "When the ship sent a boat ashore, we all ran away. When the ship sailed away, we returned to our hut and found in our underground storeroom glass beads, tobacco leaves, an iron kettle, and something else."[12]

So Steller was justified in his feelings that he and Thomas were being watched. Even so, once out of the cellar with samples from it, he sent Thomas back to the landing site with three instructions: to warn the men loading fresh water "not to feel too safe," to take cultural artifacts (salmon, bark, etc.) back to the ship, and to ask Bering (again) for the use of two or three men.[13]

He wanted the commander to see evidence of the life of native people. But he got no help. To Bering it was more important to obtain a supply of the smoked fish than to satisfy Steller's request. So Thomas, instead of returning to Steller, was obliged to lead a small party back to the cellar. Here they left Chinese silk, two kettles, two knives, twenty glass beads, and tobacco and pipes in exchange for smoked salmon.

By this time (it was about four o'clock in the afternoon) Steller had proceeded alone some three miles up the west coast, vainly hoping that Thomas and other assistants would catch up to him.

He was making important botanical discoveries. Almost everywhere he came across the salmonberry, which he called *Rubus americanus* (now *R. spectabilis*), up to six feet tall and "doubtless of superb flavor" (the fruit was not yet fully ripe). It reminded him of the raspberry and European *moschatel*. Within the rain forest of the cape he collected (and later described) two other large plant specimens, devil's club (*Echinopanax horridum*), which he named *Ricinoides Vitis folio spinoso, fructu bicapsulari* (*Ricinoides* vine with barbed leaf with bicapsular fruit); and yellow skunk cabbage (*Lysichiton americanus*), or, in his words, *Arum foliis maximis, caulescents* (Arum with very large leaves, caulescent). These and other plant specimens he carried with him until the beach he was following suddenly came to an end.

Scarcely a half mile ahead was "a steep cliff that extended into the sea beyond the beach."[14] He could go no farther. The "steep cliff" (Seacave Rock) was a final extension of the cliff he had followed. He could see that where he was, at the end of the beach, the cliff was neither steep nor high. At this point, above the cliff, rose a hill with a path going straight up.

Leaving his plant specimens on the beach, he clambered up loose rock to the top of the cliff (about 20 feet above the beach), and then climbed up the path of the hill (about 350 feet above sea level). Crossing the high, forested saddle of the summit, he noted, with only a little exaggeration, that the east side of the hill was "steep as a wall."[15] To go down the north side was to end up on top of the cliff extending into the sea. Thinking that he could proceed down the hill's south side until he could turn to the east, he started down. But he was soon stopped by thick brush.

He wanted to cross the island and, if possible, hike up the east shore to investigate his theory that a ship could find shelter in a river off the island's north end. He thought better of it. Without a path, the crossing would be too difficult. It was already too late in the day, and Thomas would never find him if he went on.

In fact, even with several assistants, Steller would not have succeeded in reaching his destination before nightfall. As Captain James Cook discovered when he stopped at the other side of the island thirty-seven years later, crossing the island on foot is difficult because of "bushy" and "woody" vegetation and steep slopes.[16]

Because he could not see the north end of the island, even from the summit of the hill, Steller did not realize that he was still about six miles from it. So, disappointed, he climbed back up the hill to a point where, from the saddle, he could look to the north and west over the smaller island and see in the distance the snow-capped mountains of the American mainland. It was depressing to realize that he could neither go farther nor expect the expedition to spend the winter here.

Just then, as he was lamenting the severe limitations Bering had placed upon him by refusing adequate time and necessary support for exploration of this country, he caught sight of smoke below him about a mile to the north, rising and blowing over a wooded knoll. "I now had the certain hope of meeting people and learning from them what I needed for a complete report," he later wrote in his journal.[17]

The knoll was on a narrow point extending into the channel between the larger island he was on and the smaller island to the west. Captain George Vancouver, fifty-three years later, called this the northwest point of the island.[18]

Steller quickly descended hill and cliff, grabbed his collection of specimens, and rushed six miles back to the creek where he had landed. The boat was just then leaving in its day-long shuttle of fresh water to the ship. With the water carriers, Steller sent news to Bering about the fire, requesting use of the boat and its crew to investigate.

While he waited for a reply, he rested, made himself some tea from the "excellent water" of the creek, and jotted down descriptions of some of "the rarest plants" among his specimens.

After about an hour the boat was back. The message from Bering was curt. Steller was to return to the ship an hour hence with the last load of water or be left stranded. According to his informant, Bering had used seaman's language. "Get your butt on board or . . ."[19]

What a "patriotic and gracious" reply! It was the deepest cut of the day. Three times Bering had denied him the opportunity to be productive in the performance of duty, and now he was being treated like a common sailor and recalled from his duty prematurely, before the end of daylight.

But at least Thomas was back with him again. He had come on the boat.

With "flight from shore" imminent, Steller sent his assistant to shoot some of the exotic birds, brilliantly colored, already observed in the woods above the mouth of the creek, while he scurried "once again on a tour to the west" to box some salmonberry bushes for the botanical garden of the St. Petersburg Academy.[20]

Thomas shot a single bird. Steller thought he recognized it as the same bird he had seen in a magnificent two-volume work, the first illustrated flora and fauna of North American wildlife, Mark Catesby's *Natural History of Carolina, Florida and the Bahama Islands,* published in London "at the Author's Expence" in 1731.

But he was mistaken. Catesby's jay (*Cyanocitta cristata*) in the painting, filling an entire 12-by-16-inch page, is the same genus but a different species. What he got is now referred to as Steller's jay (*Cyanocitta stelleri*).

"This bird alone convinced me that we were really in America," he writes.[21]

This remark, sometimes quoted as if it indicated a profound insight, simply reveals how Steller's mind often worked. Amid an overwhelming abundance of known and unknown species found on the northwest coast of North America, he snatched at identifications as best he could. A Carolina bird, imperfectly remembered, was for him, on the opposite side of a vast continent, sufficient evidence of where he was.

Steller did the best he could, and what he achieved in North America is truly impressive. But while he endeavored to be an "exact" scientist, there is no gainsaying the fact that in America, for lack of handbooks to consult and specimens to examine closely, he was often an "approximate" scientist—one who, according to modern taxonomic standards, is no scientist at all.

What did he achieve on the island? In mineralogy, practically nothing. In zoology, not much. He had specimens of salmon and jay and mere notations about foxes, seals, sea otter, whales, sharks, ravens, and magpies. In ethnology he did surprisingly well. Without seeing Native Americans or their communities, he learned that they resembled Itelmens in diet, food preparation, and implement making. Therefore he concluded they could have Asian origins, a speculation in accord with much later theory.

In botany, his favorite science, he left an extensive record of island flora in three documents produced in final form on Kamchatka from his American field notes.[22] One he titled "Mantissa plantarum minus aut plane incognitarum" (Supplement of little known or entirely unknown plants). It is the most important document, consisting of descriptions of ten plants, plus two other plants which are listed. Of the twelve, eleven were collected on Kayak Island. The dozen plants were the only ones preserved as dried specimens, hence the separate list. These are then the first specimens collected by a naturalist on the northwest coast of North America.

A second list he titled "Catalogus plantarum intra sex horas in parte Americanae septemtrionalis iuxta promontorium Eliae observatarum anno 1741 die 21 [sic] Iulii sub gradu latitudinis 59" (A catalog of plants observed during six hours in the northern part of America near Cape Elias, at 59 degrees of latitude, on July 21, 1741). Of the approximately 135 plants named, at least 9 were "observed" at a later date in another locale, and only 2 plants are described because they were collected but not admitted aboard ship: Steller's "Rubus Americanus erectus" (*Rubus spectabilis* Pursh var. spectabilis), the salmonberry; and "Grossularia Americana" (*Rubus bracteosum* Dougl. ex Hook), the stink currant. This list has sometimes been considered the only list of Steller's Kayak Island flora, with the assumption that it was produced in its entirety on the island and that it represents flora actually collected.[23]

The third list is "Catalogus seminum anno 1741 in America septemtrionali sub gradu latitudinis 59 & 55 collectorum, quorum dimidia pars d. 17 Nov. 1742 transmissa" (A catalog of seeds collected in the year 1741 in North America at 59 and 55 degrees of latitude, of which half were sent [to St. Petersburg] on Nov. 17, 1742). Of the twenty-five seeds listed, only five were collected on Kayak Island, since on July 20 seeds of most plants were too immature to collect.

From these lists it is clear that on Kayak Island Steller collected about a dozen plants and "observed," or pulled up by their roots, about 135 plants. Of these 135, most have been recently found on the island.[24] Some bear names of Eurasian plants that Steller, in his haste, obviously misidentified.

At about eight o'clock in the evening, Steller and his assistant returned to the ship with the last of thirty-five barrels of fresh water obtained that day. Steller had grave misgivings about the reception he would get.

With "a great guffaw" Bering intercepted the boxes of salmonberry bushes. Without a word he simply set them aside. There was no room for them aboard ship. They would soon go overboard.

At the same time he treated Steller to chocolate. There was no reprimand.

Under these circumstances and much relieved, Steller fell into the trap he sometimes set for himself. He became voluble about his findings and began to share ideas.

It was good, he said, to leave gifts in the cellar but it should not have been "plundered."[25] (He did not mince words!) And instead of leaving tobacco and pipes, whose use natives would not know, it would have been better to leave knives or axes, since their use would have been obvious.

Bering replied that, on the contrary, knives and axes would be a hostile sign, as if war were being declared against them.[26] Everyone except Steller was greatly amused because they knew what Steller did not know—that two knives had in fact been left as gifts and duly noted in the ship's log.

Fortunately for Steller, this teasing debate abruptly ended. Khitrovo and his party of fifteen men were coming up to the ship.

Khitrovo's findings were disappointing. The strait (Kayak Entrance) between the islands was, it turned out, scarcely deep enough to be passable, and presented the added danger of submerged reefs running out from the larger island. There was no suitable harbor but only a roadstead sheltered from many but not all winds just off the northeast shore of the smaller island (Wingham Island).[27] The inner bay (Controller Bay) was extremely shallow.

On the shore of the smaller island Khitrovo found no suitable timber for topsail yards, and because of distance he could not be sure if timber for shipbuilding were available on the mainland. Consequently, Khitrovo's sketch map (Fig. 16), showing the two islands in relation to the mainland, had limited value. Without a well-sheltered and easily accessible anchorage, with no timber for ship construction, and with no visible abundance of valuable fur-bearing animals or mineral wealth, the region was of minimal interest. Other items Khitrovo presented were mere curiosities—a basket, a shovel, a whetstone with stripes of copper, a ball made of clay with a rattle in it, a fox tail, and a paddle. He did report an abandoned hut near the north end of the smaller island where he landed, but he had not seen people.

Khitrovo and his party had come upon another Eskimo camp. Its hut was made of boards that had been hewn, possibly with a metal instrument. The floor was also made of these boards, and in one corner was a fireplace. The absence of a native craft suggests that the Eskimos at this camp were not hiding in the woods but had crossed from the smaller to the larger island when the *St. Peter* approached from the south during the previous evening. Perhaps it was their fire on the wooded knoll that had excited Steller.

Early the next morning, July 21, Bering gave orders to weigh anchor.

In his journal Steller accused Bering of having "a sluggish stubbornness and cowardly fear" of a few unarmed Americans, and "longing" too much to return to his young family in Russia. He sums up his disappointment: "The time spent for investigation bore an arithmetical relationship. The preparation for this ultimate purpose of getting to America lasted ten years. Twenty hours while the ship was at anchor were devoted to the matter itself."[28] The implication of his statement is that America would never be seen again. But it was.

In his disappointment Steller could not appreciate Bering as actually a highly competent commander, one who knew that the ship was their lifeline and that every precaution should be taken to preserve it. For his part Bering was so concerned about returning to Kamchatka safely that

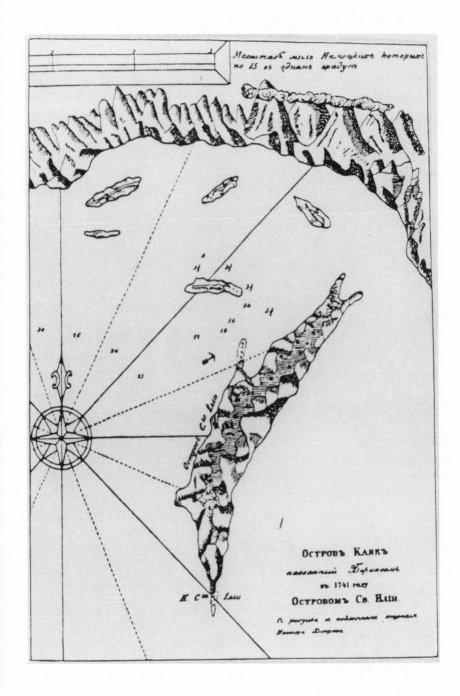

Figure 16. SKETCH MAP BY S. KHITROVO, KAYAK ISLAND, 1741 (FROM F. GOLDER, *BERING'S VOYAGES* [AMERICAN GEOGRAPHICAL SOCIETY, 1925]).

he could not tolerate Steller's zeal to write "a complete report" about Native Americans camping on Kayak Island.

Off the coast of the island, the ship was secure only as long as winds remained easterly. On July 20 the expedition was fortunate. Winds did not veer away from the east, and the *St. Peter* remained sheltered in the lee of the hill of the cape.

Bering wisely remained with the ship to check the winds. He sent out one shore boat for fresh water, essential for the return voyage. He sent out the other shore boat to seek a better anchorage as well as to complete a sketch map of the area.

He did not have a third shore boat with which to accommodate Steller. Under the circumstances, even if the ship had had provisions to spend the winter in America, there was no way Bering could agree to remain in the vicinity of Kayak Island. Lacking a safer anchorage for a second day, he made the only decision available to him. They could not take further risks. They must be away.

Preoccupied with scientific objectives, Steller was simply no seaman.

Once they were at sea again, there was virtually no communication between these two men who shared the same cabin. Bering decided that the ship had no room for the precious boxed salmonberries. Steller was about right when he said, "I myself as a protester now took up too much space."[29]

CHAPTER TEN

SCURVY

Any study of the *St. Peter*'s homeward voyage must ponder the question: What was the turning point in the fortunes of the ship and of every person on it? From the moment Bering on deck looked upon Mount St. Elias, he was determined to begin the homeward voyage without landing in the vicinity of Yakutat Bay, the large bay in view below the St. Elias Mountain Range. The stop at Kayak Island for fresh water was necessary, even at the risk of anchoring in an open roadstead. There in a single day, July 20, thirty-five barrels had been filled. Twenty remained empty. Bering must have had a restless night because Steller tells us that "two hours before daybreak, the Captain-Commander got up and, contrary to his custom, came on deck himself, and, without deliberating about it, gave orders to weigh anchor." The orders were evidently issued to Waxell, who "earnestly requested" that the ship remain at anchor until all the empty barrels could be filled.[1]

Steller does not supply as many details about Bering's argument with Waxell as he does about his own dispute with the commander the previous morning, but if the lieutenant actually said what Steller reports, then Bering obviously had not succeeded in persuading the lieutenant of the urgency of returning to Kamchatka as quickly as possible. If, as Steller says, Waxell told his commander that "nothing but a longing for home obliges us to return," then indeed he is accusing Bering of having an ulterior motive for rushing away from the island, an accusation surely offensive and unworthy of discussion.

As Steller admits, Bering "had much better insight into the future than the other officers."[2] The problem was distance. The outward voyage had been uneventful. Good progress was made with prevailing westerlies. The way homeward would face mostly contrary winds. It had taken the *St. Peter* six weeks out of sight of land to go from Kamchatka to its first American landfall. Bering understood that on the return voyage he had but ten weeks to reach home port by the end of September. His officers were apparently convinced that ten weeks would suffice to chart the American coast en route to Cape Chukotsk before they returned home. They did not appreciate the fact that continuing to follow the plan of the May 4 sea council not only nearly doubled the distance but also greatly endangered the expedition.

Thus during that first week from the island two factors combined to put the well-being of the enterprise at high risk. On the one hand, there was the intransigence of Bering's officers in refusing to consider returning to Kamchatka the way they had come—that is, in known waters. On the other hand, because of the institution of the sea council, these officers virtually held their commander hostage. Steller says they had "no use" for Bering's proposal. In his journal Waxell does not allude to any disagreement. He writes, "It was our intention to follow the land as it went."[3]

This fundamental disagreement, with a commander's hands tied as in no other navy in the Western world, doomed the *St. Peter* in stages through time lost, the onset of scurvy, and finally horrendous storms. The tragic drama of a commander no longer effectively in command (except in limited ways) and consequently of a ship out of control and (virtually) helpless began with the departure from Kayak Island, where Russia made its first known landings on American soil.

By noon of July 21, the end of the first nautical day of the homeward journey, the *St. Peter* had achieved the first 16 of an estimated 1,665 nautical miles toward Vaua Lighthouse, at the entrance of Avacha Bay, and its home port, the Harbor of the Apostles Peter and Paul. Favorable easterlies continued for the first two weeks, but the voyage did not begin well.

For Steller the next six weeks were the worst period of the sea voyage. Worse than being teased was being ignored. Bering and the senior officers rarely even spoke to him. He prepared his Kayak Island specimens as best he could. He overheard conversations. He rarely engaged in them.

The land was full of surprises. It did not trend to the north. On the second day they were diverted by an apparent barrier of three islands (later named Hawkins, Hinchinbrook, and Montague) with a bay visible between the last two. They did not see the Copper River delta, forty miles to the north, nor did they have any idea about native villages and glacially fed fiords within Prince William Sound. They were obliged to turn south to the open sea in drizzle and rain with the wind subsiding.

Once their sounding lead touched bottom for an hour at 45–60 fathoms. They were in the vicinity of Middleton Island, which they did not see.

After four days of rain and overcast skies without a landfall, Bering and his senior officers came to an agreement, reported in the ship's log for July 25, "while the misty weather prevailed, to sail SW by compass, which would take us toward Kamchatka; but when the weather cleared and the wind turned fair to sail N and W in order to observe the American coast."[4]

This was no compromise. Waxell and Khitrovo had prevailed. Turning away from the land in fog or mist was standard operating procedure for reasons of safety. It did not represent an actual concession to the commander.

On July 26, in continuing drizzle and mist, they had, as Waxell recalled, "a bad fright." Without seeing land anywhere they found themselves in shallows. Waxell writes: "We tried everything possible to escape from there, but in whatever direction we sailed, we found only shallow water. I had no idea what was the best thing to do. I decided to sail due south. For a long time the depth remained the same, but fortunately we eventually came out into deep water."[5]

Only at daybreak did they sight "high land" twenty to thirty miles to the north. This land was their only view of Kodiak Island, or possibly of Sitkalidak Island, lying against it.

A week later, just past midnight on August 2, they had another shock. According to Steller, they found, upon soundings, that they were in four fathoms. This information does not appear in the ship's log, where "30, 28 fathoms" is recorded at midnight; and an hour later, after land was suddenly sighted straight ahead, it reports that the ship "tacked to star-board" and anchored "in 18 fathoms." In his journal, written years later, Waxell remembered that "a sounding showed only 7 or 8 fathoms of water."[6] In any case, in fog and darkness the ship had come perilously close to a reef extending from the north end of the land.

By the third hour of the morning the wind had ceased blowing, and in the resulting calm the ship remained at anchor for eighteen hours. At the tenth hour of the morning the fog lifted to reveal, just "three versts away" (two miles) what both Waxell and Khitrovo referred to as Fog (or Foggy) Island.[7] Its present name is Chirikov, bestowed on it by Captain George Vancouver in 1794, though Captain Chirikov of the *St. Paul* never saw it. Situated about a hundred miles southwest of Kodiak Island, it is a treeless island of forty square miles with sandy beaches, three freshwater lakes, salmon streams, and rolling hills of native grasses, which have sustained as many as 1,200 wild cattle since they were introduced in 1888. On a stretch of black sand on its east side, small quantities of gold have been found.

The island offered Bering a rare opportunity to take on fresh water. He was probably dissuaded by the presence of the rocky reef, the exposed position of the ship in the event of a sudden storm, and the eagerness he felt to reach Kamchatka, still estimated to be 1,472 nautical miles away.

August 2 turned out to be a pleasant day. It was clear, sunny, and warm. By noon they were amused by a sea lion that swam around the ship for half an hour.

Under these circumstances, Steller was emboldened to break two weeks of silence to ask Bering for permission to "go ashore for a few hours with the small boat" to carry out his duties as mineralogist.

Bering refused the request, and according to Steller they "got into a little argument." Actually it was not much of an argument. Steller pleaded fear of reprimand from the Senate or the Academy for neglect of duty. Bering therefore called a council to make it a matter of record that Steller was not to be reproached for failing to do his work conscientiously "to the best of [his] ability at each opportunity."[8] Hardly satisfied, Steller let the matter drop.

Toward evening he caught two fish with a rod. He called them *Scorpius marinus*, described them, and preserved them in alcohol.

With a southerly wind, the ship proceeded north, away from the island. On August 4 they sighted a high volcano (Mount Chiginagak) about sixty miles away to the northwest on the Alaska Peninsula. Now the *St. Peter* turned southwest to follow the coast, but the ship was soon confronted by the Semidi Islands, a fifteen-mile-long wall of nine small islands with solitary peaks as high as 1,500 feet, extending north to south. The ship's log referred to only five of the nine islands.

The *St. Peter* passed west of Chirikov Island on its way back out to sea. Steller wrote that they had "wasted the winds," easterlies that could have driven them about a thousand miles in a straight line toward Kamchatka. Instead, they had made little progress at all, and once returned to open seas, they confronted dreaded headwinds, the westerlies.

During this first turn north toward the Alaska Peninsula, Steller saw large numbers of sea mammals—harbor seals, sea otters, fur seals, and porpoises. He linked such sightings to an abrupt change in the weather: "The more frequently they appeared and the more movement they made, the more furious the storms were."[9]

On the afternoon of August 6, sea otters, whales, and sea lions were sighted. Then a sea change did occur. In wet and foggy weather, the wind died down within an hour, and the ship, which had been moving out to sea from Chirikov Island at a speed of 3 knots, was reduced to 1 knot by midnight and to a fraction of a knot for the next twelve hours.

A worse change was heralded one hour before noon the next day. A small dead whale seemed to introduce a change in the direction of the wind from southeast to southwest all day on August 8. To continue south with that new wind, the ship was obliged to set its course southeast. As a result, it was set back 43 nautical miles (from an estimated 1,504 to 1,547 nautical miles from Vaua Lighthouse), all in a single day.

It was probably on August 8, mostly sunny with the ship drifting along at one to two knots, that a last sea mammal appeared about eighty-five nautical miles south of Chirikov Island. Steller called it a sea ape, "a very unusual and new animal" that played around the ship for "two whole hours."[10]

Steller wanted the mammal as a specimen. He shot at it and missed. Another person (unnamed) also shot and missed. The mammal did not return to the ship, although Steller claimed that it was seen "at various times in different parts of the sea."[11]

Without a specimen, Steller could describe the mammal only "imperfectly"; that is, only from observation and not from a detailed study of its anatomy. Steller did not mention the sea ape in his report to the Senate, November 16, 1742. Nothing about it appears in the ship's log or in other records of the voyage.

It was, Steller says, "about two ells long"; that is, about four and a half feet. It had a dog's head with big eyes; pointed, erect ears; and whiskers hanging down (like a Chinaman's) on both sides of the mouth. Its body was round, fat, and elongated, tapering to the tail. Its fur was gray on the back and reddish-white on the belly, but in the water it seemed to be entirely red and cow-colored. Its tail had two fins, the upper one twice as long as the lower one, like a shark's.

At first it rose upright in the water "one third of its length, like a human being." It held this position "for several minutes" while observing the men on the ship "for almost half an hour." Finally, it did "juggling tricks" with the hollowed, bottlelike end of a long piece of seaweed, antics that delighted the crew. "One could not," writes Steller, "have asked for anything more comical from a monkey."

Steller claims that the shape of the creature "corresponds in all respects to the picture that [Conrad] Gesner received from one of his correspondents and in his *Historia animalium* calls *Simia marina Danica*."[12]

Clearly his memory was faulty. The source of the woodcut is Gesner's *Icones animalium aquatilium in mari* (1560). Gesner does not call the *Simia marina* "Danish." It was the picture that came from Denmark. Most important, the shape of Steller's sea ape bears no resemblance to that of the sea ape in Gesner's woodcut. What did Steller see?

His account of the animal's behavior is entirely credible. Harbor seals, sea otters, and fur seals are all capable of the antics of Steller's sea ape. All may be seen along the Alaska Peninsula and its islands. Steller had seen them all the previous week.

The location of the ship, about eighty-five nautical miles from Chirikov Island, would make the presence of either seals or sea otters unlikely, and Steller's description, in most particulars, fits a juvenile fur seal—the doglike face, large eyes, long whiskers, and pointed ears.[13]

Whatever its identity, it proved to be another ill omen. Contrary winds, which were light throughout August 9, became moderately strong the next day. They persisted, with only occasional respite, for the remainder of the month.

After an inauspicious beginning, the return voyage now went from bad to worse. America was proving to be Bering's nemesis. Steller had wanted to stay and explore the continent. Waxell and Khitrovo insisted on charting its coast. But they could all see that the continent was armed with multitudinous reefs, shoals, and islands. America was like the devil's club (*Echinopanax horridum*) that Steller saw on Kayak Island, a sprawling plant whose roots, spikes, and leaves all bristled with sharp teeth. The continent, like the plant, seemed almost ubiquitous. Usually shrouded in mist and rain, it had more than once reappeared, unexpected and threatening. Since leaving Kayak Island, they had learned that the continent was trending southwest and consequently became repeatedly a barrier to a straight homeward course.

The time had come to rethink their plans. On August 10, after a day of strong headwinds and constant tacking in heavy seas, Bering called Waxell, Khitrovo, and Hesselberg together. They considered first their original agreement of May 4, specifically the proviso that they should return to the Harbor of the Apostles Peter and Paul "during the last days of September." They next considered their experience to date. They found that approaching the land was unsafe because of violent storms and constant heavy fog and because of the many sandbanks and islands. Then they came to a decision to suspend further exploration of America and to "steer for the Harbor of St. Peter and St. Paul along the 53rd parallel of latitude, or as near it as the winds will permit."[14]

Among the reasons for the decision was a new threat—the dreaded scurvy.

In Khitrovo's log, in which the decision appears, is the news that Matthias Betge, the assistant surgeon, has submitted a report "in which he says that there are five men on the sick list, totally unfit for duty and that, of the others, sixteen are badly affected with scurvy and if we continue at sea until the late autumn these men too will be unfit for service."[15] Among the sixteen was Vitus Bering, who had not felt well for the past two days. His illness did not affect the management of the vessel because, from the beginning of the voyage, Waxell had been in charge of routinely assigning men to stand watch, hold the wheel, and change sails. He continued to see Bering in his cabin, which remained the command center for consultations and sea council meetings.

Typically scurvy began to show up on European ships after two months at sea. On August 10 the *St. Peter* had been at sea sixty-nine days, or two months plus a week or so. Cases of scurvy often terminated in death after three or more months at sea.

That Betge rather than Steller presented the report is indicative of the latter's status as persona non grata. Steller was ship's physician, with particular responsibility for Bering's health, but also, given his superior medical education, with supervision over Betge. Yet Steller was neither asked to make the report nor consulted about it.

Once the decision had been recorded, Bering called in five men—the ensign, assistant navigator, two junior officers, and the boatswain's mate. The decision was then read to them and they agreed to it. Then all five signed the document.

Concerning the decision Steller makes two observations: first, that "the land that had already been observed at 54 degrees could stretch even farther south" (he was right; it did); and second, that "the gentlemen want to go home and by the shortest route but in the longest manner" (that is, by bumping into islands).[16]

Unknown to men on either ship, on that very day the *St. Paul* was bearing down upon the *St. Peter* along the 54th parallel, just two days' sail behind. Chirikov, starting on the homeward voyage later (July 27), had already traveled a greater distance. Lacking shore boats to replenish fresh water, he was not tempted to explore. On August 10, with both ships committed to the same resolve—to get home as quickly as possible along the same degree of latitude—the ship with the greater handicaps soon passed the *St. Peter*.

On August 17 the first "real storm" set in from the west. The next day the wind moderated. On the 19th, blessed easterly winds drove the *St. Peter* straight to the west for five hours before slackening and veering to the northwest early the next day. On August 25 a "violent" storm beset the ship.

Two days later (August 27) another council was held to consider a new factor: two-thirds of the fresh water was gone. And so "for safety's sake" the *St. Peter* turned north "to go nearer the land with a view to finding good anchorage where we might take on water enough to last until our return."[17]

Several days later, with even less fresh water, the *St. Paul* passed by its sister ship in the race for home port on Kamchatka.

Steller felt altogether superfluous aboard the *St. Peter*. The jibes and taunts continued, but they lacked the verve and sparkle they once had.

He seemed to wander about as if in some echo chamber, somewhat stupefied, hearing voices but not always comprehending the import of the words. About daybreak on August 18, for example, he "heard someone on deck" talking about land. So he got up to see land "covered by fog" but still "distinctly" recognizable "in a strange place, namely, in the south." He was sure land was there. Seaweed was drifting from that direction, and "the west wind all at once was stilled."[18]

He thought Waxell and other officers were pretending they had not seen this land so that they would not have to put it on the chart. But, unknown to Steller, they had. It can be seen on the expedition chart as a very large island (about the size of Kodiak Island) south of the Shumagin Islands. The irony of this incident is that neither naval officer nor Steller saw an island (only a fogbank). It might just as well have appeared on a map in *Gulliver's Travels* (1725).

Steller asked Waxell what land they had seen.

"It must be Juan de Gama Land," said Waxell.[19] Grim humor there. Waxell of course did not appreciate the "dreadful deception" to which they had been exposed by "that false map" with its pretended "Juan de Gama's Land."

Rather than share in Waxell's sarcasm about a fictitious land they had sought and "sailed over" on the outward voyage, Steller privately took comfort in Waxell's ignorance about other land "reaching out from east to west in the north" that had also been called Juan de Gama Land on Joseph N. Delisle's map, which had indeed misled the Bering expedition.

On August 20 Waxell "mockingly" asked, "Are you still seeing land?"[20]

Steller ignored the question, but he recalled it when they later came upon islands at 51° north latitude. He did not laugh at them then "for not being able to see farther than their disposition and experience permitted."[21]

With his enforced inactivity, Steller sharpened his mind on the human comedy he perceived was being played out aboard ship. About council decisions, first to follow the 53rd parallel and later to go north for fresh water, he writes: "The council had scarcely ended, the matter been resolved, and the document signed, when in the afternoon the wind suddenly changed, and accordingly at once the decision. But the ship had hardly been turned when the wind again blew from the west and, continuing steadily, not only forced us, indeed, to make up our minds to sail toward land but also made us actually go."[22] Thus Steller amused himself.

On August 29, with moderately strong winds and a northerly course, the *St. Peter* made good progress from the 54th to the 55th parallel. Steller noted signs of land, first fur seals, second codfish on banks as deep as ninety fathoms, and finally "a black gull," probably either a fulmar or a shearwater. At daybreak the ship sounded at seventy-five fathoms, and at eight in the morning many islands were visible about thirty miles away. Just before noon the ship headed north-northeast toward the closest one, and under clear skies in the early afternoon came in the lee of the east side of Nagai Island, thirty miles long from north to south and, with neighboring Unga Island, the largest of all fifty Shumagin Islands.

The ship anchored briefly in twenty-four fathoms while Yushin, in the smaller shore boat, checked a small bay to the west. When he reported its rocky bottom unsafe, he was sent out again about six in the evening to investigate an anchorage midway between Nagai and little Near Island. This spot was satisfactory because it was "secure from many winds," with a good bottom. The ship then weighed anchor and was towed to this new anchorage two miles farther north. Here at seven o'clock in the evening the ship was anchored in twenty fathoms. With this anchorage further penetration into a cagelike bay of islands was avoided.

To the north and east, Steller saw five islands (Nagai, Near, Turner, Little Koniuji, and Bird). The continent was but forty miles away (Fig. 17).

Bering had been bedridden with scurvy for three weeks, and twelve members of the crew were on the sick list because of scurvy.

At two o'clock in the morning of August 30, Khitrovo, as officer on watch, spotted a fire on an island (Turner Island) about eight miles north-northeast.

Two hours later, at daybreak, Hesselberg was sent off in the larger shore boat to seek water on Nagai Island. He headed for the bottom of a narrow valley fronting the ocean between a high mountain ridge and a steep, rocky hill to the north. From the ship's anchorage this valley was nearly two miles away to the northwest. Hesselberg had ten empty barrels, ten men to row and fill the barrels, and three passengers— Steller, his friend Plenisner, and Thomas Lepekhin, his servant.

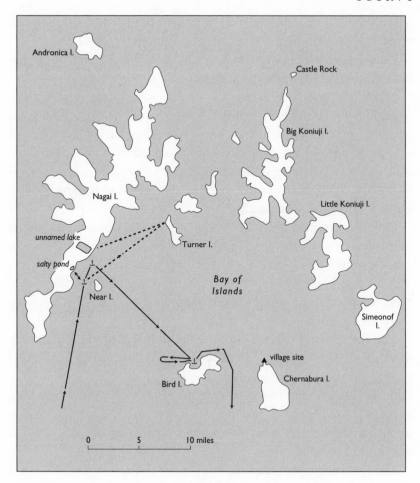

Figure 17. OUTER SHUMAGIN ISLANDS, 1741.

Waxell and Khitrovo had taken the initiative in inviting Steller to go ashore. He accepted the offer "very kindly," suspecting that he was being shunted out of the way before Khitrovo began selecting a small party to go in the smaller boat to investigate the fire seen in the night.

Steller was feeling generous, "desiring that both parties might find something useful"; that is, that he would find rare and exotic plant and animal specimens, if not also precious minerals, and that Khitrovo would have the honor of first meeting Americans. Steller assumed that Hesselberg would locate the water he was after, but he was not optimistic about his own prospects "on a barren and miserable island."[23]

Once ashore, Hesselberg found "a lake about 100 fathoms," or somewhat more than 200 yards, from shore.

Today this small lake or pond is 50–200 yards inland from the sea, depending on the end from which it is approached. It is about 200 yards from the sea at its northern end, where Hesselberg landed in a sheltered cove at the edge of a high, rocky cliff. The pond itself, up to 300 yards wide and 400 yards long on its straight eastern side, is roughly parallel to the sea. Steller sarcastically called it the "first and nearest puddle" and the "preferred salty puddle."[24]

Little has changed today. Although the land has become somewhat elevated since 1741, the water in the pond is still slightly salty because it is still within the ocean's reach. Although it no longer "rises and falls with the tide," as Steller reported, it is obvious that driftwood deposited along the pond's east edge has been swept over the sandy banks of the shore during storms.

The narrow strip of land between the shoreline of the sea and the shoreline of the north end of the pond is the first Bering Expedition landing site in the Shumagin Islands. A total of seven, and possibly eight, landings during two days (August 30–31) were made here, five or six to get water, one to take the sick ashore, and the last time to pick up Steller and his two companions and to gather up the sick brought ashore the day before.

The first landing was made at five o'clock in the morning of August 30. Steller located "several springs" with very good water, including the small stream emptying into the west end of the pond. But Hesselberg and his men had already filled their ten barrels with pond water. The veteran navigator agreed to take back to the ship a sample of spring water together with Steller's warning that the salty pond water would increase the incidence of scurvy and otherwise debilitate the crew because the water's salinity would become more pronounced through evaporation the longer it was kept.

Steller of course was mistaken about salty water being a cause of scurvy. Some eighteenth-century physicians, in fact, considered the drinking of seawater a possible remedy for scurvy. In 1747 it was one of six treatments (half a pint each day for two weeks) in James Lind's famous controlled trial in clinical nutrition.[25] These six treatments were all used in the British Navy and all had been recommended publicly. Yet seawater was no more a cure for scurvy than it was a cause of the disease. Steller had every reason to be concerned about Waxell's allowing unhealthy water to be brought on board. The quantity of water aboard ship was secondary to its quality—to its being truly fresh.

Shortly before noon Hesselberg returned to the landing to get more water and to report Waxell's judgment about the pond water. "The water is good," Waxell had said. "Just fill up with it!"[26]

Steller had meanwhile climbed over the hill to the north, about 1,000 feet above sea level, and discovered a lake, nearly two miles long and one mile wide, extending from shore to shore across the island. Because it was even closer to the east shore than the pond water, Steller proposed that Hesselberg use it instead. But the navigator now had his orders from the lieutenant and refused to have his men row another mile to the north to get it.

Steller's good advice as ship's physician would have prevented much of the suffering that occurred two months later. It was not, as he noted in his journal, a "seaman's affair" to rule in matters affecting the health of the crew, and he blamed Waxell's "old overbearing habit" for "the eventual ruin" his decision entailed.[27]

At this point Steller also expressed concern for his own health, "which had now," he writes, "fallen under foreign power," an allusion perhaps to an inkling that his own body seemed a bit sluggish because of the onset of scurvy.[28]

When Hesselberg and his crew returned to the ship with another ten barrels of pond water, Steller resolved to put the water question out of his mind and, with his two companions, reconnoiter the country.

About one o'clock in the afternoon the sick were transported ashore and escorted to a grassy slope off the northeast end of the pond. Here they had a southern exposure, where under sunny skies they could see the ship in the strait and the crew taking water from the pond below them. But by four o'clock a light rain fell, and a light wind had begun blowing up the coast from the south and the southeast.

By eight in the evening, the last landing on August 30 was made. Sometime between four and eight o'clock the sailor Nikita Shumagin died of scurvy. Steller writes in his journal that Shumagin "died just as soon as he was brought ashore," but the ship's log indicates that the news of the death did not reach the ship until ten o'clock that evening, although the men who had conveyed the sick to shore had returned by five.[29]

He was buried that same evening, very likely on the grassy slope where he died. He was the first European to be buried on the northwest coast of North America. The next day a wooden cross was erected over his grave, and the expedition named the island Shumagin (now Nagai), a name later given to the entire archipelago of fifty islands.

Steller spent about six hours exploring the island, then returned to the landing site with his two assistants soon after the afternoon rain shower. He had already built a shelter (he called it a hut), probably from driftwood, in which to spend the night. But he changed his mind about remaining onshore. It must have been Shumagin's death that prompted him "to go on the ship to bring up, emphatically and with greatest modesty once more, my opinion about the unhealthy water and the gathering of plants."[30]

His pleas, made in person rather than through an intermediary, ended predictably. Waxell "spurned and rudely contradicted" him. Instead of providing the one or two assistants that he requested, Waxell "ordered" him to gather the plants himself if they were so important. Having been addressed as if he were "a surgeon's apprentice subject to their command," Steller writes in his journal, he would thereafter take care of his own health "without the loss of one word more."[31] It was momentary pique.

Years later, in his own journal, Waxell defended his decision to take on water that he admitted was not good because it had "a faint flavour of salt water." Such water, he writes, "was always better than nothing, for we could at any rate use it for cooking" and use the remaining water for drinking. They had "no time to lose," and consequently they worked "all through the night" of August 30–31 taking on water.[32]

They had a busy day in taking on board thirty-one barrels, but the ship's log does not support the claim of continuing the water shuttle "all through the night." The last load came aboard about two hours before midnight. The boat was "tied astern" for the night, and it did not leave the ship until daybreak, about four o'clock the next morning. It is not to be doubted that Waxell "wished to replenish supplies of water in all haste" because he feared the southerly wind "could pounce" upon them and prevent their getting back out to open sea.[33]

Did Waxell use good judgment in rejecting Steller's advice about not taking the salty pond water? It is noteworthy that Waxell, in his report to the Admiralty and later in his journal, is strangely silent about the details of Shumagin's death and about Steller's advice. That the death and the advice weighed heavily upon him is suggested by action he took—too late—on August 31 in an effort to get good water.

Clearly Waxell made a mistake in having carriers take water from a pond that, according to Steller's report, had a visible outlet to the ocean and whose level was accordingly affected by the tides. Waxell, who claimed that both water samples Hesselberg delivered to him, one from the pond and the other from the spring that Steller located, were "not particularly good," tragically—and possibly out of spite for Steller—ordered Hesselberg to continue taking pond water.[34] The news of Shumagin's death that very day must have been shattering to the crew's morale, and Steller's warning, repeated as a consequence of this death, must have placed Waxell in an untenable position, one in which he could exercise his authority only arbitrarily and without reason.

On one point Waxell can be excused. He could not have known, as Steller did, that scurvy is preventable and even curable, that antiscorbutic plants known to Steller were essential for the well-being of everyone aboard. These plants were readily available ashore, even on the beach above the landing site, and his reasonable request for help in gathering these plants was urgent. Perhaps it was concerning the medicinal value of these plants that Steller found himself "contradicted," for Waxell was ignorant about any demonstrated remedy for scurvy.[35]

His ignorance is apparent in the short chapter he wrote about the disease as he observed and later experienced it himself during the homeward voyage. He offers a cogent description of the three stages in scurvy's development over only eight days. First, there is "a feeling of heaviness and weariness in all our limbs" and of wanting to sleep all the time. Second, the victim is made breathless no matter how slight his movement. Finally, limbs stiffen and swell up, the face becomes jaundiced, gums bleed, and teeth loosen. In all three stages the victim suffers from constant depression and sudden fright at the slightest noise. Waxell speculates (as do most of his contemporaries, including Steller) on the causes of the disease, such as "the continual damp raw weather," or "the continual diet of salt and dry foods," or "the often stinking and putrid water."[36] It would appear that Waxell eventually believed Steller, after all.

Ideas about staving off the disease also included bloodletting, keeping dry, getting fresh air, and staying active. Such ideas are of course wholly erroneous. Scurvy, as Steller and many others had already concluded, results from a dietary deficiency. But it was not until the early 1930s that the specific relationship between scurvy and diet was fully understood: the disease results from a lack of Vitamin C (ascorbic acid), a nutrient that must be constantly replenished because it cannot be stored adequately in the human body.

Three ironies stagger the imagination: Scurvy is among the most easily cured of all diseases known, yet from the fifteenth to the twentieth centuries more human beings died from scurvy than from any other disease. Second, certain remedies for scurvy were discovered throughout those centuries, yet tragically they did not become common knowledge. Finally, indigenous peoples, often called "savages" by Europeans, were generally not afflicted by scurvy because their diets included ascorbic acid. It was the proud Europeans, and especially seafarers on long voyages, who suffered and died because of their ignorance concerning good nutrition.

As late as 1741, British commanders were among the most ignorant of Europeans. On a voyage round the world, begun in 1740 and already overcome with scurvy in 1741, Admiral George Anson of the British navy lost 1,055 out of 1,955 men on three ships of his fleet, mostly from scurvy. It is no wonder that in the early eighteenth century, men in England were seized on city streets by roving gangs so that British naval ships might sail. It is also no wonder that James Lind, a Scottish physician, was moved to investigate literature about scurvy and to conduct his trials, showing that the juice of oranges and lemons was almost immediately effective in curing scurvy.[37]

The Bering expedition made three, possibly four, landings by the salty pond during August 31. By five o'clock in the morning, Steller, Plenisner, and Lepekhin, with the water brigade, made the first landing of the day. The water party returned to the ship at seven o'clock with eleven filled barrels, while Steller and his companions collected plants and seeds.

The last landing for water was made by ten in the morning. By eleven, ten more barrels of water filled the hold. A light wind, under partly cloudy skies, veered from the southeast to the east and freshened after ten o'clock. By three in the afternoon the boat was "sent ashore with empty casks" and returned the next hour "with the water." These notations in the log are questionable because, first, it would be the only trip from ship to shore and back, a round trip of about four miles, to be completed in about a single hour, and second, the twenty-one barrels already delivered to the ship completed the grand total of "52 casks of water" noted in the log at the sixth hour of the afternoon.[38]

By seven o'clock in the evening a last landing had been made near the pond. A storm was coming up from the northeast. Steller, Plenisner, and Lepekhin were found on the shore of the west coast of the island by a soldier sent to call them to the landing site. They were totally unaware of the rising storm because a high bluff blocked their view. They ran four miles up the west coast and then across the island to the landing site.

The situation was becoming desperate. The waves were so high that the sick, brought the day before, "could scarcely be hauled into the longboat." Steller and his two companions, collections and firearms in hand, waded through waist-high breakers and were pulled into the boat. After a rough ride to the ship, they were much relieved to be on board. The storm broke by ten o'clock, followed by a gale from the northeast three hours later. The gale lasted until late the following morning. By noon three inches of water were in the hold. The greatest worry was that Khitrovo and his party, who had left in the smaller of the two boats two days earlier, had not returned. If the gale did not abate, they might have to be left behind.[39]

CHAPTER ELEVEN

NATIVE AMERICANS

Khitrovo, who after midnight on August 30 had seen a fire about six miles to the north, proposed to Waxell that the smaller boat be used to investigate it.

Waxell demurred. It was a long way for the boat to go. In its present anchorage the *St. Peter* was not well sheltered from all winds. If a storm arose from the northeast, the ship would be forced to go out to sea. And what if a wind came up against the boat and it were unable to return to the ship?

Khitrovo said he knew the risks. He volunteered to go. Waxell knew that a future inquiry in Russia could result from failure to investigate a fire noted in the log. He decided to defer the decision to the commander.

Bering said Khitrovo should go. He should select his own men, including an interpreter in case Americans were found. He should have written orders with instructions about how to conduct himself with Native Americans. These Bering would prepare.

Khitrovo chose the constable, Boris Roselius; a soldier, sailor, and cannoneer; and Koryak and Chukchi interpreters. They carried firearms and gifts, including "½ pound Chinese tobacco, 5 copper bells, 160 beads, 20 needles, 2 *arshin* [about 56 inches] of red material, 5 small mirrors, and 5 knives."[1] They left the ship an hour or two before noon.

That morning at seven o'clock Waxell had not heeded Steller's un-
equivocal warning about bad water. Now Bering, in approving a venture
that was extraneous to their objective, had also made a decision that
could have fatal consequences. Perhaps scurvy affected his normally
cautious judgment. If Khitrovo were fortunate, he would get back to
the ship that night or the next day after about four hours of rowing
each way. If he were unlucky and did not make a timely return, he and
his men could be left behind as Waxell had warned, or the ship could
be drawn within the cage of islands in an attempt to rescue the party.

Khitrovo was unlucky, and the ship had to go to his rescue. A stop
for water, concluded in two days, had to be extended six days more,
and precious easterly winds that for four days drove the *St. Paul* rapidly
homeward threatened to destroy the *St. Peter* on Nagai's east coast.

Khitrovo reached his destination on the northwest end of a small
island (Turner Island) and beached the boat on a gentle, grassy slope
(Fig. 18). The fire was still burning. He saw "many other signs of
human beings but no human beings themselves."[2]

Unknown to him, there was an Aleut village on the other side of the
island. Did residents of the island build the fire? Perhaps. But it is also
possible that the fire was built by Aleuts who had stopped there on their
way from summer to winter quarters.

Khitrovo remained at the site overnight and the following morning.
He and his men left the island during the afternoon of August 31, the
day of a rising storm that became a gale through much of the next
morning.

As winds freshened, Khitrovo hoisted sail on the single mast so that
the boat might ride high waves that otherwise could swamp it. The
winds were east-northeast, driving them at increasing speed—not toward the ship but straight for the shore by the large lake Steller had
found (and whose water he recommended) on Nagai Island. It was a
wild ride that ended abruptly.

According to Waxell, "The large, powerful waves that were beating
on the island swamped the yawl and flung it and its crew up on to
land."[3] They crashed on a sandy beach. Miraculously, no one was hurt.
The spot where the boat and crew were hurtled upon the shore is the
third Bering expedition landing site in the Shumagin Islands.

During the first night that Khitrovo was away, a lantern on the gaff
had marked the location of the ship for him. When he did not return

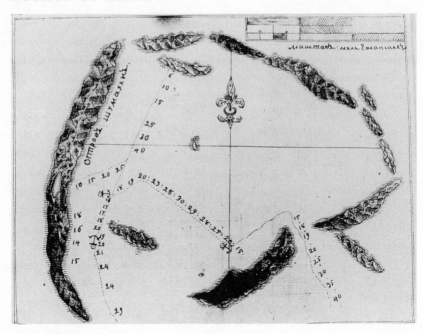

Figure 18. SKETCH MAP BY S. KHITROVO: OUTER SHUMAGIN
ISLANDS, 1741 (FROM F. GOLDER, *BERING'S VOYAGES* [AMERICAN
GEOGRAPHICAL SOCIETY, 1925]).

the second day before the storm, fears arose that the ship would be
forced to leave him and his crew behind.

Curiously the ship's log does not indicate a first sighting of Khitrovo's
party. At the fourth hour of the morning on September 1 the assistant
navigator, Kharlam Yushin, writes, "The yawl on which Khitrovo went
has not returned, probably because it could not get off shore."[4] That
statement suggests that Yushin and others aboard ship knew on what
shore Khitrovo's party had found temporary refuge.

With a gale blowing out of the northeast, there would be no way
that the small boat could be launched through the pounding surf off
the east coast of Nagai Island.

By the early hours of September 1, the bonfire Khitrovo and his wet,
freezing men succeeded in building was indeed visible from the ship.
They built the bonfire to warm and dry themselves out, "all soaked to

the skin from head to foot," and to make their presence known to the ship, because "theirs was a right desperate situation."[5]

That they were spotted on that wretched, stormy night is attested to by Steller, who writes in his journal that soon after the larger boat reached the ship, about nine o'clock in the evening of August 31, "a big fire was seen not far from the place where we had been taken into the boat," and that this place was "at the lake where I had suggested the second time that water be taken."[6] Steller supposed correctly that Khitrovo had just arrived there.

The site of the fire was between ocean and lake, about one mile north of the salty pond and three miles north-northwest of the ship's anchorage. The lake today is protected from flooding ocean tides by a sandy embankment over which no driftwood has evidently been swept. The east end of the lake is about a hundred yards from the ocean. Because of high rock cliffs rising from the ocean between the pond and the lake, it is impossible to walk from one place to the other along the east shore of the island.

During the storm and gale, the *St. Peter* was protected from east-northeast and northeast winds in the lee of Near Island. By daybreak on September 2, however, the wind shifted to the southeast, and the ship's anchorage was no longer tenable.

In thick fog Bering raised anchor and advanced three miles north-northeast to come once again in the lee of Near Island and to anchor in sixteen fathoms during the eighth hour of the evening, about a mile offshore from the stranded party. The wind was still coming out of the open sea behind Near Island when just before noon on September 2, with the sea going down, the larger boat was dispatched to shore through fog and rain.

Khitrovo and his men had already spent two stormy, wet nights by the lake. They had seen the ship set sail and then lost sight of it in the enveloping fog. The men were "in despair, believing that they must abandon all hope of being rescued." But their Chukchi interpreter, "seeing how unhappy they were, sought to give them fresh courage by telling them there was no need to despair." He said: "Even though the ship were obliged to stand out to sea, she would still come back again. And if [we] were compelled to remain some time on the island, [we] would [not] starve to death. [We have] sea cabbage [here] and an abundance of seaweed . . . good to eat. [We] could keep ourselves alive on it."[7]

Men on the ship did not know how the rescue was proceeding until the fog finally lifted by six o'clock in the evening. Yushin wrote in the ship's log that they saw "two fires on shore not far from one another."[8] One, they decided, was Khitrovo's; the other must have been built by the party sent to him.

The two parties on land were overjoyed to meet, but with "a regular gale blowing" and "a heavy sea running," they could not get back to the ship.[9]

During the night the winds continued to veer, this time from southeast to southwest, and the ship at last came under the lee of Nagai Island. Before six in the morning on September 3, "being up to their necks in the water," both parties got into the larger boat, and the boat got back to the ship and a warm welcome an hour later.[10]

By eleven the *St. Peter* sailed east-northeast from Nagai Island, seeking an exit to the open sea. Khitrovo, with sounding lead in hand, "at the first attempt left it at the bottom of the sea." Steller notes that some ordinary seamen "took it as an evil omen, recalling that just a year had passed since through his skill[!] provisions had been lost at the mouth of the Okhota River."[11]

The smaller boat remained behind. Waxell calls it "a sort of offering." Steller says it was "a souvenir" left "needlessly" behind.[12] It was left, Khitrovo said, because he could not get it through the heavy surf.

Also left were some empty barrels. Steller learned that Waxell, "beginning to tremble in the face of death," had secretly repented of his decision to take on salty water. Twice he had sent empty barrels ashore with instructions to the officer in charge to get water Steller had recommended. Twice they had failed, first on August 31, in the confusion of getting the sick into the boat, and again on September 3, when the rescue was made. Steller thought that Waxell and other officers wished to reserve such water for their private use. "Fate," he writes, "would let them partake of their biased stubbornness but not of the water."[13]

Once safely past Near Island (Steller called it "the rock"), the ship continued on a course into the middle of a vast bay encircled by islands. There was no way out. The exit to open sea was blocked by a southwest wind. Rocks like "the Twins," barely visible near the middle of the bay, raised once more the specter of submerged rock or shoals.

Every precaution was taken. Repeated soundings showed that the bay, at its deepest, was only thirty fathoms. There could be no tacking here through the middle of the night. Straight ahead was a small outer island indented on its northwest end by a rim of cliffs, and around its northern point farther to the east there appeared to be an indentation that might also offer shelter if the winds should shift from the southwest to the northwest. Nothing could be done but anchor for the night in the lee of the island and await favorable winds.

In the early evening, coming under the lee of that outer island (Bird Island), the ship anchored in twenty fathoms near the south end of a broad bay. It was out from a rock cliff just a mile and a half to the south.

Before daybreak on September 4, Yushin was sent in the boat to investigate what had appeared to be a bay around the island to the northeast. He returned three hours later with the news that the bay was in fact "an open passage" between two islands and that the depth of the water between them was only fifteen fathoms.

Upon Yushin's return, the *St. Peter* weighed anchor, set sail, and ran in a straight line to the west. Then, tacking, it ran back to the east. All day there had been no break in the stiff southerly wind. There was still no way out to open sea. In the late afternoon the ship anchored once again in the same spot off the same island nearly a hundred miles from the mainland. It was, says Steller, another "miserable" island.

They were going nowhere. They were finding nothing. They were still an estimated 1,277 nautical miles from home port. Since leaving Kayak Island six weeks earlier, they had covered only a fourth of the distance home. During the past two weeks they had made no progress at all, one man was dead, one boat had been abandoned, bad water taken on, and good winds wasted. With the autumnal equinox but six days away (September 10, Julian calendar) and winter coming soon behind, time—and provisions—were running out.

In one respect the outlook was hopeful. By September 4, nearly all the scurvy aboard ship had suddenly vanished. Men found, much to their surprise, that their sea legs were steady and their appetites strong. Even Bering was out of his bed and on the deck, beginning to feel as vigorous as he had been at the start of the voyage.

Steller had delivered them from scurvy. From the island where the sailor Shumagin lay buried, Steller had returned to the ship with lingonberries and crowberries and with scurvy grass (*Cochlearia officinalis*), sourdock (*Rumex articus*), gentian (*Gentiana algida* or *G. amarella*), and "other cresslike plants" that he knew to be "magnificent antiscorbutic plants."[14]

Starting on August 31, he fed raw scurvy grass to Bering and raw sourdock to a dozen ailing seamen. The commander was himself again, up and around "within eight days."[15] Seamen eating raw sourdock noticed a transformation in their health within three days. Swollen gums and loosened teeth were firm again. The old lethargy, the feeling of an overwhelming heaviness and weariness, of wanting to sit or lie down and not get up, was gone.

In his journal Steller makes but a single notation: "My ministrations, under divine grace, very clearly caught their attention." His status had abruptly changed from the academician the sea command loved to ridicule to the "good botanist"[16] and miracle worker they now regarded with no little awe. The belittlement and isolation of Georg Steller, which began on March 20 on Avacha Bay, ended five and a half months later off a small outer island (Bird Island) in the Shumagins.

The surest sign soon came from Bering himself.

No one aboard ship was paying much attention to the island with its high grassy hills or to the bay in which the ship was anchored. That bay was rimmed by alternating steep, rocky cliffs and gently sloping bluffs broken by a single sizable stream entering the bay south of its midpoint.

All thoughts were of the open sea, of the day's futile attempt to reach it, and of shifting southerly winds that continued to persevere and frustrate departure.

But then at four-thirty in the afternoon there was a loud noise from the island. Steller thought it was a sea lion, but it was "the screech of human voices."[17] He and others no sooner heard it than they turned and saw two *baidarkas,* or kayaks, one man in each, heading speedily from the shore toward the ship.

Everyone on the *St. Peter* was dumbfounded. All hopes of seeing Americans had been given up. Least of all did anyone expect to see them near this treeless outer island.

When they were a quarter mile from the ship, the two men began a long oration in high-pitched voices, a kind of prayer or incantation. When they were 150 feet from the ship, they stopped paddling. Now they beckoned to the ship and pointed to the shore.

The Chukchi and Koryak interpreters attempted to converse with the Americans (who of course were Aleuts), but to no avail. No word was understood. The Americans pointed to their ears, waved their hands, and pointed again to shore.

One came closer. He took some iron-colored clay and smeared it on each side of his nose from the nostril to the cheek in the shape of a pear. Next he stuffed his nostrils with grass. It could be seen that pieces of bone pierced each side of the septum. Finally, he took in hand two thin, polished spruce rods, seven feet long and painted red. Two falcon feathers were tied with baleen to the end of one and claws with feathers to the other. Laughing, he tossed these toward the ship.

Bering ordered that a number of items be attached to a board, including about five yards of red cloth, two small mirrors, three strings of Chinese beads, and twenty small copper bells. The board was then tossed to the American, who seemed pleased to receive it.

He came closer still, bound a whole falcon to another rod, and handed the end to the Koryak interpreter. Steller supposed that he wanted the Koryak to put silk between the claws to keep it dry. But the Koryak held on and pulled the American toward him.

The startled American let go and paddled back. Some silk and a mirror were thrown to him on another board. He picked these up, gave them to his companion, and again gestured for Bering and his men to follow him and his companion to the beach, where a bonfire and seven other adults could now be seen and their constant shrieking heard.

It was six-thirty in the evening.

Bering decided to accept the invitation. For the first time during the voyage, he gave orders for Steller to proceed ashore. The physician and mineralogist was now for the first time at sea fully accepted as an esteemed member of the expedition.

Besides Waxell and Steller, there were to be ten in the boat, including the Koryak interpreter.

Waxell proposed that he take all nine Americans prisoner. But Bering, mindful of his instructions to treat native peoples well "and not antagonize them in any way," forbade Waxell to carry out such a plan.[18]

Instead he ordered in writing that more presents be given. As a precaution, however, firearms and sabers were taken along, concealed under sailcloth.

When the party left the ship, it was about seven o'clock, scarcely an hour short of nightfall. They rowed south from the anchorage about a half mile to the beach within a cove of the bay sheltered from all except northerly winds. Here under a cliff along the beach the Americans had made their fire. Because of prevailing westerlies, it was the most sheltered landing spot within the bay. Here was made the fourth—and final—landing by the Bering expedition in the Shumagin Islands.

Today, whatever the tide, many rocks offshore, covered with seaweed, are visible above the water level at this location within the bay a few hundred yards southwest of an abandoned cabin on the bluff, remnant of an early twentieth-century fox farm.

Waxell decided not to beach the boat. It would have been too risky now that the ship did not have a second boat with which to make a rescue. Exposed and submerged rock was everywhere off the beach. Surf was running high and the water was becoming increasingly turbulent. Waxell dropped grapnel twenty yards from shore with cable paid out so that the boat could glide in between the rocks until it was scarcely three yards from shore. Here they were dismayed to see their presents, given earlier from the ship, strewn along the beach.

The Americans gestured for the men to proceed with the boat all the way to the shore. They were very insistent.

Waxell did not wish to give them the impression that he and his party were afraid, so he had the Koryak and two of the Russians go ashore unarmed. They were ordered not to go far and to remain in sight.

These three removed their clothes, hopped into cold water up to their armpits, and waded several steps quickly ashore, carrying clothes and boots over their heads. Once ashore and reclothed, one tied the stern painter to a rock before the three of them were led respectfully by the arm to a campfire and treated to a piece of blubber.

Meanwhile, the other half of the band gestured those remaining in the boat to come ashore too. The man whom Waxell judged to be "the eldest and most eminent of them all" picked up his kayak with one hand, carried it to the water under his arm, got in it, and paddled out to the boat.[19]

Waxell had a beaker of Russian liquor with which to greet his visitor. After demonstrating how to drink it, he presented a glass to the American, who drank it up "smartly" in a single gulp, immediately "spat it out," and "screeched most horribly."[20]

Waxell could not get him to accept a lighted pipe of tobacco or any other present.

Steller, who had warned Waxell not to give liquor or tobacco, was totally in sympathy with the American. "The smartest European," he writes, would also spit out a treat of "fly agaric, rotten fish soup, and willow bark."[21] He knew the first to be a highly intoxicating, poisonous mushroom (*Amanita muscaria*). On Kamchatka, he had learned that Itelmens and Koryaks valued all three items.

Meanwhile, the Americans continued to beckon their guests ashore. Steller observed that they "often pointed over the hill" to the northeast. He thought they were saying they lived on the other side of the island.[22]

Waxell had a copy of an English translation of *Nouveaux voyages de M. le baron de Lahontan dans l'Amérique septentrionale,* with its brief glossary of Huron or Algonquin words. From this glossary Waxell repeated *nipi* for "water." They obligingly repeated the word and pointed to what both Waxell and Steller thought was a spring-fed stream nearby. Waxell next tried the word for "meat" and was gratified when he was brought whale blubber. On the basis of these examples, Waxell believed that he had proof that they were indeed in America.[23] Not only is it highly improbable that Lahontan's words were at all meaningful apart from any sign language that may have accompanied them, but Lahontan's word list itself is suspect.[24]

With nightfall at hand, rain on the way, and water and wind rising, Waxell now ordered his three men on the beach to return to the boat. The two Russians returned right away, but the Koryak was forcibly detained. At first the Americans plied him with gifts of blubber and face paint. When these did not seem to please him, they seized him by the arms and would not let him go. Steller supposed they had "a very great liking" for the Koryak because his "speech and looks fully resembled theirs."[25]

But the Koryak was frantic. He begged Waxell not to abandon him.[26]

At the same time some of the Americans seized the painter and started to haul the boat ashore. They seemed determined to force their hospitality on these reluctant strangers. Given the maneuverability of their own craft amid rocks, they probably could not understand Waxell's concern for the safety of the boat.

For Waxell, Steller, and the men, it was not time for "angelic persuasion" or sweet talk.[27] Waxell wasted no time. He ordered two men to fire their muskets simultaneously over the heads of the Americans into the low rock cliff. The explosion of firepower stunned them, and they fell instantly upon the beach.

The Koryak sprinted to the boat, not stopping to shed his clothes and boots. As soon as he had been pulled into the boat, the painter was cut. When it was discovered that the grapnel was wedged fast under a rock, its cable was also cut.

To Steller, it was comical to see the "dismay" of their American hosts, who, standing up, seemed to scold them for bad manners.[28]

No sooner were Waxell and his party back on the ship than a storm with heavy squalls hit them from the south. It was eight o'clock. They had been near the beach but a quarter of an hour, far too little time for Steller to see what he wished.

It rained through the night.

On shore the Americans had a bonfire. It made Steller and the others "think this night about what had happened."[29] They could not know that the Russian firepower that day foreshadowed a regime some forty years later in which a few Russian intruders could control and devastate the lives of many far-flung island and coastal peoples.

Whereas Waxell's impression of these Americans was that physically they resembled Europeans, Steller notes several peculiar characteristics: straight hair, glossy and black; eyes "black as coal"; nose flat enough to appear squashed; lips thick and turned upward; and beards scant or nonexistent. Otherwise, he describes the nine individuals as young or middle-aged adults having stocky builds, brownish complexions, and average height. Only he reports the presence of women, but he makes no distinctions—their dress, he says, was the same as the men's.[30]

Their clothing consisted of a whale-gut shirt, or *kamleika*, reaching to the calf of the leg. Some tied this shirt below the navel. Others let it hang loose. Only two wore sealskin boots and trousers, dyed red-brown. Only two had a knife in a sheath on a belt. To Steller it appeared poorly made. Waxell notes that it was "about eight inches long and in front broad and thick."[31]

What distinguished these people culturally from northeast Asians was their facial ornamentation and their kayaks. Steller had previously heard that Americans who once crossed the sea to trade with the Chukchi used walrus teeth to decorate their cheeks and noses. Now he saw among this band a one-inch bone piece set crossways under the lower lip, on both sides of the nose, and even in the forehead. One man had a slate pencil, two and a half inches long, set diagonally through the septum. Waxell observes that several noses had plugs of grass. When these were pulled out, the liquid coating them was "licked up."[32]

As for the kayak, Steller provides specific dimensions. It was 12 feet long, 2 feet high, and 2 feet wide on top at the center. The craft was pointed at the bow and "cornered" at the stern. The deck was level; sides slanted toward the keel. The body was formed by poles fitted together at each end and spread apart by crosspieces. The keel was joined to the deck by "a vertical piece of wood or bone."[33] Steller, Waxell, and Khitrovo all state that the skin stretched as a cover for this boat was from a seal. In later years a sea lion skin was also used for this purpose.

Steller estimates that the hatch was 56 inches from the rear. Waxell describes it as "a raised part like a wooden bowl."[34] Fastened around this hatch was a piece of whale gut with a seam around its top. A long cord in this seam could be pulled and made watertight around the waist of a person sitting in the vessel in his long, loose whale-gut shirt with his legs pointed forward under the deck.

The kayak was so light that it could be lifted and carried with one hand, the paddle in the other hand. The paddle, says Steller, was "several fathoms long," or longer than the kayak itself. Its blades, one at each end, were quite narrow, a "hand's width." Stroking the water first on one side and then on the other, this single paddle, held in the middle, propelled the kayak rapidly for long distances in high seas. Steller marvels at the kayak's "great agility."[35]

He had seen nothing like it on Kamchatka, where the native inhabitants, being predominantly river people, used comparatively crude, open skin boats. The kayak provided evidence that Steller failed to consider: that these Americans in the outer Shumagin Islands were at home on the sea and that they lived on islands rather than on the mainland.

Their culture was accordingly distant in both space and time from that of the Itelmens. Whereas the Russians swept along coastal America by going eastward across the North Pacific, the ancestors of these Americans had some 10,000 years earlier crossed from Asia to America on or along a land bridge far to the north. Over millennia, those who occupied the outer Shumagins could be differentiated from those on Kodiak Island. Aleuts sat in their kayaks with legs extended; Koniag Eskimos knelt in theirs.

As early as 1945, most anthropologists believed that the Aleuts were an Eskimoid people who had moved into the islands from the Alaska mainland and that their language was related to Eskimo and unlike any spoken in Asia.

Waxell correctly supposed that the kayak was used to travel from one island to another, generally, he said, about 20 nautical miles. Actually much longer distances were covered, even 100 nautical miles in a single day.

How light and how fast was the kayak described by Steller and Waxell? A good guess is that it weighed no more than thirty pounds. How fast? Martin Sauer, who learned to use a kayak at Unalaska in 1790, described the frame as being "transparent as oil paper" and the speed "in a sea moderately smooth" as "ten miles an hour."[36] Thus the kayak, paddled by a single Aleut, was about three times faster than Bering's longboat, rowed by ten men.

Steller supposes that the kayak he saw was "very little or not at all different from that used by the Samoyeds and by Americans in New Denmark [Greenland]."[37]

Here again Steller's memory failed him. He was making comparisons based not on personal observation but on reading he had done in Halle or St. Petersburg. The Samoyeds, or Samoeds, lived from the land, specifically from reindeer, whereas the Greenland Eskimos (Inuit) lived from the sea, notably from seals. Whereas the Samoyed boat in no way resembles an Aleut kayak, the Greenland kayak is remarkably similar.

Steller's source was *Moscovite and Persian Journeys*, a popular book of travels by Adam Olearius (1599–1671), who obtained his information from a Danish captain, back in Denmark from Greenland. It prepared Steller for the Aleut craft he saw. Olearius provides this description of Greenland kayaks:

Their small boats with light frame are constructed partly of whalebone and partly of wood and covered with seal or walrus skins. They are shaped like a weaver's shuttle, pointed at both ends and scarcely 12 inches high in the middle, whereas a round opening nearly 24 inches wide is barely large enough for a person to get in and sit with feet stuck out in front. His cloak is fastened to the opening so that no water can get in. In travel he uses one paddle with a flat blade at each end, enabling him to recover quickly if he is turned over in a storm. If he is so inclined, he will let himself fall into the water, spin completely around, and sit upright again. He ventures several miles into the sea, knowing how to make such a fast getaway that our boats with their many oars cannot even follow him.[38]

Steller also describes the Aleut hunting hat. It was made of bark, "stained red and green" and shaped like a long eyeshade with an open crown. Set around the inside band under the visor were falcon feathers or reed grass. He notes that these decorations were confined to one side so that they did not interfere with a throwing arm on the other side.[39]

On the morning of September 5, when the wind veered to the southwest, the *St. Peter* became vulnerable in its anchorage. By two o'clock in the afternoon it was obliged to weigh anchor and move farther into the bay. At five o'clock it dropped anchor at a spot sheltered from the west, and once again, as on the previous day, kayaks came out toward the ship.

But this time seven came out, their paddlers having no apparent fear of firearms, despite the blast that had swept them off their feet the previous evening. In exchange for an iron kettle, five sewing needles, and some thread, the Bering expedition acquired two Aleut hats and a rod five feet long to which were attached "feathers of every conceivable kind." Yushin writes in the ship's log that "a small ivory image resembling a man" was fastened on the front of one of the hats. Waxell describes it as "a little human image carved out of bone, which we imagined must have been one of the idols they worshipped." Steller likewise describes it as "a small carved image or sitting idol of bone which had a feather sticking between its buttocks, which doubtless was to represent the tail."[40]

So little is known about the traditional religious beliefs of the Aleut that to ascribe any particular significance to the figurine, beyond that of decoration, could be misleading.

To the Aleuts, Bering's visit seemed timely, especially in the Shumagin Islands, where attacks by the Koniags were both deadly and frequent, destroying entire villages at a time. Each attack called for a counterattack, and even though Aleuts were victorious on Kodiak Island, Aleuts on the Shumagins suffered losses that made their settlements all the more vulnerable. They were also caught up in war with Aleuts of Unalaska and other Aleutian islands. Ivan Veniaminov (1797–1889), who first visited the Shumagins in the late 1820s, writes, "Some of the old Aleuts maintain that if the Russians had not come to these islands, it is very likely that all of them, to the last man, would have been destroyed."[41]

Aleuts met by the Bering expedition had blubber to eat and to share. Waxell saw from the boat that several of the Aleuts on shore "pulled up some roots, shook off the sand, and gobbled them up."[42] He could not know that Aleuts ate nearly all their food raw.

Steller and Waxell had little idea about the range of food items obtained chiefly from the sea, or the manner of obtaining them, or the seasons of the hunt. Not having visited families living in *barabaras,* they learned nothing about the Aleut household and community, nothing about marriage and the family, and nothing about legends and customs.

At the sixth hour of the morning of September 6, the *St. Peter* weighed anchor. With a favorable wind west by south, it sailed northeast from the bay until it turned south when it entered the channel between the two islands. The ship followed the route taken earlier that morning by the nine Aleuts, paddling in a straight line in their kayaks, headed home. That home was on a hilly point on a northwest spit on today's Chernabura Island, a point connected to the main island by an isthmus.

Steller thought he caught a glimpse of their "huts," but Waxell saw only the people: "They arranged themselves in a cluster and began screeching dreadfully."[43]

This was the Bering expedition's last, fleeting view of people whom they knew only as Americans.

A question remains. What did these Aleuts, so much at home on islands of the sea, think about the tall sailing ship and its big, fair-haired, fair-skinned men? Why did they take the initiative to come out from Bird Island and freely expose themselves?

Steller was not sure. He thought that the two men in their tiny skin boats were greeting them either as shamans, presenting a religious ceremony of prayer and incantation, or as leaders, welcoming them as friends. He writes that "both customs are in use on Kamchatka and in the Kuril Islands."[44]

Ivan Veniaminov, who lived in the eastern Aleutian Islands, 1824–34, writes in his *Notes on the Islands of the Unalashka District* that Aleuts fully expected the coming of white men. Shamans predicted that white men would come "from beyond the sea" and that "all Aleuts would become just like the newcomers and live according to their manner."[45] Veniaminov was convinced that such prophecy explained the readiness of Aleuts to accept the Christian faith. It was, quite simply, their destiny.

The ethnologist Waldemar Jochelson, who led a Russian expedition in the Aleutians in 1909–10, interprets the Aleut welcome differently. Aleuts "without any doubt have taken the Russians for unearthly beings to whom they rendered divine homage. The hawk's skin was presented as an offering and not as a token of peace or friendship."[46]

Expectations that living conditions would get better were widespread among old-time Eskimos living east of Bering Strait. James K. Wells, an Eskimo born there in Deering in 1906, writes about an old man named Ma-neal-yuk, who lived "about two hundred years ago," whose grandfather "from up above" had given him a message of hope for the people concerning changes in their future. These changes would occur when "the Big Go Around" got to their country. This particular prophecy was fulfilled, says Wells, "when the big ships started coming to every point of Alaska."[47] They were not a shock because they had been foretold and they signaled a better way of life for everyone. That "better way" was already evident during the first contact between Russians and Aleuts—the latter had knives. They did not make them. Where did they get them? The most plausible explanation is that with the product came news about the producer and about how the producer transported the product. The year 1648 may be a key. During that year and the next two, very visible events took place. Dezhnev's boat went through Bering Strait and the next year established a Russian outpost at Anadyr. Just as the Chukchi or Sirenikski Eskimos came out willingly and perhaps eagerly to trade with the Russians on the *Archangel Gabriel* in 1728, they had undoubtedly traded with other Russians stationed at Anadyr in their own territory. Therefore it is plausible that Aleuts with a few precious knives would know about Russians with ships long before those ships arrived. When at last the ship appeared, they would understandably meet it with appropriate ceremony. Veniaminov reports that Aleuts typically made an offering out in the open by tossing "a feather into the air, exclaiming *nung aqasaxtxin*, that is, 'Bring me' or 'Give me.' "[48] Instead of a feather, the Aleut in his skin boat off Bird Island had a staff to which falcon wings were attached. This staff he threw toward the ship into the sea. It was not, as Steller supposed, either "a sacrifice or sign of friendship" but an offering of thanksgiving.

There is no indication that the Aleuts regarded the Russians on the *St. Peter* as "unearthly." Steller observes that one Aleut came close to the ship "without fear." He was actually laughing when he threw the staff. Steller also writes of the "friendliness" of the small band of men and women who later beckoned them to leave the longboat and come ashore. Any Aleut fright or anger proved to be short-lived, because on the second day they once again came out to the ship with the same ceremony. For two of their hats they got the iron kettle, sewing needles, and thread.[49]

In this small way began commerce between Russians and Native Americans that would continue for the next 126 years.

CHAPTER TWELVE

CRUEL WAVES

Having emerged from the channel between Bird and Chernabura islands, the *St. Peter* came at once upon a pod of whales. To mariners the cavorting leviathans foretold a storm; one that hit furiously that first night out in open sea.

Before and after the storm, the ship ran rapidly during daylight hours, bearing southeast in the face of strong southwest winds. Its immediate objective was to get far away from the islands, and in this it succeeded. Within forty-eight hours the Shumagins were already ninety nautical miles away. A second objective was to return to the Avacha parallel, leading homeward at 53° north latitude. By the third day this objective was also reached.

There was no longer any debate between Bering and his senior officers about charting the coast of the American continent. Bering held rigidly to the goal of returning to Avacha Bay, even as his officers—given the lateness of the sailing season, the variable contrary winds, and the fear of a scurvy epidemic—spoke freely among themselves about wintering in America or even in far-away Japan.

For about two weeks, September 8–23, the ship made good progress. Because of northwesterlies, it slipped increasingly below the 53rd parallel—to the 52nd on September 14 and the 51st five days later. On the

8th it was 1,293 nautical miles from Avacha, and on the 23rd it was 771 nautical miles away, or already two-fifths of the way home from the Shumagins.

Like Bering, Steller favored a southerly route. He was aware that land continued westward out of sight to the north. He foresaw that this land, sweeping to the southwest, would yet confront them. There were constant signs of it. On September 10 horned puffins and gulls flew from the north and seaweed drifted in the sea from that direction. On the 15th, also from the north, came owls and a smaller gull he mistakenly took for a river gull. On the 16th there was more seaweed. On the 18th small snipes flew from the north. On the 19th they saw sea otter.

It was not smooth sailing. Whales sporting about again on September 13 signaled a severe storm on the 14th. Porpoises rushing about on the 15th heralded another storm later that day. Sea otter, seen on the 19th, seemed to provoke a delayed reaction, for the next storm did not blow in until the 23rd. Otherwise, though westerlies prevailed, they varied from morning to afternoon and even from hour to hour, requiring a constant adjustment of the ship's course.

These were of course unknown seas. On them the officers of the *St. Peter* had committed themselves to a terrible gamble—that the shortest way would also prove to be the quickest. There was constant fear of shipwreck, especially at night or in fog. For lack of sun at noon, observations of latitude could not be made for weeks at a time, and calculations made by dead reckoning remained uncorrected. Not knowing their exact location, the way of the winds, and the lay of the land, seamen felt apprehensive. This voyaging was grim business. With disaster looming at any time, no officer could sleep peaceably or stand watch without constant trepidation.

On September 21, under glorious sun, the *St. Peter* neared the 50th parallel with moderate northwesterly winds. All afternoon and evening, from noon until midnight, the sea remained very calm. A trysail was repaired. Thirteen men on the sick list enjoyed a respite from the rocking of the ship. Everyone had a good rest.

The next day, under more sun, the wind picked up and veered gently round the compass, from south to east to north. At noon observations of the sun revealed that the determination of latitude by dead reckoning was off by only a single minute. By afternoon the wind was generally northwest. But on the 23rd it shifted to the southwest. So for the first time in six days the *St. Peter* tacked to the northwest and ran continuously on this course for forty straight hours, recrossing the 51st parallel as the wind freshened and a storm blew in with customary rain or drizzle.

Now with the violence of the wind and the sharp rise and fall and crashing of the ship into the heaving waters of the sea, many men, says Waxell, "were attacked by scurvy so violently that [they] were unable to move either their hands or feet."[1]

Everyone feared this return of the scurvy. Only Steller, Plenisner, and Lepekhin had had a brief but timely reprieve from the steady sea diet of hardtack, groats, peas, dried beef, and brandy by sampling cresslike antiscorbutic plants during two days on Nagai Island. Only Bering and a dozen seamen on the sick list then had had Steller's prescription of raw scurvy grass and sourdock during the week after Shumagin's death. With his supply of plants soon exhausted, Steller had no way to treat any scurvy that might develop among the sixty-one remaining men.

On September 7, when the *St. Peter* had just left the Shumagins, Steller observed that "the unhealthy water already now daily reduced the number of able-bodied men, and many were heard to complain a lot about previously unheard-of adversities." In short, everyone was discouraged. The chances of getting home seemed exceedingly doubtful. Those in the initial stages of scurvy, suffering aches and pains and overwhelmed by a general lassitude, were feeling depressed. As early as September 16, twelve men were on the sick list, and seven days later, on the 23rd, "by the will of God died of scurvy the grenadier Andrei Tretyakov."[2]

He died during the fifth hour of the afternoon during a gale. When the winds let up temporarily toward noon on September 24, the grenadier's corpse was lowered into the sea. It was an eerie day, "clear with passing clouds," Yushin noted in the ship's log at noon. But how those clouds did pass! As Steller puts it, they "shot like arrows before our eyes" and even "shot out of two directions toward each other, with the same agility."[3] This display, triggered by atmospheric electricity drawn to the ship's mast in stormy weather, was called St. Elmo's fire, after the patron saint of seamen, and was considered a sign of luck.

Their luck was soon apparent, for at mid-afternoon they came quickly upon "numerous islands." With a southwest wind behind them, they were already too close to the islands to pass them on the south side.

Their only recourse was to turn back sharply to the east. Steller's words reflect a seaman's feelings: "It was most fortunate that we got to see the land while it was still day and before another storm hit because otherwise we should surely have run on it during the night . . . and been dashed to pieces on the shore."[4]

They had a close call, and they learned what Steller had predicted, that America did not extend westward from the Shumagins but in an arc southwesterly. From Kayak Island, above 59° north latitude, they had come upon Nagai and Bird islands at 55°, and now, halfway across the Aleutian chain, at little more than 51°, they had nearly run upon the same cluster of islands met with by Captain Chirikov sixteen days earlier.

For the *St. Paul* too had determined to follow the Avacha parallel homeward. It had approached Adak Island in a fog. By eight o'clock in the evening, September 9, it found itself in twenty-five fathoms. Chirikov anchored the ship and heard the pounding of the surf on a beach twelve hours before the fog began to lift. To their astonishment, the crew found themselves anchored only a hundred yards from shore.

They were close enough to see two men walking on the beach. Chirikov writes: "We called to them in Russian and in the Kamchadal [Itelmen] language . . . to come aboard. [A little later] we heard people shouting to us," but the breaking of the surf made so much noise that nothing could be understood.[5]

Having lost its two shore boats, the *St. Paul* had no way to obtain badly needed fresh water from the island. Its only hope was to get some from native inhabitants. With waves breaking over many rocks little more than a stone's throw away and with one end of the ship in twenty-eight fathoms and the other end in twenty-four, Chirikov took a calculated risk that the ship would remain sheltered from the wind.

About nine o'clock in the morning on September 10, seven men, each in a kayak, came out to look them over. Chirikov and his men gave them various gifts—bells, boxes, needles, tobacco, pipes—which they looked over with indifference, as if they had no use for them. Disdainfully they tossed a Chinese cup and two pieces of damask into the water. They let needles fall into the water and merely watched as they sank. What did these people want?

The answer was soon evident. "Among them," writes Chirikov, "we noticed several who raised one hand to their mouth and with the other hand made a quick motion as if cutting something near the mouth. This gave us the idea that they wanted knives, because the Kamchadals [Itelmens] and other peoples of this region when they eat meat cut it at the mouth."[6]

Chirikov had a knife to give them, and they were overjoyed.

Next Chirikov gave them a small barrel. They understood its purpose but refused it because they had bladders. Three paddled to the island and returned with water.

"One of them," writes Chirikov, "held up a bladder and indicated that he wished to have a knife in payment. This was given to him. But instead of handing over the bladder, he passed it to the second man, who also demanded a knife. When he got it, he passed the bladder to the third man, who [also] insisted on a knife."[7]

This tantalizing game, so profitable in knives, was not amusing to the men of the St. Paul. For whereas Bering had twice stopped to replenish the St. Peter's fresh water, Chirikov had cut water rations, and no one on the St. Paul had had a good drink of water for six weeks.

It was then that Chirikov, with some feeling, judged these playful Aleuts in moral terms. Their behavior "proves that their conscience is not highly developed."[8]

This remark is all the more ironic in view of the cat-and-mouse tactics unsuccessfully used to try to entice one or more of these people aboard ship. But the Aleuts were not inclined to take chances. They apparently feared that the Russians would use bows and arrows against them. They could not understand Chirikov's threat that he had men concealed on deck with guns loaded "in case of danger."[9]

In the end, these Aleuts proved only that they were as good as Yankee traders. They got their knives, an ax, and some sea biscuit. The Russians got some fresh water, a hat with an ivory figurine, four arrows, a bit of strange mineral wrapped in seaweed, and the roots of a plant that the Aleuts both ate and stuffed in their noses.

The morning rendezvous was repeated in the afternoon when fourteen Aleuts paddled out to the St. Paul. After several hours the visit ended abruptly when the wind rose suddenly, veered to the west, and threatened to drive the St. Paul upon rocks while the anchor cable was being heaved in.

In this extremity, Chirikov had the cable cut and sail put on, and "with God's help" the *St. Paul* beat a retreat to the southeast. It was, says Chirikov, "a narrow escape."[10]

After clearing the island by a safe margin, the *St. Paul* proceeded on a more westerly course, despite headwinds. Chirikov had the impression that the American continent was not far away, for from what other landmass could the people he saw have come? Like Bering and Steller, Chirikov underestimated the seaworthiness of the Aleut kayak and failed to consider that Aleuts were islanders.

Sighting land again on September 21 (the island of Agattu), Chirikov and his crew reached Kamchatka, entered Avacha Bay on October 10, and landed in the port of St. Peter and St. Paul two days later. He lost six men to scurvy, the first on September 16 and the last, Professor Delisle de La Croyère, on October 10. Without the services of his lieutenant, who died on October 7, and of the navigator and fleet master, who both died the next day, Chirikov and his mate, Ivan Yelagin, both gravely ill, gamely guided the *St. Paul* without relief during the last three agonizing weeks. In his cabin Chirikov worked out the courses from the logbook and passed on instructions to Yelagin at the helm. The ship reached its home port none too soon.

Meanwhile, when the *St. Peter* tacked sharply back to the east, it was running below the long southwest shore of Atka Island. No sooner had the turn been made than a new storm blew out of the south. A fierce wind became even stronger by the fifth hour of the morning on September 25, driving the ship relentlessly east-southeast in rain and heavy swells day and night.

The fortunes of the ship were now taking a horrifying turn for the worse. Eighteen days of difficult progress from the Shumagins to Atka were now matched by eighteen days during which the ship lost an incredible 304 nautical miles. (On October 11, when the *St. Paul* was nearing the port of St. Peter and St. Paul, the *St. Peter* was an estimated 1,072 nautical miles away—or three degrees of latitude directly south of where it had been on September 13, only one week out of the Shumagins.)

When the wind subsided somewhat the next day and shifted to the west, the *St. Peter* turned with it from south-southeast to south-southwest, but by evening heavy winds shifted again to the southwest and the ship was forced back to a southeasterly course. By this time sixteen men were on the sick list.

The next morning another violent storm hit. Steller was appalled. The west wind "charged," he writes, "with such terrible whistling, rage, and frenzy that we were every moment in danger of losing the mast or the rudder or even of receiving damage to the body of the ship itself . . . because the waves struck like shot out of a cannon, and we expected the final blow and death every instant."[11]

He consulted his older friend, the veteran Andreas Hesselberg, from whom he had been acquiring a growing appreciation of a navigator's skills. Hesselberg said: "During all my fifty years at sea, I have never experienced a storm like this. Nor have I heard of one so long and powerful."[12]

The next day was even worse. The ship was blown south of the 50th parallel in a storm that continued all day. In both rain and hail it became "most horrible" by ten o'clock in the morning.

A new blow hit out of the southwest at five the next morning. It was "so redoubled in violence," says Steller, that "every moment we expected the shattering of our ship, and no one could sit, lie down, or stand. . . . We were drifting under God's terrible power wherever the enraged heavens wanted to take us."[13]

Now more than half the men—thirty-eight of them—were sick. With each sharp jar of the ship they cried out in pain. The rest, says Steller, "were healthy out of necessity but thoroughly crazed and maddened by the terrifying movements of the sea and ship."[14]

Men given to cursing tried prayer, but Steller was convinced that "curses accumulated during ten years in Siberia would allow no granting of a prayer."[15]

So the ship bounced, banged, and rolled, often buried in darkness between the surging and towering waves. Nothing could be cooked. Nothing could be eaten except hardtack, already in short supply. Everyone was miserable.

The fury continued all through the day on October 1. Great waves washed over the deck. One of the lanyards to the main shroud tore loose. So did the main topmast stay. Next the gun port bulwark was swept into the sea. Boards were nailed in its place, a poor makeshift but the best that could be done.

Some officers pinned their hopes on God. If God would get them through this storm, they declared, they'd look for a harbor in America. But as soon as the storm began to abate the next day, Steller wryly noted that the same officers who had talked about wintering in America now hoped God would let them get back to Kamchatka, where they had families and property.

But these hopes were dashed when, at the eighth hour of the morning on October 2, a frightful southwester hit again. Now, says Steller, "People's minds again became as loose and unsteady as their teeth from scurvy."[16]

This storm continued for two days, but on October 4 the air for the first time became clear and very cold.

There was only a brief respite on October 5. A heavy westerly swell under very strong southeasterly winds allowed the *St. Peter* a good run to the southwest at three knots most of the evening during a downpour.

But another violent storm from the southwest struck early the next morning and continued intermittently for the next five days. Waves were once again washing over the deck. Many small sharks made their first appearance. The brandy ran out.

On the 7th, after a terrific storm most of the night, the wind let up a bit so that lower sails could be set, but little headway southwest could be made in high, westerly-swelling seas.

The 8th brought the first day-long break in storms in two weeks. At six o'clock in the morning with light wind, the *St. Peter* tacked from a southwest to a northwest course, and the next day passed the 49th parallel shortly before noon.

A terrible storm from the southwest hit shortly after midnight. With this storm, with winds veering to the northwest and becoming even more violent on October 10, the *St. Peter* was forced to swing to the northeast.

Then it seemed all too true that the winter would be spent in America. Kamchatka seemed altogether out of reach. Soon even the sails could no longer be set for lack of able-bodied men. Unless America could be regained, the voyage would surely come to a grievous end and all hands would perish. Such was the burden of Lieutenant Waxell's plea to the captain-commander, who, beset once again with a severe case of scurvy, was bedridden in his cabin.

Bering would have none of it. He ordered that money be collected from everyone in a vow to give half the offering to the Orthodox church in Avacha Bay and the other half to the Lutheran church in Viborg.[17]

This covenant was kept—by Russian Orthodox and Lutheran survivors newly returned to home port in 1742. But all funds went to the Orthodox church.

After the frightful squalls of October 10, with hail and snow and heavy seas running, sweeping over the ship's deck on both sides, the next day strangely ushered in a sea change, with stars out and then the sun. On the 11th, the wind died down to calm at midnight.

Then on the morning of October 12 the *St. Peter*, with a glorious southeast wind behind it, turned to the west, picking up unprecedented speed—four, five, six, and even seven and a half knots by seven o'clock in the morning—gaining forty nautical miles toward Avacha. The next two days, southwest winds prevailing, the ship persisted in a northwesterly course through rain, hail, and short-lived storms. Toward evening on both days a rainbow arched across the horizon. The ship gained a total of nearly ninety miles for the two days.

On the 15th and 16th, the sun shone all day. It was warm, and the sea was again quite calm. Various repairs were made to the storm-racked ship. At six o'clock in the evening on the 16th, the wind rose again out of the east, and again the *St. Peter* crested rapidly over the waves, exceeding five and six knots until the wind died down on the morning of the 17th. This magnificent ride gained 95 nautical miles. They were now 840 nautical miles from Avacha. A total of 233 nautical miles had been covered in a single week.

But good fortune did not hold. October 17 was stormy with variable winds. Everyone was exhausted or sick. Thirty-two men joined Bering on the sick list. The ship made little headway that day, and a successful race to Avacha again seemed very much in doubt.

The ship had become a hospital. On the 19th the third death of the voyage came at six o'clock in the morning; the hospital was also becoming a morgue. Grenadier Aleksei Kiselev was taken by scurvy.[18]

What Steller calls "daily deaths" seemed to follow. As the ship poked onward, corpses were wrapped and lowered into the sea with depressing regularity. On the 20th at the eighth hour of the morning, it was the soldier Nikita Kharitonov; on the 22nd, during a storm after midnight, the soldier Luka Zaviakov. The deaths could not be stopped. Men in advanced stages of scurvy could not eat with their gums swollen over their teeth and with their teeth so loose they rattled in their mouths. Their bodies hurt so much with every jar of the ship that they *wanted* to die.

It was, writes Waxell, "their only wish."[19]

Even the few seamen still on their feet were so weak that they could barely do even sedentary work. Waxell writes that "when it came to a man's turn at the helm, he was dragged to it by two other of the invalids who were still able to walk a little and sit down at the wheel."[20] Usually, he says, they begged off doing anything at all.

In desperation, Steller, who was "no seaman" but who was rapidly acquiring a seaman's outlook, was "implored" to take on a seaman's tasks. Though "it was not a part of my job description," he says, "I gave as best I could with bare hands."[21] What he "gave" was submission to orders from Waxell and other members of the sea command, the same ones who earlier had "scorned" him. He also surrendered voluntarily his status as a gentleman. "Bare hands" suggests making ship repairs and working with sails, chores in which he had little or no experience. But his Pietist outlook, as well as the urgency of the moment, moved him to action. He pitched in and did his best. Without abandoning his role as physician and naturalist, he took an early step toward unobtrusive leadership within the command by first humbling himself to the work of a greenhorn and an ordinary seaman. Steller writes that he was one of "four able-bodied men" during this most critical time of the voyage.[22]

To his credit, Waxell considered joining Steller in doing the strenuous work of a seaman. In his journal he writes: "I could perhaps have set some sails myself, but what would have been the use, when there was none able to take them in again." Most likely Waxell did not set sails because he was too sick to do so. Already he could "scarcely move about the deck without holding on to something."[23]

The same day Luka Zaviakov died, October 22, Waxell learned that only fifteen barrels of water remained, of which two were partially empty because their wooden hoops had rotted and burst, allowing water to drain out. Shortly after noon, in Bering's cabin, the naval officers in a sea council weighed four factors: the water shortage, the debilitated crew, the continuously contrary winds, and the remaining distance to Avacha (689 nautical miles). They decided unanimously to go north, to head for America for a third stop for water.[24]

They never got there.

At one o'clock in the afternoon on October 22, the ship made a port tack from a southwest to a northeast course, encountered a calm through the night, and thereafter, for nearly two days, a very strong easterly wind. As quickly as the wind shifted, the officers put off their decision to seek water.

On October 23 the St. Peter ran four to five knots for twelve continuous hours and registered 123 nautical miles toward Avacha for the day. The next day, driven by even more powerful easterlies, it ran another 70 nautical miles. The following day, October 25, with northerly winds, the ship gained an additional 59 nautical miles, reaching an estimated 446 nautical miles from Avacha.

During this extended run to the west, they were surprised to see, at seven o'clock in the morning on October 25, a "high, rocky, treeless," and snow-covered peak thirty-two nautical miles northwest by north.[25] This was 4,004-foot Kiska volcano, on twenty-three-mile-long Kiska Island, trending southwest and northeast. They called the island St. Markiana. An hour before noon on the same day they again sighted the volcano. This time it was eighty nautical miles away. At four o'clock in the afternoon, Khitrovo thought he had sighted another island. At this time, however, only Kiska volcano could have been visible to him.

Ever since the easterlies on October 23 had put off the officers' decision to go north to secure water, the St. Peter had continued on a westerly course, crossing the 50th parallel on October 24 and the 51st parallel three days later. A substitute plan proposed by Waxell was in effect: to move up to the 52nd parallel, follow it steadily, and land in the Kuril Islands or Avacha Bay, depending on the winds off Kamchatka.

This plan, not adopted formally, seemed reasonable to Steller. On the 27th, with a strong southwest wind and a starboard tack, the St. Peter adjusted its course west-northwest and by noon the next day had nearly reached the 52nd parallel, only 400 nautical miles from Avacha. It now proceeded westward along this parallel.

The cooper Stepan Buldirev died October 28, at three o'clock in the morning.[26]

With the wind dying down in the early morning, the St. Peter, enveloped in fog and drizzle, was moving slowly and cautiously. At seven in the morning the wind became very light and the fog lifted. Nearly straight ahead, only three nautical miles away, lay a small, solitary island.

Bering named it St. Stephen's; today it is Buldir Island. Steller describes it as "not very high but low land whose shore was flat and sandy." He was thankful for God's providence. "We would have been done for," he writes, "if we had come here a few hours earlier in the gloomy night or if God had not even now pulled up the fog."[27]

He was preoccupied with the ship being wrecked in the night because of seeing the nocturnal ancient murrelet (*Synthliboramphus antiquus*) flying aboard ship. He had seen that bird around Avacha Bay the previous spring and knew its habits. Also, this bird probably gave him the impression that Kamchatka might not be as far away as the officers calculated. He was eager for the ship to make progress.

Khitrovo had proposed that they drop anchor off Buldir and haul water from shore. "Fortunately," says Steller, this "disastrous plan" was rejected, presumably by Bering. "We all together consisted of ten weak men still able to give a hand who would not have been able to retrieve an anchor from the bottom."[28]

At noon the island was about four nautical miles away to the northeast. Near it Khitrovo supposed that there were "three small islands." Yushin, in the ship's log, also notes that near the island were "three small islands to the east not far apart."[29] Did they actually see islands? Buldir itself is a nearly circular island only three to four miles in diameter. Possibly the two officers saw the few islets extending northwest off Buldir's western point, north by east from the ship.

On October 29, with a southeasterly wind becoming a gale, the *St. Peter* ran westward, covering 100 miles in twelve hours. Yushin estimated that at noon they were only 279 nautical miles from Avacha.

At ten o'clock in the morning everyone saw a "low island" directly to the west only five or six nautical miles away. Bering named it St. Abraham. Today's Shemya, the easternmost of the Semichi Islands, it is four miles long and two miles wide. Once the ship had tacked to the north for two hours and the island could be viewed to the west-southwest about nine nautical miles away, Yushin observed "a projection like a cape" near the island. Steller identified it as the second of "two adjacent islands separated by a narrow channel."[30] In fact, he probably saw Alaid and Nizki islands as a single long island, cut off from Shemya by a strait only two miles wide. The three islands together trend generally east and west a total of twelve miles. The Semichi Islands were the ship's last landfall in the Aleutian Islands.

Steller claims that these "were taken to be the first two Kurils by the Kamchatkan inhabitants" aboard ship, and he himself believed they were right. But his four reasons for believing so are extremely tenuous: the abundant sea otters, a sudden west wind, the observed latitude, and the fog "in the west over the land."[31] The habitat of the sea otter, like that of the ancient murrelet, abundant or not, extends far to the east. The westerlies, sudden or not, are prevailing winds, encountered for the past three months of the voyage. The latitude observed for October 30 was not "50 degrees and several minutes," as he supposed, but 52°27', which was later discarded for a reckoned latitude of 53°4'. In short, the *St. Peter* was on the Avacha parallel, and the two northernmost Kuril Islands near the 50th parallel were more than 520 nautical miles away.

Steller even argues that the ship's future course north and west to Bering Island would show "without any doubt that we had been at the first two Kuril islands."[32] Perhaps for once Steller as deckhand was indulging in the wishful thinking of some of the crew, not realizing that the Kuril Islands swing away to the southwest from the Kamchatka peninsula, much as the Aleutians do from the Alaska peninsula.

He fully shared any rage of his disappointed comrades when "against all reason" the ship turned north as the wind suddenly became westerly. Steller may likewise have expressed the dark suspicions of his fellow malcontents that "there was concealed behind the decision a very secret reason for personal intentions: they wanted to go north to be able to pretend an urgent necessity for sailing into the mouth of the Kamchatka River and not to Avacha."[33]

Waxell turned north to get around the islands. Once the *St. Peter* reached the 53rd parallel in the early afternoon of October 30, it tacked alternately southwest and northwest through the next day before turning north-northwest on November 1 and generally west-southwest through November 4, on which day it was by observation at 54°30' north latitude.

These were days of extreme travail. The "daily deaths" resumed. On October 31, at eight o'clock in the morning, the soldier Karp Pashennoi died; on November 2, also at eight o'clock in the morning, the carpenter Ivan Petrov; on November 3, just after midday, the drummer Osip Chentsov; just before midnight the soldier Ivan Davidov; and, at the fifth hour of the morning, the grenadier Aleksei Popov. On November 5, at the fourth hour of the morning, the grenadier Ivan Nebaranov was the last one to die at sea.[34]

Fortunately the terrible storms had ended, yet the ship was managed "with great difficulty." Men such as Yushin functioned in agony, being, as he says "altogether exhausted from scurvy." They remained at their stations "only because of extreme necessity." The ship, says Waxell, "was like a piece of dead wood, with none to direct it. We had to drift hither and thither at the whim of the wind and the waves."[35]

On November 4, at seven o'clock in the evening, the ship's sail was shortened because, as it was announced, Kamchatka was at hand. After so many weeks at sea, such news was hard to believe. But at nine o'clock the next morning, land appeared, as foretold, on the horizon. Khitrovo estimates that it was twenty-eight nautical miles away. Yushin reports it was sixteen nautical miles, and writes in the log: "On this land there is a mountain ridge covered with snow. We think this land is Kamchatka."[36]

It was incredible. "The half-dead," says Steller, "crawled out to see it. From our hearts we thanked God for his favor. The very sick captain-commander was himself not a little cheered. Cups of brandy, here and there secretly concealed, were produced to sustain the pleasure."[37]

Sketches of Avacha Bay made their appearance, and the land ahead was said to agree perfectly with the sketches. The capes, the Vaua Lighthouse, and the harbor mouth were all identified. The ship's course was then set farther to the north toward a cape considered to be Isopa, just south of Avacha Bay.

Having rounded that cape about nine o'clock in the morning of November 5, the *St. Peter* entered what appeared to be a broad inlet. Here at noon an observation of the sun placed the ship halfway between the 55th and 56th parallels, or more than 100 nautical miles *north* of the Avacha parallel.[38]

The land had fooled them. There was great consternation. Was this land Kamchatka?

The ship tacked to the southeast, returning close to the entrance of the supposed inlet at five in the afternoon. A storm appeared to be rising. Once again the crippled ship reversed direction. Some sails were furled, but not enough. During the night, in rising strong wind, shrouds of the mainmast were badly torn.

Waxell had had enough. He told Bering that the ship was now nearly a wreck.[39]

During the *St. Peter*'s voyage from August 30 to November 6, 1741, 12 men died, and 20 more were yet to die, leaving 46 survivors. Thus, on November 6, 15 percent of the *St. Peter*'s complement of 78 had perished. On January 8, 1742, at the end of the period of deaths, the *St. Peter* had lost 41 percent of its men.

The *St. Paul*, completing its voyage on October 12, 1741, lost 21 out of 76 men, or 28 percent of its crew.

PART THREE

SHIPWRECK AND SURVIVAL

CHAPTER THIRTEEN

DECISION TO LAND

Bering Island

At the behest of his officers, Bering called a sea council and invited everyone who could get to his cabin to attend.

According to Steller, the outcome of this council had already been determined. Steller believed that Khitrovo had persuaded Waxell and many of the other seamen that the ship should be anchored in the broad bay they could see about fifteen nautical miles to the west. In that bay the sea voyage could be terminated.

The meeting took place at seven o'clock in the morning, November 6.

First, Bering presented his view. No one was surprised that he insisted on proceeding directly to home port in Avacha Bay. His argument can be summed up in these words: We have already endured much. We still have six barrels of water. We can use the lower sail on the foremast. We don't have far to go.[1]

Waxell and Khitrovo, next in rank, responded with arguments already well rehearsed: almost everyone has been sick for a long time and there is no one to mind the ship. The time is late and the weather severe. The mainmast is useless and the shrouds are ruined. Help from the Lower Kamchatka Post is nearby. We need only send for horses.[2]

Some seamen said they would put their signatures to a decision to land "if they could be assured positively that this land was Kamchatka."[3]

Khitrovo said that "if this were not Kamchatka, he would let his head be chopped off!"[4]

Bering told his adjutant, Dmitry Ovtsin, formerly a lieutenant, to speak next.

He said that he supported his commander's recommendation.

He paid dearly for that support. Waxell and Khitrovo ran him out of the meeting with their epithets of "dog" and "son of a bitch" ringing in his ears.[5]

Bering was too sick to control the proceedings.

Steller, who was next in rank (his social rank was nearly equivalent to that of lieutenant), did not wish to suffer Ovtsin's fate. He quoted himself as saying: "I have not been consulted about anything from the start, and my advice will not be taken if it is not just as you would want. Besides, the gentlemen themselves say I am no seaman, so I would rather say nothing."[6]

Bering could not insist that Steller express an opinion about what should be done. But he did ask that Steller, as physician, prepare a written statement concerning the health of the crew. This much Steller could not refuse.

So it was agreed to run the *St. Peter* into the bay and seek refuge on land.

Bering was resigned. With so many lives and her majesty's ship at stake, a sea council augmented by all the available crew had appropriately made a decision. Now it had to be carried out, whatever the consequences.

Steller, for his part, viewed the sea council as an outrageous farce. Too many men were desperate, their minds still as loose as teeth from scurvy. And some of those who had any sense had been bullied.

There had earlier been the voice of Khitrovo, bragging so unashamedly: "If there had been a thousand navigators, they could not in their reckoning have hit it within a hair's breadth like this. . . . We are not even [two miles] off."[7]

If Khitrovo were the foolish prophet, then Waxell was the foolish mariner in giving up on the ship prematurely. After sailing so far, they were expecting to see Kamchatka. They also, Steller said, entertained the false notion, based on the experience of the first expedition, that no island could be found this close to Kamchatka.[8] In their present exigency, so much depended on sober judgment and prudent action.

The decision was made. It seemed to Steller that no one cared any more about anything. And now they were headed straight for shore.

From all indications, Steller concluded it was an island. If earlier he had joined other seamen in mistaking the Semichi Islands for the first two Kurils, this time he stood alone in viewing the land before them with a cool eye. He reasoned as follows: The mainland from Cape Lopatka to the Chukotsk peninsula trends northeast. This land, as far as he could see from south to north, trends northwest. Then there was this question: If the point of land they had already passed were a cape of Kamchatka, why did it seem to be longer than Cape Shipunski, the longest on Kamchatka? Finally, Steller observed that, after all the wild speculation about recognizing points of land near Avacha Bay, no one— no seaman, no native of Kamchatka—was now professing to identify features of the land before them.[9]

Later they learned that what appeared to be an inlet was actually a broad channel between Copper and Bering islands. Isopa was actually the southernmost point of Copper Island. Had a rising storm not kept the *St. Peter* from seeing beyond Cape Manati, the southern point of Bering Island (Fig. 19), men on the *St. Peter* might then have known that the ship had come upon two large islands, not the Asian continent. Even as late as the sea council, Bering and his men were prevented by fog from seeing that the "inlet" was in fact a channel.

The two islands, together called the Commander Islands, can be regarded geographically as the last distant links between America and Asia. On a map of the North Pacific Ocean they resemble nearly parallel slivers, with Copper Island southeast of its wider sister island. Viewed from the east, they are off the deep end of the Aleutian chain, 200 nautical miles from Attu Island and half that distance from the Kamchatka peninsula of the Asian mainland. They are usually too blustery, foggy, and wet for a pleasant sojourn. Until the era of ships and planes, they were desolate, solitary places, uncharted and forgotten or unknown. They were, and still are, islands at the end of the world.[10]

On a map the Commanders may be viewed pictorially as the last wisps of a beard blown out in an arc from the chin of Alaska, whose face farther north goes nose to nose with Chukotka. By itself, Bering Island, seen up close, resembles a spike, slightly bent near its southern point (Cape Manati) and not at all level across its northern head (from

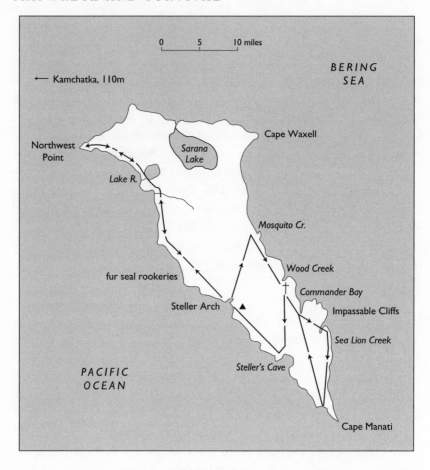

Figure 19. BERING ISLAND, 1741–42. THE BROKEN LINE INDICATES THE
ROUTE OF STELLER'S FIELD TRIPS, MAY–JUNE 1742.

Northwest Point to Cape Waxell). The spike looks battered—hit too
hard too often, its shape hammered by Arctic storms and misshapen by
frequent earthquakes.

Mednyi, or Copper Island (so called because low-grade copper deposits were found there in the eighteenth century), is twenty nautical
miles southeast from Bering Island but trending in the same northwest
direction. Whereas Bering is fifty-five miles from top to bottom and
roughly twelve miles across its middle, Mednyi is nearly as long but
half the width, a nail without a head and with a blunt bottom point. Its

western side is straight-backed, its eastern shoreline marked by seven broad bays. Both islands are rocky and precipitous, with high barren spines covered by snow six months of the year.

Yet such remote, forbidding ground has both a history and a natural history. In 1826, Russians transplanted Attuans and Atkans to the Commanders to manage fur seal colonies, but these native peoples (according to their traditions) had already been there years before on extended *baidarka* hunts. Yet neither Aleuts nor Russians were first. In the summers of 1979 and 1981, Russian archaeologists, excavating the 1741–42 winter camp of the Bering expedition, turned up stone and bone tools (scrapers, blades, and spalls) of an ancient camp of Neolithic inhabitants who had once lived in subterranean dwellings in the same sandy ridge chosen by the Bering expedition.[11] It was simply a matter of making the same wise choice thousands of years apart—of selecting a site where a nearby high bluff cut off Arctic winds, where fresh water and salmon in season were close by in the Commander River, and where the sea was but a few minutes away.

There was an abundance of mammals: sea otters, seals, sea lions, fur seals, and that most gentle and humanlike creature, the giant manatee, *Hydrodamalis gigas*, otherwise known as the sea cow. In his reports Steller gives the impression that Bering Island was a sea mammal Eden (he did not get on Mednyi). It was a birthing place. Sea otters regularly came ashore to pup and to rest, fur seals and sea lions mingled by the thousands in rookeries along the western shore, and seals and sea cows ringed the island in shallow water, the latter clustering in groups near the mouths of streams, the youngsters snuggled protectively between mother and father, all the family chomping endlessly on seaweed. They ate so much that their adult bodies were thirty feet long and twenty feet in diameter. They were four-ton balloons, with small, thick head, two short forefeet, two flippers, and one long tail appended. Steller says that these sea cows were sometimes so close to shore that he could tap their heads with a pole.[12]

Perhaps for a few years it was an Eden for wildlife, but for the Bering expedition the place was hellish. Going in to land was itself a bad dream.

At four o'clock, an hour after the sea council, the ship tacked for the last time, and with a strong wind from the north headed west-southwest for a broad bay. Main yards and main-topmast both lowered, it crept toward the bay ever so slowly.

Finding himself alone on deck as the ship neared the beach, Steller learned that Waxell and Khitrovo were both sleeping. Alarmed, he rushed to Bering, who had the officers called to the deck.[13]

They hove the lead: thirty-seven fathoms. An hour later they hove again: twelve fathoms. At nine fathoms they dropped a small bower anchor and paid out its cable. The ship was headed straight for shore, just a quarter mile away.

At six o'clock the cable broke. "The ship," Steller says, "was tossed back and forth like a ball" by heavy surf. "Twice," says Waxell, "the ship bumped on rocks."[14] It seemed as if the bottom of the ship would be smashed to pieces.

To Steller it was bedlam. The ship bounced on the reef as the surf crashed against the ship. With all the racket and the cries and moans, it was impossible to know who might be giving orders and who might be receiving them.[15]

Steller heard someone laughing, asking, "Is the water very salty?" and he wondered what the man was thinking. Did he suppose that death would be "sweeter in sweet water"? He heard another man cry out, "Oh, we are done for! O God, our ship! A disaster has befallen our ship!"[16]

Steller noticed several seamen tumbling corpses overboard "head over heels." These corpses had been kept for several days for proper burial ashore. Now they were dumped unceremoniously in the shallow waters of the bay. Steller thought that these men were superstitious, blaming the dead for the terror they felt.[17]

Then above the din came the shout of an officer who, it seemed to Steller, was "terrified and gripped by fear of death." This man wanted the anchor cable cut and a new anchor thrown into the pounding surf. It was dropped in five fathoms, but to no avail. The cable again broke. In scarcely twelve minutes two precious anchors had been lost.[18]

Now Steller was aware of the calming presence of Adjutant Ovtsin and the boatswain. They stopped the casting of any more anchors. Their counsel was to let the ship float. Incredibly, the waves instantly lifted the ship over the rock reef and into calm waters four fathoms deep with a sandy bottom. Here, 600 yards from shore, the last anchor was dropped.

The voyage into unknown seas was finished. Sixty-six survivors rested on the deck of the ship under a moonlit sky. What Waxell called "God's miraculous, merciful assistance" was all the more wonderful when later came the revelation that nowhere else round the 140-mile coast of Bering Island could a ship breach the encircling outer reef but the portal through which the *St. Peter* so helplessly chanced to come.[19]

Now it was a question of time before a storm would plunge the ship in one of two directions—out toward sea, irretrievably if it did not crash on the encircling reef, or lifted up and driven upon the shore.

CHAPTER FOURTEEN

DEATH CAMP

After a day of confusion and terror, the ship sat tranquilly like a dark bird upon the water through a night with bright sky and light northwest winds. These favorable conditions held all the next day, November 7.

Yet the situation of the Bering expedition was desperate. Besides the twelve men who had died on the return voyage, thirty-four were totally disabled by scurvy. Many others were so sick that they could scarcely get about. Bering was incapacitated by the disease. Those remaining who were still quite healthy included the Steller trio—Steller himself, his friend Plenisner, and his servant, Thomas Lepekhin, no doubt well fortified with the antiscorbutic herbs they had gathered on Shumagin Island. Those who very likely had benefited from Steller's botanical largesse other than Bering included Matthias Betge, the assistant surgeon, and 12-year-old Laurentz Waxell, the lieutenant's son.

While Bering was gravely ill, Steller became very active on shore, determined to save as many men as possible. Both Waxell and Khitrovo remained mostly aboard ship for two weeks, and then when they did come ashore both were severely stricken by scurvy.

The immediate objective was to get to shore to try to save Bering and all the other scurvy-afflicted men: first, to find fresh water to replace the remaining brackish water taken from Shumagin Island; second, to get fresh meat; third, to gather antiscorbutic plants; and last, to locate a spot where the sick could be sheltered and tended.

Though quite ill himself, Waxell accompanied Steller as co-leader of the landing party, consisting of Plenisner, Thomas, young Laurentz, a cannoneer, two cossacks, and several of the sick. In the boat, leaving the ship shortly before noon, were also the oarsmen, the baggage of those who were to stay ashore, and sail for a tent.

As they approached the beach, they saw sea otters coming toward them from the land. It seemed strange that they should be on shore and so tame and curious.

Once ashore, the oarsmen tended the boat and the sick. The cannoneer and cossacks went hunting in one direction, Plenisner hunted by himself in another direction, and Steller, Thomas, Waxell, and his son headed for the mouth of a small meandering river debouching into the sea at the northwest end of the bay. Here, above the mouth, between the river and a steep bluff marking the north end of a long valley, they came to a promising site, consisting of parallel dunes. Between the dunes were deep hollows over which sail could provide a roof. The site offered proximity to fresh water, shelter from the wind, ready access on firm ground to the beach, and sand, which could be easily shaped and through which the urine of the sick could quickly pass. The chief disadvantage of the entire bay area was the absence of plentiful driftwood for fuel.

While the Waxells returned to the landing site to lead the sick to their new home, Steller and Thomas scouted the area for plants, took notes, and toward evening returned to the camp. Here he found the lieutenant "very weak and faint."

They indulged in tea and conversation.

"God only knows if this is Kamchatka," Steller said. "What else would it be?" asked Waxell defensively. "We will soon send for post-horses but will let the ship be taken to the mouth of the Kamchatka River. The first priority is that we save the men."[1]

Then Plenisner showed up with a half dozen ptarmigan. Steller contributed nasturtiums and brooklime (*Veronica americana*) for a salad. With this fresh food, intended specifically for Bering, Waxell and his son returned with the oarsmen, arriving on board ship about eight o'clock in the evening.

Steller was now briefly in charge of the camp. When the two cossacks and the cannoneer came in with only the pelts of two sea otters and two seals, Steller reproached them for discarding the meat. They dutifully went out to get another seal because they supposed it would taste better than the otter.

Meanwhile Steller prepared ptarmigan soup. After supper Plenisner constructed a hut between the dunes. It was made of driftwood and old sail. Here they all slept overnight.

Good weather continued the next day, November 8.

In the morning Steller and Plenisner agreed to divide the hunt. Plenisner would shoot birds, Steller animals. They would meet at the camp before noon.

Steller and Thomas followed the beach to the southeast. They collected plant specimens and chased an otter, and Thomas shot eight Arctic foxes (*Vulpes beringensis*). Steller could hardly believe how numerous, fat, and unafraid they were.

Also, for the first time in his life, he saw manatees. They were offshore, only their rounded backs showing as they fed on seaweed under the water. Were these beasts known on Kamchatka? Thomas did not think so. And if this land were Kamchatka, where were the trees and shrubs? Then he noticed, over the land to the southwest, clouds reflecting the image of the sea. More and more this land appeared to be an island.

After lunch at the camp, Steller, Plenisner, and Lepekhin decided to hunt for driftwood by following the shore in the other direction, to the northwest. They found not the least bit. But they saw more sea otters, shot more foxes and ptarmigan, and stopped by a small stream for a tea break, thanking God for plentiful fresh water and terra firma. They also reflected on strange events and—once again—on "the unjust proceedings of various men," including of course Waxell and Khitrovo of the naval command.[2]

That evening in camp, having eaten, they saw an Arctic fox approach and run off with two of their ptarmigan. It was only the first of many thefts.

Steller now began to consider how the Bering expedition could best survive a winter on this land if indeed it were an island. It seemed to him that men would need to stand together as comrades, sharing equally, setting aside considerations of rank and learning.

He knew that Thomas was beginning to feel weak, sick, and depressed. Thomas asked him why they had to go on this voyage and endure such misery.

Steller replied, "Cheer up! God will help. Even if this is not our country, we still have hope of getting there. You will not die of hunger. If you cannot work and wait on me, I will wait on you. I know your honest heart and what you have done for me. Everything I have is also yours. Just ask and I will share with you half of all I have until God helps."

But Thomas was not easily consoled, nor did he quite understand what Steller was saying. "All right, sir. I will gladly serve you. But you are responsible for having led me into this misery. Who forced you to go? Could you not have enjoyed good life on Bolshaya River?"

Steller laughed goodheartedly. "Thank God, we are both alive. If I have dragged you into this misery, then you have also in me, with God's help, a faithful friend and benefactor. My intentions were good, Thomas. So let yours be good also. After all, you cannot know what might have happened to you at home."[3]

In this way he made a start toward a new relationship with the young man who had been his servant.

Next he approached Plenisner. They agreed to build a new dwelling, to be partners pledged to each other no matter what happened. Steller could tell that his friend was not yet ready to agree that they were on an island; he was going along with the idea of being on an island to avoid being disagreeable. In any case, sharing a dwelling obviously appealed to him. It would symbolize their commitment.

On November 9 the weather was tolerable, with easterly winds. In the morning the two friends gathered wood and scouted for a site. Upstream from their first camp and closer to the bluff, they picked a place on a sandy ridge.

The pesky foxes were everywhere around them. The temptation to purge them from the vicinity of their future home was too great to resist. So the two men went on a rampage, Plenisner with an ax and Steller with his long knife. They hacked and stabbed, killing as many as sixty foxes. It was only the beginning of a brutal campaign to run off the maddening little animals.

That evening the two men returned to the original camp, where they found Bering resting under a tent in a hollow specially prepared for him; separate quarters were provided the ten other sick men. Boatswain Nils Jansen had died that morning on the ship and been buried ashore.

Bering had come to his own dwelling in a makeshift litter carried by four men. He was flat on his back. Steller was "amazed at his composure and strange contentment."

Bering asked Steller what he thought about this land.

Steller said it did not look like Kamchatka. He explained that the animals were too abundant and too tame to be living where people also lived. But Kamchatka must not be far because plants Steller had observed here were the same ones he had seen there, whereas plants peculiar to America were not to be found here. Then Steller told him about the manatees, unknown on Kamchatka, and about clouds to the southwest reflecting images of the sea. He showed Bering a poplar window shutter with cross moldings that he had found only that morning farther up the river. Apparently it had come ashore some years ago to be later carried by a high tide that also washed sand over it. He was sure it was of Russian workmanship, coming perhaps from a storehouse built at the mouth of the Kamchatka River. If so, he thought that this land could be on Cape Kronotski. But he said he was not convinced that they were somewhere on the cape because of another artifact found the day of the landing. Steller pulled out of his pocket a piece of a fox trap. Instead of the iron teeth used by the Itelmens, it had the teeth of a shell, called *Entale*, not found on Kamchatka. Steller supposed that it had drifted to this place from America.[4]

Listening to these extended explanations, Bering understood what his physician was saying, and he tacitly concurred. He solemnly remarked: "I doubt the ship can be saved. May God spare us the longboat."[5]

That evening, after eating with Bering some of the ptarmigan that Plenisner had shot earlier that day, Steller invited the assistant surgeon, Betge, to become the fourth resident of the dwelling that he, Thomas and Plenisner were planning to build.

Betge accepted the invitation gratefully. Meanwhile, he agreed to tend to the captain-commander as well as the thirteen other scurvy-stricken men in the camp near the shore.

Steller and Plenisner proceeded to erect a small hut, covered it on top with Steller's two overcoats, and plugged holes on the sides with some of the dead foxes lying about in heaps. But about midnight a violent wind, bringing snow, blew off the overcoats and chased all three occupants from the hut.

The trio were a strange spectacle, running along the seashore, picking up driftwood, digging a pit like a grave, making the frame of a tepee over one end of the pit, covering the frame with clothes, coats, and blankets, and building a fire at the other end.

With thanks to God, they slept very well in their "grave" the rest of the night.[6]

The next day, November 10, Steller caught a seal. At the new building site he cooked its fat with peas and shared the meal with his three companions, including Betge, who had made two shovels and had started to dig.

In the afternoon, Waxell, Khitrovo, Constable Roselius, and three of the crew showed up from the ship, carrying Bering on a litter from the first campsite. Steller and his companions treated them all to tea and joked about the "grave" they were building.[7]

Bering, accorded a front or northernmost residence on the sandy ridge, once again had a tent of sailcloth erected for him, but now there was space also for his two servants.

At the same time, others of the rank and file who still had strength enough to dig prepared a square pit in the slightly frozen sand and erected a double sail as a roof. This dwelling, called "the barracks," became the infirmary, the new home for the sick.[8]

Having enlarged their dwelling by digging and acquiring more driftwood from the beach for a roof, the Steller group acquired a fifth member, Boris Roselius, whom Bering sent with two natives of Kamchatka to follow the beach to the northwest to look for inhabitants who might help rescue the expedition. They set off that same evening.

They were gone four days.

On November 12, Waxell and Khitrovo returned to the ship in the morning. Steller supposed that they preferred the comforts of the ship to camping on shore, but Bering no doubt depended on them to safeguard the ship and supervise the transfer of men and supplies to shore.

In the afternoon the boatswain, Aleksei Ivanov, came ashore with five men to continue work on the barracks. At the same time they started work on a fourth dwelling of their own, identified as Ivanov's place. Thus within a week without storm or gale, twenty-seven men were already residing on land in four dwellings on the same sandy ridge about ten yards from the foot of the high bluff. From this ridge the river was but ten yards to the east and the seashore but another sixty yards. Here the men had a view of the wide bay with the *St. Peter* anchored another 600 yards away down the shore.

Though neither Bering nor any of the thirteen men in the barracks had yet recovered, the good news was that fresh air and Steller's fresh soups and salads had apparently arrested the rapid rate of dying among the men on land; it still continued on the ship, where that night the trumpeter Mikhail Toroptsov passed away. His was the fourteenth death, leaving thirty-seven of the living still on the *St. Peter*.

That afternoon, with conditions in the camp much improved, the Steller household, minus the absent Roselius, went hunting along the coast to the northwest, clubbing four sea otters near a creek thereafter called Sea Otter Creek. That evening Steller made a variety of dishes from the meat and organs of the otters. The men dined "with thanks to God" and "prayers that God might not deprive us of this food in the future."[9] The obvious alternative to sea otter meat was the flesh of the ubiquitous, hated Arctic fox.

Steller observed that the men's values had already changed. Precious otter pelts were wasted for want of time to dry and prepare them. They were discarded and chewed up by the foxes. On the other hand, they prized many things that were previously of little consequence, such as needles, thread, shoelaces, awls, poles, shoes, shirts, socks, knives, and axes. If these were lost, their living would become even more precarious. Already their guns were becoming useless. With the humidity and the habitual drizzle being transformed into wet snow, it was difficult to keep gunpowder dry.

Steller reminded himself frequently that naval hierarchy and social preferment had nothing to do with survival skills in a wilderness environment. He therefore resolved to set aside his own status as a gentleman and to encourage others also, whatever their former station, to do what they could to contribute to everyone's benefit with whatever strength they still had. Accordingly, he persuaded his own household to enter "into a community of goods," to share equitably in necessary tasks, and to resolve all questions by consensus.

To preserve the utmost dignity of each man, and hence his loyalty, it was agreed that, according to Russian custom, a first name plus the patronymic rather than a familiar nickname would be used. They soon saw that Pyotr Maksimovich was more obliging than Petrusha had been earlier.[10]

Steller also had the wisdom to realize that a more democratic regime was not sufficient without a common belief that, with God's providence, the expedition would survive the winter, isolation, and deprivation, to say nothing of scurvy, and that whatever the setbacks and heartaches, they would get home again. He had learned what faith could do: The Halle orphanage in which he had been a student teacher had demonstrated what wonders could result when, in faith, a common goal was reached through willing hands superbly organized and universally supported. But for Steller, on what proved to be an island, the challenge was even greater than it had been for August Hermann Francke, the founder of the orphanage. The goal was certainly compelling—survival and deliverance—but the hands were impaired by illness, fear of the unknown, and unfamiliar (and for some, demeaning) tasks.

Beginning with Thomas and now with his growing household, Steller assumed an insistent and visible pastoral role. In confronting those twin personal disasters of depression and death, he put on a face of earnest resolve, gentle admonishment, and even unfailing cheerfulness. He became physician to both body and soul. The expedition historian Gerhard F. Müller, who later interviewed survivors, made this statement in his history of the Bering voyages: "Men could not lose heart because they had Steller with them. Steller was a doctor who at the same time administered to the spirit. He cheered everyone with his lively and agreeable company."[11]

Bering refused to adapt to a varied subsistence diet. When that evening Steller visited the captain-commander, showed him a nursing sea otter pup, and recommended that it be prepared for his supper, Bering was shocked. "I wonder at your taste," he said. Steller told him that his taste adapted itself to the circumstances of time and place.[12] But Bering insisted on sticking to a diet of ptarmigan, with which he was well supplied. Fortunately he had recovered from scurvy a second time. Earlier he had lost four teeth, but now his remaining teeth were solid and his gums firm.

But still he remained constantly immobile, too weak even to get on his feet. He suffered from exposure to the cold weather and humidity. Steller understood too that he was grieving and suffered internally; he noted a dark discharge from the commander's anus. He saw the ravages of lice. But fortunately Bering's head remained clear. He constantly gave orders and received reports.

Steller was not only his physician but also his confessor. Bering said that he was grateful for the "good fortune" that had been his lot from youth. That fortune, he said, lasted until "two months earlier," no doubt at the time scurvy struck him a second time and, together with the worst storms at sea, confined him to his bed.[13]

For the next three days the weather was worse, with hail, snow, and wind. The longboat remained on shore. The only communication was a signal from the ship. Lanterns hung from shrouds at night indicated a desire for the boat to come. There was a shortage of fresh water; on November 14 only one barrel was left aboard ship.

During this period of being cut off from the ship, construction continued on the sandy ridge. On the 15th the weather was better. The four households were divided into three parties: the first took the boat to the ship with a barrel of fresh water and prepared to take most of the sick back with them to the camp. A second party, seeking driftwood, found large logs three miles to the northwest near a stream thereafter called Wood Creek. They dragged the logs all the way back to the camp. The third party consisted of two stay-at-homes. A sick cannoneer busied himself with construction of a sled with which to haul wood and supplies. The other, Steller, took charge of cooking for the entire camp and also looked in on the captain-commander, since his two servants were sometimes away when he wanted a drink of water.

During the afternoon of the 15th, death, an old horror, appeared when men were moved from the ship to the shore. The moving of the sick men from the ship seemed to begin auspiciously. They got out of their bunks, dressed themselves, and seemed pleased that they might recover on the shore. However, three died instantly on the deck, and a fourth died in the boat. Never before had so many men died on the same day.

What Steller called "depressing and terrifying sights" were "everywhere" to be seen. The four dead men, lying unattended on the beach with no cover under the open sky, were attacked by foxes. Before their corpses could be buried, foxes had mutilated hands and feet. The foxes were numerous, bold, and malicious. According to Steller, they "dragged apart all the baggage, ate the leather sacks, scattered the provisions, stole and dragged from one man his boots, from another his socks and trousers, gloves, and coat. . . . They even dragged off iron and other implements that were of no use to them."[14]

It was bad enough that some men cried because they were cold and others because they were hungry and thirsty and yet could not eat anything because of the ravages of scurvy—"gums swollen like a sponge, brown-black and grown high over the teeth and covering them." But those "wicked" foxes—the more they were slaughtered and tortured, the more determined they seemed to become.[15]

When the dead were buried and the sick were finally helped to get from the shore to the camp, the foxes continued to harass the men all along the way. They even got into dwellings at the camp and "dragged away everything they could get to." The craftiness of these creatures and "their monkey tricks" made Steller and others want to laugh and cry simultaneously. Some of the stronger men raged against them. Some foxes were running around partially skinned. Some had eyes gouged. Others had tails cut off.[16]

Even though the barracks had been finished that day, there was not room for all seven newcomers. Lying on the ground, they wailed and complained bitterly, calling for God's vengeance upon Waxell and Khitrovo, who had brought misfortune upon them. Men pitied each other but could provide no assistance.

Steller's household took in one of the sick, Midshipman Ivan Sindt, and he fully recovered within three months. Steller himself nursed the many sick, often providing fresh water and warm soup.

At this time Khitrovo begged fervently to be admitted into the fellowship of the Steller group, but with space no longer available and with so many objections to him, he was summarily refused.

The return that same day of Roselius and the two Kamchatkans cast heavy gloom over the camp. Many of the men had believed with Waxell and Khitrovo that help was close at hand. But after hiking about twelve miles along the shore to the northwest, the three men had seen no forest and no sign of a habitation.

After a miserable night of hearing complaints and curses in the barracks where they were obliged to sleep, the two senior officers were glad to return to the ship in the morning. However, the ship itself was in bad shape. For ten days there had been six inches of seawater in the hold. Now the sea often washed over the deck. With strong winds rising, the men feared that at any time the anchor cable would break.

During the morning of November 17, the Siberian soldier Sava Stepanov, aboard ship, became the sixteenth fatality. Though the boat had iced up overnight, the dead man was taken ashore for burial. Then, starting on the 18th, strong winds and high waves again raised fears for the ship. Over the sides the sea poured relentlessly. Men on board were frantic—so much seawater, and on the 19th only four buckets of fresh water left to drink. On both days the ship signaled for the boat to come, firing three guns and flying a red flag from the main shrouds.

That day another man died aboard ship. He was lowered into the sea at midnight. Only his given name, Nikita, is known today. He had been a servant of Adjutant Ovtsin.[17] The next morning came the first death among those ashore. It was a sailor, Mark Antipin.

Thus the dying continued from day to day, and the ship with its drenched provisions and doubtful seaworthiness represented a fading hope of deliverance. Men who had valiantly operated the shore boat, wading into a frigid sea up to their armpits, were becoming exhausted and ill.

Finally, at noon on November 21, Roselius was able to lead boatmen to the ship. They found Waxell in the galley, where he had taken up quarters to be warm away from the stench and filth of the hold. He could not even move. Two men got him to his feet but he could not take even a few steps, though steadied by a man on each side. Dragged between the galley and the gangway, he fainted three times. Once ashore, four men carried him all the way to the camp. Here he was once again given a place among the patients in the barracks.

Khitrovo, too, was beset by scurvy. He could still walk, but only with difficulty.

All the men were got off the *St. Peter*. Before they left the ship, Roselius and a Siberian soldier dropped a reserve anchor, kedge, and grapnel, everything and anything that might serve to hold the ship. They struck yards and topmasts, anything that might catch the wind. Now, as the boat left, the ship was subject to the vagaries of the weather.

Bering had clung to the faint hope that the way out from the land was still, in some fashion, the way they had come in. On the morning of November 22 he ordered Waxell to consult with all the surviving officers ashore about the best way to save the ship. It took but a day for them to reach a conclusion and to present a written report to the captain-commander. They agreed that at high tide the ship should be run upon the beach and secured with hawsers. Bering then ordered Khitrovo to take charge of beaching the ship.

The order was not carried out. For two days the seas were too rough to get out to the ship. On the 26th Khitrovo could hardly walk. He asked Ivanov, the watch for the day, to tell Bering that an effort would be made that day to lay up the ship. Bering told Ivanov that if the ship could not be beached, provisions should be brought to shore.

Later, when Khitrovo hobbled down to the boat on the beach, Ivanov informed him that he had only five able-bodied men, and one of these, after getting wet while pushing the boat into the surf, had gone back to the camp. At this point Khitrovo called off his return to the ship. He doubted that the four remaining men were strong enough to weigh the best anchor, and he observed that the northwest wind might drive the ship directly upon a very visible reef. Khitrovo conceded that he might have called upon additional able-bodied men, so he stressed the issue of the ship's safety in reporting first to Waxell and then to Bering. The matter of getting provisions from the ship was not pressed. No one had much heart left. The three senior officers were very ill. Other men were ill or exhausted. Impending doom settled over the camp. Steller, convinced that Khitrovo was more lazy than sick, had no sympathy at all for him. But he was particularly concerned about Waxell, fearing that he would die, and that if Bering died, the command might devolve upon Khitrovo. In such a case, Steller doubted the expedition could be saved.[18]

Contributing to the gloom was the death of two men on the 22nd, one a sailor, Semyon Antemev, and the other Andreas Hesselberg, the 70-year-old navigator, whom Steller greatly admired.[19] Hesselberg was put to rest in a new grave site established at the north end of the same sandy ridge that provided shelter for the living. This grave site, with the graves of five other men, was not of course discovered until 1991. A concerted effort in 1992 to find the graves of the remaining nine men buried ashore was unsuccessful. Most likely all of them were claimed by high tides that swept over an eroding shore.

During the night of November 28, when the prospects of the expedition seemed bleakest, a violent storm broke the anchor cables and set the ship on the beach near the bank of the small river below the camp, as Steller writes, "better than human industry could perhaps have accomplished it."[20] With the ebb and flow of the tides, however, the ship sank in the loose sand about eight feet up to its gunwales and filled with salt water. The salt water ruined all the remaining gunpowder and penetrated five tons of rye flour stored in leather sacks. The flour could be rescued and consumed, but the loss of gunpowder was a terrible setback in the constant hunt for meat. Even so, the beaching of the ship was a great relief. Except for the household chores of cooking, hunting, and getting driftwood, the men relaxed for two days.

Then on December 1 Bering sent out a new search party of three men, led by the sailor Timofei Anchugov, to go southwest to look for forests and to determine, if possible, whether the land were on the Asian continent. He still hoped, against all odds, that they were on Kamchatka.

This party was gone four weeks, encountering many obstacles in getting past cliffs. They saw many herds of sea otters but no forests. Anchugov had no proof, but he supposed that the land was an island.

CHAPTER FIFTEEN

BERING'S DEATH

During the first week of December, Bering became reclusive as he lay in his hollow in the sand. He wanted no one, not even Steller, to assist him, even though sand had caved in from the sides and covered his lower extremities.[1]

"The deeper in the ground I lie, the warmer I am," he said.[2]

Bering died December 8, at the fifth hour of the morning, two hours before daybreak. It was Steller's judgment that the commander would have lived if the expedition had reached Kamchatka's Harbor of the Apostles Peter and Paul, where he would have had a warm room and fresh food. In his journal Steller writes that "he died more from hunger, cold, thirst, vermin, and grief" than from scurvy or any other disease.[3] Though scurvy undoubtedly weakened him, his teeth at death were firm. His recurrence of scurvy at sea had been cured on land by Steller's salads and Plenisner's ptarmigan. The immediate cause of his death was heart failure. What Steller described as "hunger, cold, thirst, vermin, and grief" were contributing factors. Also contributing was his last bout of scurvy, which left him helpless.

As his father confessor, Steller writes well of Bering at the time of his death. Although Bering had "too great an esteem for the officers under his command," he "wished nothing more than our deliverance from this land," writes Steller, "and, from the bottom of his heart, his own complete deliverance from this misery."[4]

In death the captain-commander was tied to a plank and carried but eighteen paces from his dwelling to his grave, next to Hesselberg's. A coffin was constructed around the corpse. Because the boards were a bit short, the head of the deceased was bent forward and his knees raised. The plank on the bottom and two crosspieces on top secured the side boards, which were nailed into thick end boards. No lid was provided. A thin strip of wood over the top was nailed to two crosspieces. Over the open coffin a cover of sailcloth was finally attached.

Waxell, as new commander, led a brief service with rites similar to those of the Lutheran Church. He took as the theme of his eulogy "He died like a rich man and was buried like the ungodly."[5] The theme probably combined two thoughts: Bering displayed his rank as a nobleman through his splendid dress and his many possessions in nine sea chests; and he had the misfortune to be put into unconsecrated ground in an uninhabited place hitherto unknown to Europeans.

Steller was not pleased with the theme. He took silent exception to it. He was thinking about the men their commander had raised up "in the swampy areas around Okhotsk and on Kamchatka . . . whoever had fallen into a morass." But "they leaned so hard on him that he himself had to go under," and "he took to his grave everyone's receipted bill." In this dark reflection, Steller shifts from "they" to "man," and the identity of the man becomes clear when he concludes by saying, "It was this man who later contradicted him in everything, became the author of our misfortune, and after Bering's death his greatest accuser."[6] Whatever else is being alluded to, the one person who, according to Steller, "became the author of our misfortune" was Khitrovo, whom Bering had promoted before the mast to lieutenant and who in the last sea council had opposed his commander and insisted that the land before them was Kamchatka.

Steller was also thinking about Bering's last days. He recalled Bering's "composure and earnest preparation for death and his blissful end itself," and concluded that "he might well not have found a better place to prepare himself for eternity than this deathbed under the open sky."[7]

Steller has no comment about Bering's dying "as a rich man," and Waxell, in his final report and his later journal, makes no mention of his leading Bering's funeral service. Even though it is not known how the new commander developed his theme, his words were undoubtedly respectful, and the theme itself, as Steller gives it, makes an important distinction. Bering was rich, and, given his habits in support of his station in life, he did not, and perhaps could not, adjust to being on an uninhabited island where camping and hunting and gathering were absolutely essential to sustain human life.

Aboard ship, where his aristocratic garb was a sign of his command, it was different. He was effectively in charge. During the outward voyage he persuaded his officers to make a detour to be certain that they had not missed land shown on J. N. Delisle's map. There was later no argument among officers about eating thick mush to conserve a dwindling supply of fresh water, nor was there any dissent about changing to a more northerly course to seek land for fresh water.

Off Kayak Island he orchestrated the movements of the two shore boats, deftly deflecting Steller's protests with humor and even a bit of mischievousness. He scarcely missed a beat in directing the proceedings. With the assistance of a trumpeter, he sent off Steller and the water-seeking party with a resounding flourish. Steller did what Bering probably feared he would do on the island; in his zeal for exploration, the adjunct of natural history left the shore, where he was visible, entered the woods, and stayed there for hours, and later he hiked up the shore and climbed a hill where again he was out of sight for an hour. Then in the late afternoon Steller requested the boat, which was busy shuttling water from shore to ship, so that he could go off on a special mission on the chance of meeting the possibly dangerous natives whose fire he had seen. Under these circumstances, Bering ordered Steller back to the ship with a few choice words in seamen's language—and back he came, quickly.

From Kayak Island, Bering's control unraveled. First, he was constrained by the sea council plan of May 4, 1741, an agreement he could not ignore as long as Waxell and Khitrovo insisted on following it. As a consequence, they missed favorable easterlies when the ship turned into bays of islands to chart the coast and obtain fresh water. Then real trouble began: scurvy and mounting deaths from it, terrifying storms, and islands they avoided bumping into only by the grace of God. Almost every major decision Bering wanted to make was thwarted: first, to make haste to return to the harbor from Kayak Island; second, to take a southerly route he knew to be safe (they had come out on it) instead of following the 53rd parallel directly toward Avacha Bay but blocked by the Aleutian Islands; and third, to resume the voyage rather than land when they were already close to Kamchatka and the harbor. With any one of these new plans for action, Bering would probably have saved the ship and many lives, but because of the plan of May 4, he could make only recommendations to his three senior officers.

For their part, Waxell and Khitrovo saw the discovery of a new part of America as an opportunity for further exploration and mapping of the coast. Moreover, they did not doubt that the American continent lay somewhere north of the islands, just as it had been north of the Shumagin Islands. This misconception, shared by Chirikov, became fixed on later Russian maps of Russian discoveries (Fig. 20).

Because his officers were within their rights in opposing him, Bering was stoically resigned to his fate but never ceased to act within his authority to try to save the expedition, even as he lay dying on Bering Island. Scurvy twice struck him down and literally laid him low. From about October 8 he began a slow descent toward death after only about five weeks of recovery. His order about taking a collection of money was an act of faith to which his men apparently assented. But the die was cast. They had too far to go, and scurvy and forces of nature overwhelmed the expedition. As Bering remained immobile, he was carried from his cabin bunk to a sandy house pit, almost at last a descent to his grave.

According to Müller's official history of the Bering expeditions, based partly on interviews, Bering was "very fond" of Steller toward the end.[8] He appreciated his physician's loyalty and attention, his observations of nature, his organizational skills, and his readiness to serve as confessor. Even so, there remained a respectful distance between them and tacit agreement when, during his last week, Bering wished to be left alone to prepare for death. That he valued his physician is shown by his bequest of his two servants to Steller's care. In a way it was a debt extinguished, a fulfillment of a promise for assistance not granted off Kayak Island but finally granted on Bering Island.

Resurrected, Bering in his bronzed new sculptured image is superbly handsome, rugged, and reserved, with a placid, faintly whimsical demeanor (frontispiece). In an active, highly responsible life, he was the emperor's man, a man's man, and a family man. It is fitting that across the North Pacific region there are important landmarks memorializing

Bering—the sea, the strait, and the island where he is now reburied. It seems appropriate that the two men who bridged Asia and America, one a Nordic explorer with an Atlas physique, the other a German scientist, agile and audacious, be seen in their contrasting characters.

Like the mythical Atlas, Bering carried exceptional burdens. He bore those burdens with patience and resolve, and he labored mightily. He—unlike Steller—retained in the wilderness the politesse, noblesse oblige, and fastidious taste of his social rank. To go native was for him unthinkable. He could not change. He was, as Waxell said, a "rich man." His wigs and fine clothing had virtually no survival value on the island. Waxell also perceived that his late commander felt he had fallen into a desolate and ungodly place, a forsaken island and finally an unseemly hole in the ground. So however kindly Steller felt toward his dead commander, Waxell's differing perspective about Bering underscored the reality of a man who, in departing from them, was unprepared for the wilderness test that now confronted his expedition. It remained for both Waxell and Steller, men selected by Bering, to meet the immediate challenges of supplying the elusive basic requirements of food, warmth, health, and hope.

The dying was not over with Bering's death. The same day the commander was laid to rest, Nikita Khotyantsev, his former adjutant, died and was buried on Hesselberg's other side. Through Steller's light cooking of fresh meat in soups, most of the sick, including Waxell and Khitrovo, began to recover by the end of the year. In December six men died, in January only two. The last death was that of an ensign, Ivan Lagunov, on January 8, 1742. His was the fourteenth burial on the island. No deaths occurred thereafter. Thus the immediate goal of ending the sea voyage at Bering Island had at last been reached—to save the men, thanks chiefly to the botanist and physician who also served as pastor, cook, nurse, and cheerleader. With the two remaining senior officers severely stricken themselves, Steller was quite free to do what he considered to be in the best interest of all the men. He led by example in the expedition's adaptation on land to a cooperative, more nearly democratic way of living in order to accomplish many onerous necessary tasks efficiently. And it was Steller who, besides remedying scurvy, chose both the site and the mode of safe wintering that probably saved the remaining members of the expedition stranded on Bering Island.

Bering was consistent in his taste. As for Steller, his taste changed

Figure 20. MÜLLER MAP OF "DISCOVERIES MADE BY RUSSIAN SHIPS ON UNKNOWN COASTS OF NORTH AMERICA WITH ADJACENT LANDS," 1754 (COURTESY OF THE JAMES FORD BELL LIBRARY, UNIVERSITY OF MINNESOTA

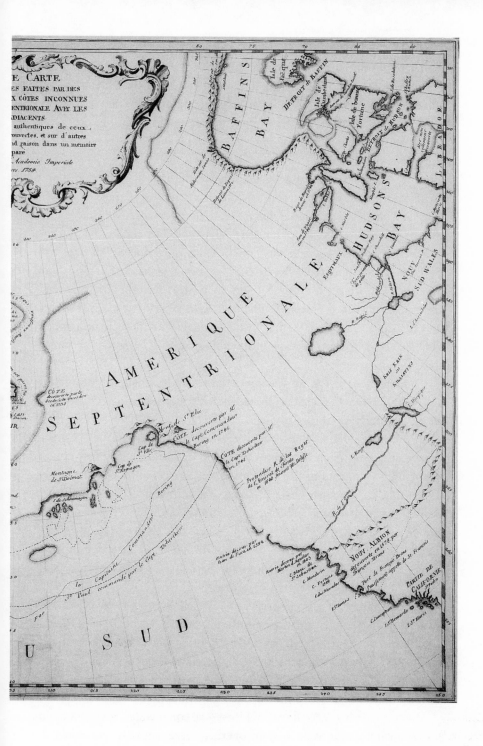

with circumstances as the world turned. He was of a different breed. He was a man of the world, a rare man of European culture and education who was at home everywhere. On the frontier it mattered little to him what he wore or how he ate as long as his dress was serviceable, he had cup, plate, and spoon, the water in his cup was fresh, and the food—however he ate it—was reasonably edible. What mattered was a diligent pursuit of his science of natural history, response to his continuing curiosity about peoples and cultures, and a consistent Christian standard of social justice and decency for everyone everywhere. Otherwise, he was eminently adaptable. His success in adapting to a wholly subsistence diet was later demonstrated during his hikes with Thomas to the north and south ends of Bering Island. The only food they ate was what they found (eggs in a nest), caught (sea mammals and fish), or picked (sarana bulbs and wild celery leaves). Most days they feasted. Several days they went hungry. For more than a month they survived, trusting always in the abundance of Creation for tomorrow's food.

Coming to America, he was prepared to study at length flora, fauna, and peoples. On Kamchatka he had quickly befriended native communities by studying their languages and customs and by serving their interests. His anger at Bering for refusing him access to the American continent sprang from his deep caring for an extraordinary first contact opportunity available to the expedition and his commitment to prepare, if possible, a "complete report" about the land and its people. Even if Bering made the right decision in avoiding landings on the mainland and in leaving Kayak Island precipitously, one must sympathize with Steller. Everything considered, Bering with his heavy responsibility was a man to respect. Steller in his love of the natural world and in his care of his companions was a man to praise.

Just as Steller was well prepared, Waxell was likewise capable of leadership as Bering's successor on Bering Island. To begin with, he had a good reason to recover from scurvy and earnestly to reunite the survivors to find a way out of their daily trials. He was a father whose preteen son, Laurentz, was with him, the two of them sharing a single person's portion of bread during their two simple meals each day.

Much preferring Waxell over Khitrovo as commander, Steller set aside his complaint about Waxell as an overbearing antagonist. No doubt the new commander had learned well from Bering the importance of keeping records of all deliberations. No doubt on the island Waxell learned quickly from Steller the wisdom of abandoning a naval hierarchical command structure in favor of giving everyone an opportunity to work toward consensus in group decision making. As in many aboriginal societies, the survivors on Bering Island became united under their new chief and were given courage by their physician, who was also their spiritual adviser. Waxell and Steller together completed the Bering expedition from Bering Island as Bering himself never could have done. Under these two men many others (most of whom are known today only by name, position, and expedition exploit) exerted themselves heroically in concert toward liberating them all from the island.

That story remains to be told.

CHAPTER SIXTEEN

HOW BERING'S MEN
GOT OFF THE ISLAND

In late December and early January, as Waxell, Khitrovo, and many others slowly recovered from scurvy and as the burials came at longer intervals and finally came to an end, the forty-six survivors could at greater leisure try to reconcile themselves to their losses and ponder what might lie ahead. For more than five months the *St. Peter* had been their home at sea. Now, only 200 yards in front of their camp, it was a wreck mired down in sand on the beach not far from the mouth of the small river. They had lost their commander and two-fifths of the ship's complement within five months. They had temporary shelter, plentiful fresh water, and a ration of flour for daily use, but some men did not have adequate clothing to keep warm and dry in the damp, subfreezing winter. Each dwelling had a fire pit, but firewood was so scarce that it often had to be reserved for cooking meat.

Every day was a struggle, even as the nightmare of death retreated. The hunt for meat and wood took survivors farther away each day, usually along the shore to the northwest, since the shore to the southeast was cut off by cliffs after a half-dozen miles. Deep snow confounded the search for driftwood. They had to look for telltale signs. Where the surface of the snow was uneven, they dug. Sea otters were no longer tame and readily available on land in the vicinity of the camp. Without gunpowder, seals were no longer a dependable source of meat.

The cherished hope of the expedition was that help would come. In the meantime, their lesser hope was to find out where they were. Each search party sent out, first by Bering and then by Waxell after the captain-commander's death, carried with it the expectation that circumstances would somehow improve and that someday they could leave this land for home.

After Bering's death and burial, his personal possessions were restored to his cabin on the ship, and the two servants moved into Steller's dwelling.

The camp was divided into two parts. Four dwellings (variously called huts, yurts, dugouts, pits, hollows, and "graves") were lined up side by side, only a few yards apart and about ten yards from the bank of the river. At the north end the barracks, formerly the infirmary and now called Waxell's dwelling, included Khitrovo, Waxell's son, and about five other men. Next to it Quartermaster Luka Alekseev's dwelling, the largest of the four, housed about a dozen men. Then came Steller's dwelling, which also housed five German speakers and five others, three of whom were natives of Kamchatka. The last dwelling at the south end, Boatswain Mate Aleksei Ivanov's dwelling, included Assistant Navigator Kharlam Yushin and about three others.

The second part of the camp consisted of a single dwelling 160 yards upstream on a sandy ridge at the foot of the high bluff (a short distance southwest of the high steel cross erected in 1966 as a memorial to Bering). This dwelling, Dmitry Ovtsin's, housed a dozen men, mostly of the rank and file. The location of this dwelling is significant because it represented a threat to Waxell's leadership. Ovtsin, a former lieutenant demoted to sailor, had been restored to some dignity and granted a servant (who soon died) as Bering's adjutant. Waxell did not continue Ovtsin in this position and he reverted to his status of sailor.

The first three dwellings of the first group opened to the east; that is, to the river and a view of the bay. Ivanov's, the southernmost unit, was entered from the south. At the entrance of each dwelling were several barrels used to store meat safe from foxes. Anchored in the ground next to the barrels were tripods on which clothing washed in the river could be spread to dry. On relatively calm days, coats, hats, and blankets could be hung here as well, out of the reach of marauding foxes.

Most roofs were of sail. Waxell's was set at an angle of 33° to provide a runoff for rain and snow. Such sail had to be replaced from time to time because mists from the sea kept it damp and subject to rot. Then the wind tore the sail and even, billowing under it, blew it to the ground. Steller's dwelling resembled a shack. It had support posts for a level roof fashioned from driftwood. No other dwelling was so cozy and snug.

By mid-January men who had been deathly ill were on their feet again and beginning to walk. Among those feeling much better were both Waxell and his partner, Khitrovo.

On January 18, in his first major act as commander, Waxell called a meeting of all the men, both officers and crew, to inspect the ship to determine if it were still seaworthy.

Waxell and Khitrovo had already declared the ship unfit for further service, of course, and all those assembled knew that it had serious defects. Waxell called the meeting for several reasons. First, the *St. Peter* was government property. Any alteration or disposition of government property could bring severe punishment. Second, he sought consensus, the new democratic way of doing business advocated by Steller. If there were dissenters, he would learn their identity and their arguments and thus be able to make a rebuttal in writing. Finally, a paper trail was a safeguard if a government inquiry should ever be held.

The "Statement on the Condition of the Ship," drawn up the same day, noted a variety of deficiencies. The bottom of the ship was damaged and the rudder lost. Not a single anchor was left and there was no hope that one could be recovered on the sandy bottom of the bay. Rigging and shrouds "snap and tear" and cables were no longer reliable. The ship was so deeply buried in the beach sand that it would be impossible to move it. Finally, the hull was cracked below the water line.[1]

When Waxell called a meeting on the day the statement was completed, the statement was read and signed by all but one man, the sailor Dmitry Ovtsin. He was ordered to put his objections in writing. He did so five days later, offering a somewhat optimistic point-by-point assessment: The condition of the bottom could not be known until snow and ice were gone. A new rudder could be made. Anchors might be found in the bay next summer. Rigging could be repaired or replaced from stores. It was too early to ascertain whether the ship could be floated. The hull as well as the bottom could be repaired.[2]

Two days later, a rebuttal was drawn up, read, and signed by all men except Ovtsin. It called attention to the January 18 inspection of the ship, in which everyone participated. Consequently, all of Ovtsin's views were rejected, with the further observation that "even if the ship were sound it could not be floated since we have no anchor, no timber, and not enough men for such work."[3] The rebuttal, however, makes an important concession to Ovtsin: the ship should be inspected again for its seaworthiness after water in its hold could be removed.

Meanwhile, assuming that such later inspection would again find the *St. Peter* unfit for duty, the men agreed to consider, with Ovtsin dissenting, that in March the ship should be dismantled and "out of the wreck some kind of small vessel should be made" to carry the survivors back to Kamchatka.[4]

After nearly three months on land, the expedition under Waxell was contemplating positive action if help were not forthcoming. Waxell had succeeded in rallying the men to a plan for future action and in doing so had met the first test of his leadership.

Even winter was beginning to seem almost bearable. The snow had an insulating quality. Men lying under an open sky remained still as the snow fell. Waxell writes that "those who had a blanket or a rag were as happy as [if] they had a house."[5]

Sometimes the wind was so strong that walking in it was quite impossible. At these times men who had to leave their dwellings to answer the call of nature were whirled away, and once their mission was accomplished, some were obliged to crawl back to their shelters.

On February 7, shortly after noon, the expedition experienced its first earthquake. It lasted, according to Steller, "six full minutes." It was preceded by "a strong subterranean wind" and culminated in "a violent hissing and roaring—ever stronger the closer it came" to the camp. The shaking itself was powerful enough to move upright posts in Steller's dwelling and to cause sand on the walls of all dwellings to cascade down and cover men sleeping or resting on the floor.[6] Steller rushed out to observe the sea. He could detect no movement, no tsunami.

Only once did he see the aurora borealis. Almost every day throughout the winter was cloudy or snowy.

Until March, when snowfalls became less frequent, most travel was along the shore, where six- to eight-foot tides left a broad walkway. Elsewhere, on level ground, Steller estimated that the depth of the snow was six to nine feet.

Mealtimes came but twice a day, at noon and in the evening. There was little variety in the menu. The principal meat was boiled or roasted sea otter. Steller found it "rather good," but for taste and tenderness he preferred the meat of females and young nursing otters. Waxell, for his part, disliked the sinewy quality of otter meat. "It was like a piece of leather," he writes, "and has to be chewed, chewed and chewed again, before it becomes slightly softened and can be downed bit by bit."[7]

On January 29 a sea lion was killed near the camp. Its meat was far superior to the otter's. Steller compared it to veal. Also in January a dead whale nearly fifty feet long washed up on the shore about three miles from the camp. Its blubber was slightly rancid. Men carried the blubber on their backs, cut it up in camp into small squares, boiled the oil out, and swallowed bits of nerves and sinew without chewing. As long as it lasted, that whale was called the "provision store."[8]

Meat was supplemented by rye-flour cakes, called *kolachi,* fried in whale oil. First the flour was stirred into warm water in a wooden bowl and left for a few days to ferment. Then it was spooned into a frying pan and fried. Each cake was small enough to be consumed in five bites or spoonfuls. Waxell and his son shared equally a single allotment of flour (thirty pounds per month). The one who had three spoonfuls at midday had only two in the evening.[9]

These fried cakes were a treat despite the condition of the flour from which they were made. That flour, according to Steller, suffered from a "particular calamity." After being stored for several years in leather sacks, it got soaked by the salt water that filled the hold when the ship was driven ashore in the storm. Consequently, "it became a tincture of all kinds of materials contained in the ship—gunpowder and other trash—and had to be consumed without much anatomical speculation." Until men got used to it, "it caused such gas," says Steller, that "stomachs swelled like drums."[10]

Barley groats, boiled in water and eaten as hot cereal, lasted only two months, December and January.

After Bering's death, his private stores of food and drink were put into provisions for general use. Waxell and Steller added their own private supplies at the same time. Cocoa and brandy having already been consumed, these private supplies consisted of various teas enjoyed at Christmas and other holidays.

Water, of course, was the chief drink. It was taken from the small river that meandered by the camp. Because the river never completely froze over, water was always available. After consuming brackish water for three months aboard ship, the men appreciated the quality of the river water. "It was really good and healthy water," says Waxell, "and must have contributed greatly to our recovery."[11]

Another drink was crakeberry tea, made from bushes dug out of the snow and cut up and boiled thoroughly back in camp.

Steller describes in considerable detail the sea otter hunt, or *promysel*, undertaken at first chiefly on moonlit nights after the evening meal. He writes: "We usually went two, three, or four persons together, provided with long and sturdy birch poles. We traveled quietly along the beach against the wind as much as possible, looking around diligently everywhere. When we saw one [otter] lying or sleeping, one person very quietly went up to it, even crawling close to it" while the others cut off its path to the sea. When he was close enough, the person stalking the otter would pounce on it and beat it repeatedly over the head. If it got away, the others would close in upon it, driving it inland against a wall of snow until, exhausted, cornered, and hissing like a cat, it could be pommeled to death.[12] If the men came upon a herd rather than a solitary otter, each man would go after the otter closest to him, so that several might be taken all at once.

But as time passed, the otters became wary. When they came ashore they looked around everywhere and pointed their noses in the air to smell danger they could not see. Steller observed also that herds posted otters to stand watch. Sometimes it seemed that foxes would deliberately awaken otters before men could reach them.

Soon they had to hunt on the darkest nights or during inclement weather, when otters least expected danger. Too, the hunters expected to go greater distances to find otters—in January four to six miles up the shore to Whale Creek, and in February twelve to twenty miles, as far as the Great Cliff.

Steller greatly admired this sea mammal for the beauty of its glossy black pelt and its human characteristics. He noted that otters stayed together as families, the male caressing the female, who sometimes would teasingly push him away. "Not even the most loving human mother engages in the same kind of playing with her children. . . . When the young are taken from them, they cry aloud like a little child and grieve in such a way . . . that within ten to fourteen days they dry up like a skeleton, become sick and weak, and do not want to leave the land."[13]

They killed otters out of necessity. "This animal deserves the greatest respect from us all," he writes. "It served us almost solely as our food and at the same time as medicine for the sick."[14] As thankful as they all were for bountiful fresh water, he, unlike Waxell, seemed to know intuitively that fresh meat was more important than fresh water as a remedy for scurvy. For this reason, like aboriginal hunters, he felt respect for the otter as the primary source of sustenance and good health throughout a long winter.

The Steller household was well organized. With five German speakers and five Russian speakers, work was accomplished by pairing a "German" with a "Russian" for hunting, cooking, and gathering wood. The two cooks endeavored to have meals ready on time or whenever their comrades returned from foraging for wood or meat. Two or four hunters worked together, as did four or six wood gatherers. Just as hunting without guns was a cooperative enterprise, so was the collecting and hauling of wood. If a driftwood log were found, four or six men were needed to lift and carry it to camp. At other times the finder of heavy driftwood returned immediately to camp to recruit others, who brought axes, chopped as much wood as they could carry, and roped the pieces to their backs.

In January and February men went four to six miles from camp for wood and in March as far as ten miles. So, as time elapsed, this resource, like the sea otters, became increasingly distant.

Although it was everyone's intention to operate as democratically as possible, in practice the rank and file still tended to defer to their superiors. For example, Steller's partner, Thomas, as fellow cook, insisted on performing such menial tasks as lighting the fire, fetching water, and washing and putting away cooking and table utensils. Not only was the head cook thus distinguished from his assistant, but he also gave orders "so that everything might proceed properly."[15]

This arrangement made good sense for several reasons. Steller was skilled as a chef. Thomas continued to do work that was familiar and satisfying. Finally, Thomas demonstrated his awareness that he owed Steller gratitude and respect for sharing what had once been his private property, whether it were tea, a blanket, or an overcoat.

Other households followed the example of Steller's. Men were daily assigned the same chief duties, but the burden of supporting the entire camp fell disproportionately on Steller's household largely because of what he called "a new, worse epidemic," by which he meant "dissolute gambling with cards." According to Steller, "Nothing went on in the dwellings but card playing, first for money, now held in low esteem, and, when this was gambled away, the fine sea otters had to give up their precious pelts."[16] At morning roll call men talked about last night's winners. The heavy losers sought to recoup by gambling with sea otter pelts.

It pained Steller to see these precious mammals killed indiscriminately, with meat often wasted. Some men were so addicted to gambling that they began to steal pelts simply to stay in a game. Such pilfering, according to Steller, led to "hate, quarrels, and strife."[17]

Waxell did not discourage the gambling, which he euphemistically called card-playing. In his journal he justifies the pastime: "Far from forbidding those under my command to play cards, I was glad that they found something with which to pass the time and help them overcome the melancholy from which most of them suffered badly." His allowing card-playing was, he says, an example of the "mild" nature of his command. He not only allowed it but also sold ten decks of playing cards at one ruble apiece. He found them on January 4 among Bering's possessions. But using cards, he says, was justified by circumstances: It was "represented to me," he says, "as something at variance with the commands of Her Imperial Majesty and therefore I, as the senior commander, ought to forbid it. My answer to this was that the regulations . . . against playing cards had been made without any thought of our pitiable circumstances."[18]

The one who protested to Waxell was Steller. Waxell, he claims, allowed gambling for two reasons—to distract men from blaming him and Khitrovo for their being stranded and because he enjoyed gambling himself. Though Steller's Pietist faith did not tolerate gambling, his concern was based on practical considerations rather than on religious principle. Gambling kept men preoccupied when survival chores needed to be done. Gambling resulted in the wasting of sea otters. Gambling caused dissension when unity was vital in achieving the goal of leaving this place.

Waxell's policy of relaxing discipline and promoting fraternization through cards can be partly defended by the situation in which he found himself at Bering's death. He was still very ill, even despairing for his life. Some of the men playing cards at that time could not work anyway because of their illness. There is finally the larger question of the effect of blame heaped upon Waxell and Khitrovo for promising relief that never materialized. Very likely Waxell could not have exercised his authority as commander to stop an activity that was already a consuming passion with most of the men. Despite Steller's repeated objections, the gambling continued throughout the winter and into the spring.

On February 1 a violent storm and a very high tide lifted the *St. Peter* and drove it farther up on the beach, exposing most of the hull. This event raised hopes that a similar tide might launch the ship back into the sea. If the ship were dismantled, however, its new high-and-dry position would facilitate the work.

Toward the end of February, Waxell sent Assistant Navigator Yushin with four men to explore the coast to the northwest. In six days they walked forty miles to a northeast cape. Here they were caught in a blizzard on a rocky bluff and stopped by cliffs extending into the sea. During their return they hunted sea otters. On March 8 they were back in camp.

Two days later Waxell called a new council, which unanimously agreed to send Boatswain's Mate Ivanov with four men to explore a different route. They were to go along the shore northwest only as far as Wood Creek and then proceed overland up the creek to the south. Leaving camp on March 15, they succeeded in reaching the sea on the other side, but when they followed the shore to the south, they were soon stopped by cliffs. When they returned on the 19th, they reported two curiosities. The first was an animal they had never seen before but which Steller knew, from their description, to be a fur seal. The second was pieces of a sloop that Ivan Akulov said he recognized as the very one he had built the previous winter on Avacha Bay.

On March 27 Ivanov and the same men set off again with instructions this time to go north after going overland. If the men reached the mainland in this direction, two were to return to inform the camp while the others were to continue to Avacha Bay. If the men came to the end of an island, all should return.

This time Steller and three members of his household made the overland trip with the Ivanov party. The hills and the distance made for a fatiguing journey, but Steller's party was rewarded by the discovery of plentiful sea otters, still tame and easily killed. Only ten were taken, the maximum number that four men could carry back over the hills to the camp.

On April 1 a second hunting party from the Steller household, led by Roselius, attempted another crossing. A violent northwest storm surprised them above the mouth of Wood Creek the same evening. The wind was so strong that none could stand upright or see more than a step ahead. They were stopped. Worse, six feet of snow fell that night. The men lay under the snow until morning, when the storm ended. With stupendous effort they dug themselves out and in single file slogged through the deep snow down to the beach.

Back in camp, anxious about their comrades, Steller and his remaining housemates cleared the entrance to their dwelling just in time to welcome three of the party, "senseless and speechless, and so stiff from the cold that, like immovable machines, they could hardly move their feet." Betge, who was totally blind, stumbled along behind the others. The fourth man, Midshipman Sindt, was missing.

Steller, assisted by the others, immediately undressed the three men, wrapped them snugly in bedding, and with hot tea "and other remedies" revived them sufficiently so that now the household's concern was wholly centered on Sindt. He was soon found, dazed and wandering about the beach. Steller was fearful that Sindt would lose both his hands and feet because he had lain in a creek the whole night. His body now was "hard as a stone" and his clothing was frozen to his body. But despite Sindt's miserable condition, Steller, as physician, was able to save him, or, as Steller the Pietist writes, "God restored him without any injury whatsoever."[19] Betge too was most fortunate. After eight days of convalescence he fully recovered his sight.

After this scare, the Steller household resolved to wait for better weather before attempting another crossing. They could not wait long because on April 5 the camp was out of meat.

This time, on a sunshiny day, Steller, Plenisner, Thomas, and one of Bering's former servants went overland, reached the shore on the other side, and killed as many otters as they could carry. They were sitting around a campfire by a cliff, planning to spend the night, when a violent northwest snowstorm hit them before they could find shelter. Thomas was pinned under so much snow that he could not move. Steller sat dumbly in the snow and "sought," he writes, "to warm myself and drive away death's bitterness by constantly smoking tobacco." The two others ran back and forth, like long-distance runners, barely keeping on their feet because of the wind. At daybreak these two forced Steller to get up out of the snow, and together the three men tried to find a cave or other shelter. No luck. After much looking around, they came back "half dead" and "full of despair."[20]

Finding Thomas, they could not pull him to his feet, so they had to dig him out.

Now, with Thomas ambulatory, they split into two parties and in the continuing storm made another attempt to find shelter and save their lives. In half an hour Thomas, who earlier had been content to die peaceably under the snow, found "a very wide, roomy cave in a rock," which Steller supposed had been created in a great earthquake.

Bringing into it both wood and meat, they found everything they needed: shelter from wind and snow, plenty of space, a storage room out of the reach of foxes, and even "a naturally made fireplace" to heat the cave and cook without the annoyance of smoke, which could rise above the cave through a narrow crevice.[21]

For the discovery of the cave they thanked God. Under its protection, they recovered from their ordeal in no time at all. They spent three days in the cave, resting up and hunting enough sea otters to replace those they had left behind during the storm. On the fourth day they returned home to the camp, where everyone was elated to see them and to hear the good news about the cave. Because Steller's party had found it, it was henceforth known as Steller's Cave and the bay it was on was called Steller's Bay. Such nomenclature indicates the respect that the physician-naturalist enjoyed in the camp.

While Steller and his party had been recuperating their first day in the cave, another hunting party led by Yushin had, unknown to everyone else, been trapped for seven days without food and wood in a crevice where they had taken refuge from a rising tide in the first storm that also caught Roselius and his companions. Yushin's party got back to camp just three days before Steller's.

And just two days before Steller's party returned, Ivanov also was back with all four members of his party and with reliable news that the land they were on was indeed an island. Ivanov had rounded the northwest cape of the land, proving that water was on all sides. This news, predicted by Steller and later believed by others, actually now came as no surprise.

They knew they were on an island opposite Cape Kronotski on the Kamchatka peninsula. They also supposed correctly that the northwest point of the island was approximately on the same parallel (55°25'N) as the mouth of the Kamchatka River. They knew that the southeastern point of the island (54°31'N), though inaccessible to them because of cliffs, was the closer of the two points to their camp.

Steller greatly underestimated the distance of their island from the American continent. Whereas Yushin reported on March 8 that when he and his party were about thirty miles northwest of the camp, he saw land he thought was an island about forty nautical miles to the east, Steller, when looking eastward from the bluff near the camp, said he saw mountains "very clearly" some sixty to eighty nautical miles away. He thought these mountains were too high to be on an island and therefore must be on a promontory of the American mainland. Thus he conceived of America and Asia as being opposite each other with a "channel" running between them; and in that channel, he believed, the island on which they were stranded was closer to the American mainland than to Kamchatka.

Waxell had a similar view. But while Steller declared that the channel could have been crossed "within three or four days" on a northeast course from Avacha Bay, Waxell thought that the American continent could be reached "in eight days" from the same starting point. Had they realized that a sea rather than a channel separated Kamchatka from America and had they known the width of this Bering Sea (as it was later named), a better estimate for the crossing would have been about three weeks, or half the time it took the *St. Peter* and *St. Paul* to sail from Avacha Bay to American landfalls in the Gulf of Alaska.

With everyone safe and sound and back in camp—Yushin on April 5, Ivanov the next day, and Steller on April 8—and with definite information that they were on an island, and with snow rapidly disappearing at lower elevations, the time had come to decide upon a course of action for escape from the island.

So on April 9 Waxell called a meeting and made a brief speech: "The time [has] come to consider how we [are] to escape from [this] wretched [place]." He said he wanted every man to give his answer plainly so that they could agree finally on the best of different opinions. "Our plight [is] the same for the lowliest seaman just as much as for the first officer. . . . [We all long] for safe deliverance, [and] we should all stand by each other. If we [do] what lies in our power to do, God [will] give it his blessing, for God helps all who help themselves."[22] Deliverance. Standing together. Doing what was possible. God helping. With such words Waxell expressed Steller's message, making it his own and that of his command. Survivors were to have both will and faith.

Three proposals were considered. First, as Waxell reports, "some suggested that we should make a sort of 'deck' of sailcloth over the [longboat] to render it fit for an ocean voyage as best as we could and send it due west with five or six men on board so that they might reach Kamchatka, give news of us there, and obtain for us necessary assistance."[23] This suggestion was not immediately rejected, but it presented difficulties and uncertainties. The boat might founder. It might not find help. It would split the survivors into two groups. It was agreed that the longboat should be sent out only as a last resort.

The second proposal, advanced by Ovtsin and supported by several members of his dwelling, was to raise, repair, and launch the *St. Peter*. Both familiar and new reasons were cited for the rejection of this proposal. The ship could not be repaired, for its hull leaked so badly that the level of water inside remained the same as that of the sea. Even if repairs could be made, there was no way to get the ship on rollers for lack of a sufficient number of men and of even one log from which to make the many rollers. Besides, digging a canal for the ship was impossible. As soon as a ditch were dug at low tide, it would fill up again with sand at high tide.

Waxell and Khitrovo then made the proposal they knew had the most support: to dismantle the ship and use the timbers to construct a new, smaller vessel. Waxell argued that "it would be a great relief and comfort for us if we who had survived so many sufferings should find consolation together."[24] Waxell got what he wanted, unanimous support for breaking up the ship. Even Ovtsin signed.

The next day, however, Ovtsin handed Waxell a written protest in which he and another person (unidentified) objected to the decision reached and pleaded that it be reconsidered. Waxell obligingly called another meeting, read the protest, and asked that each person express an opinion. The outcome was predictable. The decision was overwhelmingly reaffirmed and a plan to carry out the work was agreed upon. Yushin would lead a party to hunt and supply the camp with meat. The meat would be divided equally. Ten sacks of flour would be saved for the projected voyage to Kamchatka and the monthly allotment to each person accordingly reduced from 30 to 20 pounds per person for May and June.[25] The ten sacks remaining after June's allotment amounted to 900 pounds, or 20 pounds per person for the hoped-for resumption of the voyage.

Fortunately there was in camp one man, the sailor Sava Starodubtsov, who knew something about shipbuilding because he had worked at it as a laborer at Okhotsk. Starodubtsov told Waxell, "If you will give me the proportions of the new ship, I will build it and make her so solid that, with God's help, we should be able to put to sea in her without risk."[26]

Twelve days, April 10–21, were devoted to preparations. Everything stored in the ship was removed and collected in one spot on the beach. Tools were cleaned and whetstones cut to sharpen them. A forge was erected near the ship to make crowbars and large hammers. Driftwood, suddenly visible again as snow melted and disappeared, was gathered, carried to camp, and now used to produce charcoal.

The master organizational plan devised by Steller called for twelve men who could best work with ax, crowbar, and hammer to work on the ship every day under Starodubtsov's direction. Other men were divided into three teams of about ten men. Each team in succession hunted for two days, rested and cooked for the camp for the next two days, and assisted the shipbuilders for two days before beginning another rotation. Hunters brought meat to a central location, where an officer distributed it to cooks in such a way as to ensure that men working exclusively on the ship would get equitable portions.

This plan was modified when it was realized that on the hunting rotation two men could do the killing for two days while the eight other men could be carriers, making one round trip each day between the hunting grounds and the camp, twelve miles distant on the other side of the island. The distance each way was reduced to six miles when a new trail, going upstream directly behind the camp, was established.

Although the hike was strenuous and the boots of some men were wearing out, some thirty men completed the trip between April 21, when dismantling of the ship began, and May 5, when construction of the new ship began. This hike of twelve miles on each of two successive days over hills and across valleys with snow still on the ground most of the way was testimony to the improved health of the men.

Waxell gave Steller credit for everyone's complete recovery from scurvy. "As soon as the snow was gone and green shoots came out of the ground, we collected and used quantities of herbs and plants. In this Adjunct Steller gave excellent assistance, for he was a good botanist. He collected and showed us many green herbs, some for drinking, some for eating, and by taking them we found our health noticeably improved. From my own experience I can assert that none of us became well or recovered his strength completely before we began eating something green, whether plant or root."[27]

Meat remained the mainstay of diet, and men became emaciated when sea otters disappeared within a daily hunting range from the camp, especially in early April. But suddenly, on the eve of pulling the ship apart, two male fur seals, each more than 700 pounds of meat and fat, were taken on the other side of the island on two successive days, April 18 and 19. They were enough to feed the entire camp for a week. Unfortunately, this new meat had a nauseating smell. Many men vomited and suffered from diarrhea. Luckily, on April 20 a large whale, about a hundred feet long and quite fresh, washed up on the shore just three miles northwest of camp. In two days so much oil was taken from the whale and stored in barrels that the camp never ran out during the spring and summer.

With all this meat so fortuitously available, the *St. Peter* was speedily dismantled within two weeks. On May 2, 1742, the deed was done. On that day the decision was made to build the new ship on the beach directly in front of the last resting place of the old one. From this position, the men believed, it could be easily launched.

On the morning of May 5 the keel of the new ship was laid and the stem and sternpost were installed on the keel. The ship was to be 36 feet long with a 12-foot beam and little more than 5 feet high. In the afternoon Waxell declared a time of celebration. He made a drink for the entire command, using whale oil, rye flour, and crakeberry tea. He made plenty of the mixture, enough for all the company to drink until midnight, giving the men good cheer, though the cheer was mixed, says Steller, with "longing" for departure from the island.[28]

The next day the men were thankful for the celebration. But then for several days the work had to stop. Southeast winds brought in rain that pounded the camp. At the same time, warm weather melted the snow pack at higher elevations. The river that normally meandered by the camp, only a few feet deep and about five yards across, now rose rapidly and flooded over its banks. On May 11 the four subterranean dwellings dug into the sandy ridge near the river started to fill with water from one to two feet deep.

It was an emergency. Using surplus timber from the wreck, men took time out to build summer dwellings aboveground. Taking time from planking the new ship was a serious matter, but other teams that also took a break from hunting caused renewed hunger in the camp. Men resuming work on the ship complained that they were starving for lack of meat. Some asked for permission to hunt. "This request," says Waxell, "was grievous news."

The men hunting fur seals on the other side of the island and carrying the meat back to camp across hills and valleys had their own problems. First, the fur seals were hard to kill. "The beasts," says Steller, "are so tenacious of life that two or three men beating only their heads with clubs could scarcely kill them with two hundred blows, and frequently would have to rest and refresh themselves two or three times." Steller spares no details: "When the cranium is broken into little bits and almost all the brains have gushed out and all the teeth have been broken, the beast still attacks the men with his flippers and keeps right on fighting."[29]

Second, not only were boots worn out by the overland hike, but shirts had become tattered. Some men were barefoot. Finally, there was the meat itself. Compared to the meat of sea otter, harbor seal, and sea lion, the flesh of the fur seal made most men gag.

More and more men looked longingly at the giant manatees feeding on seaweed day by day right before their eyes several fathoms offshore all across the bay in front of their camp. No one had ever seen them elsewhere before, but from his reading Steller knew they were manatees, or sea cows.

The immediate challenge was to capture one of these beasts clustered offshore. These mammals were huge. The largest sea cow, says Steller, was "four to five fathoms" (24 to 30 feet) long, "three and a half fathoms" (21 feet) around the middle, and the heaviest adult, according to Steller's estimate, was "200 puds" (7,200 pounds, or nearly four tons).[30]

After gazing upon these monsters for more than seven months, the men stopped everything on May 21 to try to land one sea cow on the beach. Waxell says he had the men make a large iron hook and attach a heavy cable to it. The idea was to hook into one sea cow in the surf and pull it out of the water by brute force, a tug-of-war between a single sea cow at one end and as many as forty men at the other.[31] The sea cow won each time. Invariably the men ended up in the surf. But with so much meat staring them in the face, they could not give up. They changed hooks, devised new stratagems. Nothing worked.

The main problem, other than the sea cow's strength, was its thick hide. Actually, as Steller later discovered, it had a double hide. The outer one was "an inch thick, having a consistency almost like cork" and "the look of the surface of a thimble." The inner hide was "thicker than an ox hide, very strong and white in color."[32] They simply could not penetrate this double hide, and many experiments ended with the sea cow getting away. Finally Steller figured out how the beast might be taken. It would require the use of the longboat, badly damaged on rocks the previous fall. To repair it took a month.

Toward the end of June a two-sided assault was made. A harpooner in the boat was accompanied by five other men who rowed behind a beast while it was foraging for food. To one end of the harpoon was affixed a long rope held by more than thirty men on shore. As soon as the harpoon had struck, the men on shore started to pull it toward the beach while men in the boat stabbed parts of the body with bayonets. Once enfeebled by the blood gushing from its wounds, the mammal could be beached at high tide and then butchered when it was stranded as the tide receded.

All the men were ecstatic about their new food. After it had been several days in the sun, the fat, Steller says, was "as pleasantly yellow as the best Dutch butter," and the boiled fat "excels in sweetness and taste the best beef fat and is, in color and fluidity like fresh olive oil, and of exceptional good savor and nourishment." He adds, "We drank it by the cupful without feeling the slightest nausea." In a lamp it burned clear without smoke or odor. The flavor of the fat was reminiscent of almonds and "far preferable to that of any other quadruped."[33]

The fat was not the only good news. The milk given off from two four-inch teats, he says, "in taste, fat, content, and sweetness excels the milk of land animals but is otherwise not different." The meat, he says, is somewhat tougher than beef and therefore must be cooked longer. But when it is done, its taste, he claims, cannot be distinguished from that of beef. And it can be kept in the open air without spoilage, a discovery that Steller attributes to the intake of salt in its seaweed diet.

The new food marked a turnaround in the fortunes of the expedition. According to Waxell, before the sea cow harvest, "we never had enough to eat, and otherwise I should not have been able to feed the carpenters and so we should have had to spend yet another winter on the island." Everyone, says Steller, "increased notably in vigor and health."[34] Each person was free to cook as much sea cow meat as he wished as often as he wished. One sea cow fed the camp for two weeks.

Thirteen sea cows were killed. The second one was taken on July 12, and the third was probably the 1,200-pound calf Steller caught on July 18. The fourth was taken on July 27, the fifth on July 29. Finally eight sea cows were slaughtered on July 31, providing more than enough food for the planned voyage.

From June to August, the men were also treated to fresh salmon darting upstream by their dwellings. Each haul of fish netted them choice fillets for eight days. With scrap wood from the wreck, they had plenty of fuel. The major crises were overcome. The way was clear to plan for a late-summer departure from the island.

Progress on the ship was phenomenal. By mid-July the best planks had been used to complete the hull of the new vessel, with some deck planks used to complete the top of the hull. By August 13, all preparations for leave-taking were made. Steller, the only person not directly involved in tasks associated with construction, gave Waxell credit for his constant "friendly encouragement" to all the men. Each day Waxell, as commander, was the first to greet them. There was much improvising. "For the keel," Waxell says, "we used the old ship's mainmast which we sawed off three feet above the deck. . . . The remaining stump had to serve as the new vessel's prow. The sternpost we made from a capstan we had had on the old ship." Fortunately some parts were transferred without modification, including the main-topmast, a large topsail-yard, the topgallant-mast, and the jib-outrigger. The inside of the hull was makeshift, "lined," says Waxell, "with holed planks from the old ship. These were full of nail- and bolt-holes and much splintered and cracked from being wrenched loose . . . but they did much to make the vessel solid and stout, being fixed to each rib with good iron spikes and nails."[35]

The ship had a single cabin in the stern for Waxell, his son, Khitrovo, and Steller. At the bow was the galley. The other men were to sleep in the hold.

From the beginning of construction it was realized that only a minimum of provisions, baggage, and ballast could be transported. Everything and everyone would fit very snugly. Steller could see very soon that he would be unable to take his mounted sea cow calf.

Given the nature of inside planking, it was essential that the hull be watertight. There was plenty of hemp and old rope for caulking but very little pitch with which to seal the hull. The men cleverly extracted tar from ropes that had never been in the water. Each rope was cut into lengths about a foot or less to facilitate unraveling of the strands. These went into a large copper kettle that had a lid with a hole in the center. A wooden vessel was then set well into the ground and covered with its lid, also with a hole in the center. The copper kettle was then inverted so that the holes in the two lids were lined up, earth was packed around the lower part of the kettle to protect the wooden container, and finally a fire was started around the exposed upper part. As expected, the heat melted the tar and the tar trickled down into the wooden vessel. In this way they obtained enough tar to seal the bottom of the ship, leaving the hull above the gunwales to be greased only with tallow.

At this time Steller began to revise and enlarge documents other than his diary. Though he did not find any valuable minerals, he described streams, a few lakes, cliffs, rock reefs, hills, and vales. The resulting descriptive essay he later appended to his revised journal, dated 1743. He also prepared a catalog of plants and a long list of descriptions of fifty-one plants. Finally he made extensive notes on four sea mammals— the sea otter, sea lion, fur seal, and sea cow.

Early in the summer Ivanov, in the longboat in the bay, made a lucky find on the sea bottom—the 8-pud (288-pound) grappling. Later both he and Yushin kept looking for anchors the *St. Peter* had lost in the bay, but they never found any.

Khitrovo made a list of all government items to be left on the island. He listed 2,071 items under such categories as artillery and artillery supplies, corporal's supplies, and navigator's supplies. They included such items as cannon, falconets, axes, crowbars, hammers, saws, rigging, lanterns, compasses, sounding leads, watch glasses, flags, pennants, a large copper kettle, Chinese cotton fabric, tobacco, thimbles, copper bells, mirrors, and knives. Also left on the island were some of Bering's belongings, sorted into three chests.

In July, Ivan Sindt had the job of preparing a list of the total weight allowed for each person's baggage and provisions, including not only personal items but also each person's share of sea otter pelts. Allotted 28 of nearly 900 pelts, Steller acquired nearly 300, having either purchased them with tobacco or received them as gifts from men who credited him with saving their lives.

With Khitrovo's inventory and Sindt's weight list in hand, Waxell on August 1 called a meeting of all men to formalize decisions already made about what to take and what to leave. The men were very willing to sign their names to a document that made various points. First, only one trip from the island should be made and no man should be left behind. Second, only a very small part of the supplies should be transported with the men to avoid overloading the ship. Third, no one should remain on the island to guard government goods because the island had no inhabitants. Last, only enough iron should be taken to serve as ballast and also only things necessary to sustain life, such as barrels of fresh water and sea cow meat. Waxell and the men made no promise to return to recover items of great value, such as cannon. He intended only to construct a storehouse to keep the items secure from foxes and sheltered from the weather.

During the first week of August a storehouse and two ovens to make biscuit were built. Wooden hoops for barrels had rotted. They were replaced by new hoops of iron.

On August 8 everything was in readiness. The ship, poised on the bilge block, was dedicated to the holy apostle Peter and named after him. It was a single-masted hooker on which forty-six castaways were now committed to cast themselves on the sea.

The critical moment had come. It was flood tide. Men prepared the cables. The ship slid down the ways. Then it happened. Boards on the platform gave way and the hooker stopped. The platform was built too low. Winches were used to raise the platform so that the mistake could be remedied by pushing a few thick planks in on the sides between the ship and the platform.

Then at flood-tide the next day, at five o'clock in the afternoon, the ship "with the help of God" hit the water, becoming moored in eighteen feet of water and held by the grappling.

That evening Waxell had another party of tea and cakes, but this time the celebration was short. There was yet too much to do, and no one could predict how long the calm weather would continue. Everyone worked through the night and then for three more days and nights.

On August 10 ten barrels of water were stowed on the little ship. They were followed by a single barrel of salted beef, which, Steller says, "had been spared even in our often-urgent need on the return voyage from America."[36] In addition to these barrels were added 900 pounds of rye flour, 72 pounds of dried peas, and for every man 4 pounds of butter. Besides these provisions there came on board 187 bits of iron (grapeshot), two jacks, two pumps, three small cannon, and several hundred cannonballs for ballast.

On August 11, under Ivanov's direction, the mast was set in place, the ship was rigged, sails were bent on, the rudder was hung, and the ship was made clear to set out to sea.

On August 12 it was time for baggage. First it was weighed. Any excess over the weight allowed for each man was left behind. There were no arguments.

At four o'clock on the afternoon of the 13th a wooden cross was erected over the grave of the late captain-commander. It was the most prominent landmark, bespeaking Russia's claim to a new land. Yushin calculated its latitude: 55°5'N. By prior agreement the island was named for the late commander: Bering Island. Subsequently other local landmarks were named for him too: Komandorsky Camp, Commander River, Commander Bay, Commander Islands.

That afternoon the men left their dwellings for the last time. Only when they boarded the hooker did they realize how crowded they would be. In the hold, three men had to share spaces for two. For lack of space, pillows, bedding, and clothing were thrown overboard. Looking back to their camp from the ship, the men saw foxes claim their dwellings as their own, relishing scraps of fat and meat left behind.

Toward midnight on the 13th, with anchor weighed, the hooker St. Peter, a most humble and nondescript vessel, was ready. With a draft of 5 feet, she sat low in the water, all of 4¾ feet at the stern and 4½ feet at the bow. In the continuing calm, the new ship was rowed by use of sweeps nine miles out from the bay into the channel, where a gentle north wind caught the sail and drove the ship southward. At a speed of only two knots, the hooker with the longboat in tow soon passed Cape Manati.

Men felt exuberant. The weather was bright and pleasant. They were leaving an island they had known all too well as a place of suffering and death, struggle and travail. "God's grace and mercy became manifested to all," writes Steller, "the more brightly considering how miserably we had arrived there on November 6. . . . The more we gazed at the island on our farewell, the clearer appeared to us, as in a mirror, God's wonderful and loving guidance."[37]

On the very first day under sail, August 14, there were already three inches of water in the hold. The next day, in the face of a strong headwind, the longboat in tow began to strain the ship. It was cut adrift. Finally, shortly before midnight a very bad leak was bringing water into the ship faster than it was pumped and bailed out. Sail was quickly taken in. Cannonballs and grapeshot were thrown overboard. Starodubtsov found the leak just where he suspected it was, in an open gap high on the hull from which the seas had washed the caulking away. The leak was plugged quickly from the inside. It was covered with wood cleats. Still the pumps had to be kept going.

Two days later, on August 17, land was seen through mist and fog. They were but a few miles from the Kamchatka mainland near Cape Kronotski. Then progress became difficult, the hooker bedeviled by calms and contrary winds. After eight days of tacking and a full day of rowing without a break, during the early hours of August 25 the ship entered Avacha Bay past the lighthouse. There an Itelmen came out in his boat and told them disquieting news. They had all been given up for dead, and all their personal possessions stored at the Harbor of the Apostles Peter and Paul had been sold off and carried away. It was the custom whenever men died or were lost at sea.

The next night, at the second hour past midnight, they came into the harbor and up to the dock. For the detachment stationed there, this little ship never seen before resembled a ghost.

For the survivors of the Bering expedition it was a shock to return with scarcely any personal possessions and find at last nothing at all of what they had once owned and left behind. It was an even greater shock to be plunged all at once into what Waxell calls "veritable overabundance," into storehouses full of provisions and into luxurious quarters both dry and warm. Steller says, "We were all so accustomed to misery and wretched living that we thought that the previous circumstances would always continue and thought we were dreaming the present ones."[38]

During their first hours ashore the men learned that Chirikov's *St. Paul* had returned to the harbor on October 12, 1741, and that the following spring, on June 2, 1742, Chirikov and his men had left Avacha Bay to search for Bering and the *St. Peter*. They reached Attu on June 9 and actually sighted Bering Island (they named it St. Julian) on June 22. It was a rare beautiful day during which Steller was observing sea lions on the beach of the island's west coast. A point kept him from seeing the *St. Paul* coming up from the south. It got close enough so that Chirikov could see "many fur seals," a "steep shore," and "much snow . . . on the mountains." Chirikov estimated the length of the island "from east to west" to be "about thirty minutes," a poor estimate (it is about one degree or sixty minutes of longitude, or fifty-five miles long), but it is likely that Chirikov was not far enough west to see the full length of the island.[39] Unaware of the presence of forty-six men, Chirikov sailed back to Avacha Bay and arrived in the harbor on July 2. Ten days later he left for Okhotsk, leaving his ship there with twenty men while he and others made a long trek as far as Yeniseisk in Siberia, and from there several years later back to St. Petersburg.

Waxell and Ovtsin in particular were interested in the whereabouts of Captain Chirikov, who with the death of Bering became commander of the Second Kamchatka Expedition, of which the voyages to North America were the culmination.

The next day the men met in the chapel built in the spring of 1741. There, says Steller, "we heartily thanked Almighty God in a common prayer for his gracious protection, our miraculous preservation, and our happy return to Asia." The men did more than pray. Ovtsin, who now found out for the first time that his former rank as lieutenant had been restored as early as February 19, 1741, even before the voyage had begun, was suddenly senior officer among the survivors, having longer service in rank than Waxell. So it was up to Ovtsin to fulfill the vow made at sea at Bering's behest, that the survivors should make their offerings in gratitude to God. With Bering gone, the men agreed that both Lutherans and Russian Orthodox should unite to contribute their gifts to the chapel in which they now found themselves. Ovtsin later arranged for a memorial plaque bearing "a silver mounted image of the apostles Peter and Paul with the inscription, 'an offering in memory of our miraculous rescue from a barren island, and our return to the coast of Kamchatka, by lieutenant Dmitry Ovtsin, and the whole company, August 1741.' "[40]

CONCLUSION

Anna Bering had spent the winter of 1740–41 in Yakutsk. On February 9, 1742, she reached Tobolsk,[1] where she probably for the first time heard the astounding news that Russia had a new empress, Elizabeth, daughter of Peter the Great, who came to the throne in a coup that swept "foreigners" from positions of power: Biron, duke of Courland, former lover of Empress Anna; Munnich, field marshal and first minister under Ivan VI; and Ostermann himself. In Tobolsk customs officials made a thorough inventory of all her possessions, sealing and putting them under the protection of soldiers who escorted her to Moscow. Here she certainly heard the full story and probably for the first time realized that she would no longer enjoy the support of influential friends in St. Petersburg.

News traveled slowly. Empress Anna had died on October 17, 1740. Bering on Kamchatka had addressed his comprehensive report of April 18, 1741, to a monarch already six months dead. Succeeding Anna was an infant only two months old, Ivan VI, her grandnephew and the grandson of her sister, Catherine. This succession was deftly master-minded and executed by Ostermann, who got Empress Anna to sign the necessary papers only the day before she died. At the same time she designated Biron as regent until the new emperor came of age. Biron lasted twenty-two days.[2] A detachment of guards, led by Munnich, entered the palace before daybreak on November 9, arrested Biron in his bed, and carried him off still wrapped in a blanket. A proclamation of the Senate and Holy Synod named the emperor's mother, Anna Leopoldovna, as the new regent. Munnich became her first minister. But not for long. Ostermann soon won her confidence and replaced Munnich by imperial order on January 28, 1741. Since Anna as regent had little interest in ruling the nation, Ostermann reached the pinnacle of his power as sub rosa emperor of Russia.

But the guards were restive. As never before, Germans headed the state. Ostermann of course was German. Anna Leopoldovna had a German father and a German husband. Consequently, little Ivan VI was the most German of all Russian emperors. All these German connections rankled many Russians. It was alarming how distant was the blood relationship of the monarch to Peter the Great, given the presence of the mature Elizabeth, Peter's own daughter.

Anna Leopoldovna herself spurred Elizabeth to action. On November 23, 1741, Anna warned Elizabeth that Ostermann was aware of a plot against the throne. The next day the guards heard that they were about to move to the Swedish front. If Elizabeth were to avoid permanent consignment to a nunnery—or worse—she had to act immediately.

The next day after midnight, accompanied by gentlemen of her household, she went by sledge to the guards' barracks. As she entered the building she held a large silver cross in both hands. She was welcomed by acclamation and oaths of support. At the head of 300 guards she rode to the palace where the regent and emperor were sleeping. They were arrested in their beds. Elizabeth, lifting the curtain on the crib of Ivan VI, reputedly said, "Poor child, you are innocent indeed!"[3]

The next day Ostermann, Munnich, Biron, and others were arrested. Ostermann was charged with concealing the will of Catherine I, designating the order of succession, and of manipulating the succession of Anna Ivanovna and Ivan VI, who were not included in that succession. He was also charged with deliberately bypassing the obvious prior claim of Peter's own daughter, Elizabeth. For these crimes Ostermann was to be beheaded and his corpse broken on the wheel.

On the morning of January 17, 1742, the beat of drums rolled through the streets of St. Petersburg to announce the next day's execution of enemies of Empress Elizabeth. On the 18th crowds gathered in the square on Vasilevsky Island, where a regiment encircled a scaffold on which the execution block had been placed.

At the stroke of ten o'clock in the morning, Ostermann came from the fortress into the square. He was pulled on a sledge by a horse because he was, he said, too lame to walk. Four soldiers lifted him out of the sledge and seated him on a chair on the scaffold.

His wig was removed. The secretary of the Senate took a scroll in hand and read his sentence. Ostermann's shirt was then unbuttoned and his neck bared. With his head still bereft of the wig, he was laid face down on the block. One executioner held his head by the hair. Another bared the ax. Minutes elapsed.

The secretary of the Senate then took a second scroll and proclaimed, "God and Her Majesty have spared your life. Your sentence is commuted to exile in Siberia." Wig restored and shirt buttoned, Ostermann was lifted back on the sledge. His only sign of emotion was the trembling of his hands.[4] No one was executed. Unlike Anna Ivanovna, Elizabeth Petrovna shed no blood. After a short time in prison, Ostermann and his wife entered Siberia just as Anna Bering was coming out.

Anna's journey took twice as long as she had expected, two years and one month. She spent nearly six months in the home of a Lutheran pastor in Moscow, eleven of her sealed trunks on four sledges in the yard.[5] She had attested that all these goods were for her personal use, though in her correspondence she had already promised a valuable pelt to the professor's wife and a basket of precious green tea to her "dearest friend," the wife of the Austrian resident in St. Petersburg.

On September 15, 1742, Anna left Moscow for St. Petersburg, accompanied by her two servants and two children. The news awaiting her at home was devastating. Her dear papa had died. Ostermann was in exile. Nikolai Sebastian von Hohenholz no longer had channels of influence within the Russian government; moreover, he was deeply involved politically in the War of the Austrian Succession, which had begun in 1740 when Prussia seized Silesia. Finally, Aleksei Ivanov, a special courier who arrived in St. Petersburg on September 4, 1743, brought Anna the very worst news—the death of her husband. A widow, she no longer had status or expectations. What was left for her was an award of 5,000 rubles, a small pension, and a claim on the goods belonging to her husband and sold at auction in the Harbor of the Apostles Peter and

Paul and in Yakutsk. Eventually she also received items of gold and silver that Bering had carried aboard ship in nine sea chests, including a gold watch, silver spoons, a silver tray, a silver tobacco box, and a silver-studded sword with silver-inlaid sword belt—all remembrances of the promised better life that now would never come.[6]

The woman who was ever ready to offer cash for services to improve the prospects of her two older sons soon had to petition the Admiralty College for money. Her last letter, dated March 27, 1745, begs payment "without delay" for some of her late husband's goods sold at auction because she has, she writes, "the greatest need for the money."[7] She had a mounting obligation to Professor Sigismundi in Reval for years of instructional fees and boarding expenses for her two sons. She possibly had reimbursements to make to "dear Badska" for favors she had sought for her son Jonas. Perhaps she was also in debt to her two sisters. Short of funds, how and where would she live? How would she launch her two younger children into a society now prejudiced against foreigners?

The brave woman who for more than a decade had wandered across the face of an empire, longing for the scintillating life of the capital and the security of a hereditary estate, now found her ideal world in ruins. Nothing was sure or settled or even safe. Peter's city without Peter was no haven for Western Europeans. A letter written in December 1741 by a foreign resident reflects general unease: "All of us here live constantly between hope and fear, since the soldiers, getting ever bolder, utter threats which, thanks only to Providence, they have not yet carried out. We poor foreigners tremble for our lives."[8]

Anna certainly knew that Viborg, her hometown, was also hostile to people like her. In 1743 soldiers publicly demanded that their foreign officers be summarily put to death. When their demands were ignored, they mutinied. They were quickly put down with overwhelming force, but thereafter the town remained threatening.[9]

Anna quickly faded from view. Friends and family soon passed away: Ostermann died, still in exile, in 1747; Hohenholz died two years later. Her only brother, Bendix, having left Viborg, died in 1752 and he had no son. Both Anton and Helena von Saltza died in 1753, and Eufemia early the next year. In short order the entire generation of a family was gone.

Ivanov delivered to the Admiralty College Waxell's report about the voyage to America, dated November 15, 1742. This report and news of

Bering's death hastened a decision already being considered: On September 25, 1743, the Senate ordered the termination of the Second Kamchatka Expedition and the return of all participants.

Survivors of that second expedition who retained their share of the precious sea otter pelts from Bering Island were of course eager to dispose of their small fortunes. These pelts excited everyone at the harbor. Steller decided to leave his cache of some 300 pelts there. Expedition members knew that whenever they reached Irkutsk they could get the highest value in Siberia at the Chinese trading post near the border.

Steller was the first to leave Avacha Bay. He and Thomas hiked overland 140 miles to Bolsheretsk, arriving September 5, 1742. There he wrote his report of November 16 and continued his work of describing the land and peoples of Kamchatka. He spent much of his first year revising his journal and other documents. He reopened a bicultural school at Bolsheretsk for Russian and aboriginal students, hired a schoolmaster, and at first supported this project from his own resources. He eventually recovered his pelts at the harbor in Avacha Bay, traveled north as far as the Olyutor River, nearly drowned when he attempted to cross the ice to Karaginski Island, and as person in charge at Bolsheretsk caused an uproar by releasing natives arrested by Russians.

He never got back to St. Petersburg, where presumably he would have been able to edit and publish his findings. At 37 years, on November 12, 1746, he died of a fever at Tyumen, in Siberia. Of his voluminous writings, *De bestiis marinis* (Beasts of the sea) was published in 1751; an unauthorized collection of his reports about Kamchatka appeared in Germany as *Beschreibung von dem Lande Kamtschatka* (Description of Kamchatka) in 1774; and his journal, rewritten and reorganized, was published as *Reise von Kamtschatka nach Amerika* (Voyage from Kamchatka to America) in 1793.

Waxell was determined to follow Chirikov. Finding many cracks in the bottom of the hooker *St. Peter*, he and his men caulked and repaired the ship on August 28–29, 1742, loaded the vessel the next three days, and sailed south from the entrance of Avacha Bay on September 2. But the very next day, the hooker, already leaking badly, returned to the bay and the harbor for the winter. Reaching St. Petersburg in 1749, Waxell and Khitrovo corrected and completed the expedition's charts.

In 1744 Waxell became a captain second class, and five years later captain first class. He completed his journal by 1756, leaving it in manuscript when he died in 1762. Khitrovo also became captain first class, in 1749, and advanced to rear admiral in 1753. He died three years later.

Chirikov complained to the Admiralty when, after news of Bering's death, Spangberg immediately took over command of the expedition. Their rivalry soon ended when the expedition officially terminated. In 1745 Spangberg returned to St. Petersburg without permission, a liberty for which he paid dearly—he was sentenced to death. Two years later he was pardoned but demoted to the rank of lieutenant.

At Yeniseisk, Chirikov was in charge of various affairs left over from the expedition, including an accounting of various auctions held to dispose of Bering's possessions. When in 1746 he was ordered to return to St. Petersburg, he left Waxell in charge. In the capital he was made director of the Naval Academy and promoted to captain-commander. Unfortunately, never having fully recovered his health since the voyage to America, he died of tuberculosis in November 1748, leaving a widow and four children and a heavy debt they could never repay.

Spangberg regained his rank of captain first class in 1751. He died in 1761.

Of the four officers, Waxell gained the greatest reputation. Though Chirikov and Khitrovo outranked him in the end and Spangberg outranked him during the Second Kamchatka Expedition, his account of that expedition, written in German and left in manuscript, was used by historians in Russia as late as 1851. Then it was lost until 1938, when it turned up in a Leningrad bookstore. Soon published in Russian, Danish, English, and Swedish translations, it is valued today, together with Steller's account, as a primary source of the history of the expedition. Waxell also had the good fortune to have three sons who in 1778 were granted patents of nobility in recognition of their father's service. By the time Waxell died, in 1762, his eldest son, Laurentz, born in 1730, had already attained his father's highest rank, captain first class, in the Russian navy.

As soon as Anna and her siblings passed from the scene, the reputation of Vitus Jonassen Bering began a slide of 250 years into virtual obscurity, essentially for two reasons. During Empress Elizabeth's reign, 1741–61, prejudice against foreigners and people with foreign names was widespread in Russia, even as Peter the Great, the emperor who had enlisted foreigners, was venerated and idolized. Anna Bering could receive no estate for her husband's services. Her brother, Bendix, left Viborg, never to return. Her son Thomas left Russia in 1752 to enter the service of the duke of Holstein. He returned to Russia in 1761, at the end of Elizabeth's rule.[10]

Despite changing times, the children and grandchildren of Vitus and Anna Bering did well. Only Thomas was in the civil service, as assessor; the other two sons had careers in the Russian army. Jonas became a colonel; he was commandant in Ukraine until 1784. At the age of 63, he was murdered. Anton retired in 1796 as riding master in the cavalry. Their sister, Anna, married a lieutenant general, Fromhold Georg von Korff, in 1750, was widowed in 1758, and was buried near Moscow in 1786. Of the grandchildren, two distinguished themselves in the Russian navy. Alexander Bering served in the Black Sea and the Mediterranean, becoming a captain-lieutenant in 1811. Christian Bering followed his grandfather to the Pacific Ocean, served in the Joseph Billings expedition of 1785–94, and became captain-commander in 1799.[11]

The second reason for Bering's eclipse was the Russian government's reluctance to divulge information concerning the Second Kamchatka Expedition. Though this expedition had officially ended in 1743 (but was prolonged unofficially for several years more), only snippets of news were published abroad, and they were based on unofficial and largely unreliable sources.[12] In 1740 a Dutch representative in St. Petersburg learned that Spangberg had discovered thirty-four islands on which the Russians met friendly people but could not communicate with them. This report appeared first in Amsterdam and soon afterward in Paris and London. In 1743 the first report of Bering's death appeared. He had been wrecked on an island where "the larger part of the crew" died with him. Survivors got off the island and back to Kamchatka by building a smaller boat from the wreck of the larger one. Steller is cited as the source, with the implication that only Chirikov had reached America. Steller of course was still on Kamchatka, where it was unlikely that he met or wrote anyone who could pass on such distorted news. When he heard about it by letter from his brother Augustin in 1745, he was incensed. "I should like to know," he writes, "who has been making me out a sailor and a windbag."[13] He feared that some personal enemy was exposing him to the charge that he had broken his pledge to keep Russian discoveries secret.

In 1748 appeared what has been called "the first—though very brief—official factual report on the voyage of Bering to America."[14] It was written anonymously in both German and Russian. The German version, published in Frankfurt, was titled *Leben Herrn Georg Wilhelm Stellers*. It was written in response to a biographical sketch by Steller's brother Augustin in 1747 after he learned about Steller's death. Unable to find out the circumstances or even the place of his brother's death, Augustin suspected foul play and raised questions about Russia's responsibility for the death. The story appeared in a literary journal and reached an educated readership throughout Germany.

Many Russian professors and ministers continued to respect their Western European mentors, looking to Berlin, Halle, Paris, and London for encouragement and approval. It was bad enough that Augustin's story was misleading about Steller's role on the Bering voyage, but Russia's prestige would suffer if dark thoughts about Steller's death persisted. The challenge for Russia was to defend the national honor by setting the record straight without dignifying Augustin's story with a direct reply, without at the same time arousing any further controversy in the international scholarly community, and without propagating information that would compromise imperial interests in the North Pacific Ocean—the reason for secrecy ever since the second expedition had been authorized. Indeed, Russia enjoyed a world monopoly on pelts of sable, sea otter, and fur seal between the voyage north of Japan by the Dutch Captain Vries (1643) and the third voyage of British Captain Cook (1778).

Through the *Leben*, Russia for the first time revealed, in sketchy outline, major events of the expedition to America, with a chronology that was in some instances inexact: June 4, 1741, Bering left his home port on Kamchatka; June 18 (*sic*) he sighted America; July 20 he explored an island (Kayak) near the mainland; September 4 he met people resembling Itelmens but speaking a different language; November 5 the ship was "beached" on an island (Bering Island); December 8 Bering died; August 17 (*sic*), 1742, survivors left the island on a new ship built from the old one; and August 26 (*sic*) they arrived safely in the same harbor on Kamchatka. Details are brief; some are inaccurate. For example, the sea did not bring "pieces" of the ship ashore but in a storm lifted the entire vessel intact high on the beach of Commander Bay. No mention is made of sea otters, sea cows, fur seals, or foxes.

The writer was probably Gerhard Friedrich Müller. There are several clues. He was German; there is a reference to "we Germans." He was very likely present when Steller arrived at Yeniseisk in 1738; the *Leben*'s author is familiar with the naturalist's movements and activities in Siberia and the "extensive instructions" he received from Müller and Gmelin before his departure for Kamchatka. The author regards Steller as their "assistant" and not the independent investigator he considered himself to be. Gmelin did not write the *Leben* because in 1747 he was on his way to Germany and he did not return to Russia. In 1747 Müller was appointed rector of the university in St. Petersburg and Russia's first historiographer. At the same time, as a participant with Steller in the Second Kamchatka Expedition and as a fellow of the British Royal Society, he would be particularly sensitive about criticism of the Academy's achievements in Siberia. Writing the *Leben* would give him an opportunity to show his loyalty to Russia. That nation, he says, provided necessary support so that Steller could "immortalize his name." Russia, he says, cannot be blamed for secrecy "if, after having spent large and almost immeasurable sums toward useful discoveries, it forbids those who spent them and who are well paid to promptly write everybody all about them."[15] Altogether the *Leben* is a curious mixture, a disarmingly factual narrative interspersed with testimony on Russia's beneficence.

Secrecy concerning the voyage to America persisted despite the very limited information made available in the *Leben* and despite bits of other information leaked in Denmark, England, and Germany between 1747 and 1752.

Bering's reputation was poorly served by the publication in Paris of Joseph Nicolas Delisle's *Explication de la carte des nouvelles découvertes au nord de la Mer du Sud* in 1752. The French cartographer, back in France in 1747 after twenty years with the Russian Academy of Sciences, clearly broke his oath by publishing two maps and an explanation of them. Delisle made two false claims: that Bering, upon leaving Kamchatka, got no farther than the island where he died, and that Delisle de La Croyère deserved equal honor with Chirikov for having reached America.[16]

Russia authorized a response in French published in Berlin as *Lettre d'un officier de la marine russienne à un Seigneur de la cour concernant la carte des nouvelles découvertes au nord de la Mer du Sud.* In the *Lettre* Müller poses as a Russian officer, using Waxell's journal as his source. His sarcasm, as translated in the English edition, is unmistakable: "Here I am obliged to give Mr. de l'Isle's dry and slender account a little more nourishment, by adding a relation of the voyage of Mr. Beerings [*sic*], and the other officers in this expedition. I am the better able to do it, as I myself had a share in it, and can appeal to the journals and charts of each of the ships."[17] As in the earlier *Leben,* the *Lettre* summarizes the voyages of Bering and Chirikov as well as voyages of Spangberg to Japan and the various voyages down Siberian rivers to the Icy Sea.

Delisle's *Explication* finally brought an end to Russia's policy of secrecy, and Müller had the task of producing a first official map and history. The map was completed in 1754; only a small number of copies were printed (see Fig. 20). With few changes the same map was published in 1758 in the completed history, titled *Nachrichten von Seereisen, und ʒu See gemachten Entdeckungen, die von Russland aus langst den Kusten des Eismeeres und auf dem ostlichen Weltmeere gegen Japon und America geschehen sind,* published in St. Petersburg as the third volume of *Sammlung russischer Geschichte.* In 1761 its English translation was titled *Voyages from Asia to America . . .* and its French version in 1766 was *Voyages et découvertes faites par les Russes. . . .* A definitive English translation with an extensive introduction was issued in 1986 as *Bering's Voyages: The Reports from Russia.* The "reports" used by Müller include chiefly journals by Waxell, Steller, and Peter Chaplin, a midshipman who took part in the first expedition.

Müller's history seems purposely to avoid any sustained focus on Bering. Even in a section titled "Bering," the name itself is used solely in the first paragraph and "the captain commander" in the second paragraph; later the passive voice obscures the agent of any action, as in "it was decided to go to sea again." The section is more about Khitrovo and Steller (and the continuing voyage to the Shumagin Islands) than about Bering. One has the impression throughout the history that Bering as commander initiates action and then remains withdrawn and relatively inactive while subordinates carry out their duties. Müller does not explain why Bering went to Yekaterinburg and Irkutsk. He indicates Bering's support of explorations down the Lena River and his supervision of provisions sent to Okhotsk, but he does not mention Bering's other major responsibilities at Yakutsk, namely, the building of an iron foundry and the search for a feasible southern route to the Sea of Okhotsk. Müller's limited knowledge and lack of understanding are reflected in his indirect criticism of Bering when he writes that "everything proceeded so slowly [in Yakutsk] that no one could predict when the voyage to Kamchatka would begin." Upon Bering's death, Müller briefly reviews the commander's career and praises him in a single sentence, "He combined the skill proper to his office with long experience, which made him especially deserving of such an extraordinary business as the discoveries that were twice entrusted to him."[18]

This infrequent reference to Bering has a precedent in Waxell's account, also written in German. Though Waxell is frank in expressing his opinions, sometimes passionately, he shows obvious and proper restraint concerning his commander. About a dozen references to him are respectful and matter-of-fact, and he never alludes to his dispute with Bering upon leaving Kayak Island. But there is a single deviation. Waxell states that during the sea voyage of the First Kamchatka Expedition its "members . . . never sighted land" in the direction of America. "In my opinion," he writes, "this was because they had not gone far enough to the north."[19] Waxell would have been well advised to delete this opinion. He did not participate in this voyage. He seems to think that finding America was its chief objective. Apparently he did not realize that the expedition reached 67°24'N, from which additional progress to the north would not necessarily take the *Archangel Gabriel* within sight of America.

For insight into Bering's character and achievement among primary sources, a biographer has invaluable documents in Bering's own reports of the expeditions through April 18, 1741; in his recently discovered personal letters and those of his wife, written in February 1740; and in the findings of the scientists who recovered his remains in August 1991. As noted earlier, these sources leave a short but critical gap, the last eight months of Bering's life, including outward and homeward voyages of the *St. Peter*. Fortunately, the earnest and irrepressible Georg Steller was a cabin mate of his commander. Unlike the dilettante James Boswell, who courted Samuel Johnson and recorded conversations of that great essayist and lexicographer, Steller was a single-minded scientist determined to fulfill usually self-assigned duties that Bering could not always accommodate. Steller's judgment of his commander could be appalling, as when in the preface to his manuscript journal of 1743 he asserts, "Because the Captain-Commander did not accept the least advice from me—he had too much regard for his own opinion. . . . The aftermath and divine judgment showed only too clearly how different my reasoning was from his unfounded presumption."[20] It is astonishing that here Steller not only considers his views superior to Bering's but also is confident that God punished his commander for impeding his (Steller's) work. Here is Steller's Pietism at its worst; the man of God presumes to pronounce God's judgment. Yet the context of such a remark must be understood. Steller had not obtained permission from St. Petersburg to go on the voyage to America. He had heard news of the accession of Empress Elizabeth and the arrest of Germans who had served Empress Anna. Steller had good reason to be apprehensive. Even so, his remark is revealing. As an independent operator from the Academy, he presumes also that his scientific work should take precedence over Bering's other responsibilities. The question begs to be asked: Who had "unfounded presumption"?

On the other hand, Steller was singularly compassionate, tireless, and effective on Bering Island. He was Bering's confessor. His eulogy of his dead commander is warm and sincere. His remedies for scurvy saved many lives. Here was his Pietism at its best. In other words, Steller's remarks about Bering must be interpreted in the context of a given situation in the light of each man's motivation. Unlike Müller and Waxell, Steller frequently feels free to fault or commend his commander. Without Steller we would know little about Bering on his last voyage.

In the late eighteenth century Steller's views about Bering received little attention, and Bering himself was almost forgotten at a time when Russian fur traders returned to Bering Island in 1743, Attu in 1745, Atka in 1747, Umnak in 1759, Unalaska in 1762, Kodiak in 1763, Kayak in 1783, Sitka in 1799, and Fort Ross (California) in 1812.

During most of this time Russia had no institutional presence in America. Russian traders came toward America and returned to Asia, small bands in small sailing ships, trading such items as beads, cotton cloth, knives, and kettles in exchange for sea otter and fox pelts. It was sometimes a bloody business on both sides, Russians massacring Aleuts and Aleuts stealthily getting revenge. But usually the sides cooperated, the Aleuts hunting sea otter to acquire desired trade goods. During the second half of the eighteenth century, as many as a hundred Russian ships traded at various times along the Aleutian Islands, the Alaska Peninsula, Kodiak Island, Cook Inlet, and Prince William Sound.[21] For the merchants the trade was highly profitable but also risky, given the vagaries of weather and the rapid decline of sea otter. Over the years, as ships were wrecked and voyages extended, single merchants gave way to partnerships, and small companies yielded to a few larger ones. These firms began to stake out territory, establish forts and settlements, and conscript Aleuts and Eskimos to do the hunting.

One of them, the Shelikhof-Golikov Company, had big plans. It sought a monopoly over all of Russian America. Grigory Shelikhof, who with his wife, Natalia, actually lived for two years on Kodiak Island, 1784–86, returned to Russia to continue a campaign for an imperial charter granting his company sole rights to Russian American trade. When he died, his wife pursued those appeals. Much was promised—support of Orthodox missionary priests, benevolent rule over native peoples, and extension of trade to Britain, Japan, China, Korea, India, and the Philippines. In 1799 Emperor Paul finally granted the desired charter, and the Russian-American Company, with headquarters in St. Petersburg, became in fact the first single continuing Russian institutional presence in the New World and its chief manager, Aleksandr Baranof, in effect ruler of Russian American colonies.

It was a one-way movement from west to east with more Russians coming again and again after Bering had pioneered the way, exposing the last great expanse of a rich continent to European civilization. By any measure, the cost was horrendous to Native Americans. Russians, Spaniards, British, French, and New England Yankees were relentless. Disease decimated indigenous populations as guns never did.[22] The new era on the west coast of North America dominated by European cultures was neither kind nor pretty.

Just as news of Columbus's first voyage of 1492 triggered almost immediate further Spanish as well as Portuguese, French, and British exploration of the Americas, so news about Bering's voyage to North America's northwest coast prompted Spain to establish missions in California and persuaded Spain, Britain, and France in the late eighteenth century to sponsor voyages of exploration between California and the Bering Strait. Since 1500 world political and economic power has shifted from Spain to Britain and from Britain to the United States. Within the United States that power has begun to shift in the twenty-first century from the east to west coast, that is, from the Atlantic (Columbian) "pond" to the Pacific (Beringian) "lake." It can be argued that what

Columbus started as an explorer in the Americas, Bering finished—granted that neither explorer could possibly predict the direction of future political and economic development. What can be said confidently is that the Bering expeditions, and particularly the second one, initiated a rush of Europeans into a last very habitable region of the Americas and changed that part of the world forever. And now at last the man who led the expeditions that charted much of the Pacific lake and made his impact felt on much of the land around it has himself a new face, a new image, a fortuitously improved reputation, and with his wife, Anna, a partially recovered family story.

What seems unusual for their era was their solid partnership. Though long apart, they seem not to have lived separate lives, hers subordinate to his. Their goals were the same, both for themselves and for their children. They had the same religious faith. They were evidently entirely open to each other. He missed her and the children. His "longing for home" was apparent aboard ship. He was surely proud of her bravery, strength, refinement, cleverness, and eloquence. His good fortune until his sixtieth birthday—until the last four months of his life—was that he still had good health; and to the very end of his life he had purpose, position, wealth, clarity, and to all appearances the abiding love of an intelligent woman.

Notes

Complete authors' names, titles of books and articles, and other publication data are given in the Bibliography. Titles of books and collections of documents or papers cited frequently are abbreviated as follows:

Divin, GRN Divin, *Great Russian Navigator*
Fisher, BV Fisher, *Bering's Voyages*
Frost Frost, *Bering and Chirikov*
Golder, BV Golder, *Bering's Voyages*
Hintzsche Hintzsche, *Reisetagebücher*
Krasheninnikov, EK Krasheninnikov, *Explorations of Kamchatka*
Kushnarev, BS Kushnarev, *Bering's Search for the Strait*
Lauridsen, VB Lauridsen, *Vitus Bering*
Len'kov, KC Len'kov et al., *Komandorskii Camp*
Lind and Møller, KK Lind and Møller, *Kommandøren og Konen*
Müller, BV Müller, *Bering's Voyages*
Pekarskii Pekarskii, *Archival Research*
Pierce Pierce, *Russia in North America*
Pokrovskii, BE Pokrovskii *Bering's Expeditions*
RP *Russian Penetration of the North Pacific Ocean*
Smith Smith, *Science under Sail*
Smith and Barnett Smith and Barnett, *Russian America*
Stejneger, GWS Stejneger, *Georg Wilhelm Steller*

Steller, J Steller, *Journal of a Voyage with Bering*
Waxell, AE Waxell, *American Expedition*
Wood Wood, *History of Siberia*
Zvyagin et al., VJB Zvyagin et al., *Vitus Jonassen Bering*

INTRODUCTION

1. J. N. Delisle, *Explication* (1752), cited in Urness, "The Setting," in Müller, BV, 50; A. Sokolov, quoted in Divin, GRN, 138; Golder, BV, 1:34; and Ford, *Where the Sea Breaks Its Back*, 51.

2. See, e.g., Waxell, AE, frontispiece.

3. A. K. Stanyukovich was expedition leader; V. N. Zvyagin was forensic physician.

4. The Russians did not have the advantage of an unabridged edition of Steller's journal.

5. Zvyagin et al., VJB, 65–67, 72–73.

6. Steller, J, 131. On Nov. 11, 1741, Steller refers to his dwelling as a "grave."

7. Ibid., 113.

8. Ibid., 124.

9. Madsen et al., "Excavating Bering's Grave," in Frost, 229–30.

10. The archaeologists from the Horsens Historical Museum were O. Schiørring, O. Madsen, and S. G. Petersen. The archaeologist from the National Museum was S. E. Albrethsen.

11. Albrethsen, "Vitus Bering's Second Kamchatka Expedition," in Jacobsen, *Vitus Bering*, 90.

12. Frost, "Vitus Bering Resurrected," 91, 94.

13. Zvyagin, "Reconstruction of Vitus Bering," in Frost, 262.

14. Golder, BV, 1:33–34; Introduction to Waxell, AE, 31–32.

15. Hintzsche and Nickol, *Grosse Nordische Expedition*, 75, 299.

16. Golder, BV, 2:159 (the translator is L. Stejneger); Steller, J, 141 (the translators are M. A. Engel and O. Frost).

17. Steller, J, 134.

18. Zvyagin et al., VJB, 74.

19. Steller, J, 141. Waxell's list appears in Golder, BV, 1:281–82. See also lists in Len'kov et al., KC, 9–10. Waxell omits two individuals.

20. Lind and Møller, KK, 97–100.

21. Pokrovskii, BE, 125 (italics added); Steller, J, 93–94 (italics added).

22. L. Pasenyuk, Foreword, in Zvyagin et al., VJB, 7.

23. Albrethsen, "Vitus Bering's Second Kamchatka Expedition," 90–91.

CHAPTER 1. VITUS BERING SIGNS ON WITH RUSSIA

1. When Peter returned from Western Europe in 1698, he ordered that male inhabitants of cities and towns be clean-shaven; only the patriarch and two elder courtiers were excepted. See Cracraft, *Church Reform*, 1, 9, 149, 175; Hughes, *Russia in the Age of Peter the Great*, 410.

2. Weber, ambassador of Hanover, was in Russia from 1714 to 1721. See Massie, *Peter the Great*, 765–66.

3. Armstrong, *Russian Settlement*, 61; Fisher, *Russian Fur Trade*, 49–92.

4. Lind and Møller, KK, 143–46; Steller, J, 49–50.

5. Stejneger, "Witus Jonassen Bering," 295.

6. Urness, "Captain-Commander Vitus Bering," in Frost, 12.

7. Alekseev, *Destiny of Russian America*, 4; Steller, J, 138; Urness, "The Setting," in Müller, BV, 16.

8. Massie, *Peter the Great*, 71–75, 124–32.

9. Urness, *Bering's First Expedition*, 252.

10. Bridge, *History of the Russian Fleet*, 26; Urness, "Captain-Commander Vitus Bering," 13–14.

11. Bridge, *History of the Russian Fleet*, 25.

12. Hughes, *Russia in the Age of Peter the Great*, 13, 333–34.

13. Lind and Møller, KK, 90.

14. On Anna's family, marriage, and age see ibid, 51–58.

15. O. Bering, "Bering-Slaeghten," Horsens *Social-Demokrat*, Dec. 16, 1941, 13.

16. Urness, "Captain-Commander Vitus Bering," 14.

17. Ibid., 15.

18. Kushnarev, BS, 22.

CHAPTER 2. NEVER ON LAND HAD SO MANY GONE SO FAR

1. Kushnarev, BS, 20.

2. Goldenberg, *Gvozdev*, 17, 19. See also Urness, "Captain-Commander Vitus Bering," in Frost, 33–35.

3. Kushnarev, BS, 20; Barratt, *Russia in Pacific Waters*, 17.

4. Kushnarev, BS, 20.

5. Steller, J, 58.

6. Fisher, "To Give Chirikov His Due," in Frost, 38; Divin, GRN, 34.

7. Kushnarev, BS, 182n19.

8. Ibid., 29.

9. Ibid., 9–10.

10. Urness, "Captain-Commander Vitus Bering," 27–29.

11. The lieutenant's last name is Safonov (Kushnarev, BS, 31).

12. Ibid., 35. Kerner lists Siberian forts and their founding dates (*Urge to Sea*, 185–90).

13. Kushnarev, BS, 35.

14. Ibid., 36.

15. Ibid., 55.

16. Garrett, *St. Innocent*, 39.

17. Kushnarev, BS, 67. The corporal's name is Ivan Anashkin.

18. Ibid., 63, 69, 71.

CHAPTER 3. INTO THE ICY SEA

1. Kushnarev, BS, 85. In 1738 Ushka had 51 payers of tribute or about 200 residents (Murashko, "Demographic History," 19).

2. Kushnarev, BS, 93–94.

3. Krauss, "Bering 1728 and Gvozdev 1732," in Smith, *Science under Sail*, thinks the expedition met speakers "probably of the Sirenikski Eskimo language first documented in 1895 [and] extinct in 1997."

4. Fisher, *Voyage of Semen Dezhnev*, 172, 185.

5. Krasheninnikov, EK, 3.

6. Semyonov, *Conquest of Siberia*, 109–10.

7. Belov, *Russians in the Bering Strait*, 28; Fisher, *Voyage of Semen Dezhnev*, 276.

8. See, e.g., map appended to text in Demin, *Semen Dezhnev*.

9. Kushnarev, BS, 102, 106.

10. Parkinson, "Variability of Arctic Sea Ice," 341–42, 346, 349–50.

11. Golder, *Russian Expansion*, 149.

12. Beaglehole, *Life of Captain James Cook*, 618–19.

13. Cook, *Journals*, 3:418n, 427.

14. Kushnarev, BS, 107.

15. Ibid., 109; V. Bering, "Report," in Golder, BV, 1:18.

16. Fisher, "Finding America," in Smith and Barnett, 19–20. Fisher, reflecting Sopotsko's views, mentions the *Archangel Gabriel*'s "back-and-forth" course as a clue that Bering was seeking America. However, the actual course of the ship was predominantly to the north, without sustained movement east or west.

17. Kushnarev, BS, 113.

18. Ibid., 114.

19. Their titles indicate their thesis: Lauridsen's *Vitus Bering: The Discoverer of Bering Strait* and Kushnarev's *Bering's Search for the Strait*.

20. See, e.g., Imbert, "Bering and Chirikov," in Frost, 64.

21. "Report from Captain Vitus Bering," in RP, 81, 84–85.

22. Krasheninnikov's *Explorations of Kamchatka, 1735–1741* is available

in English. Messerschmidt's Siberian studies are collected in five volumes (*Forschungsreise durch Sibirien, 1720–27*). An English translation of *Beschreibung von dem Lande Kamtschatka* is available (*Steller's History of Kamchatka,* trans. Margritt Engel and Karen Willmore [Fairbanks: University of Alaska Press, 2003]).

23. Her lover was Ernst Johann Biron (Buhren) and her commander in chief was Count Burkhard Christoph Munnich.

24. Lind and Møller, KK, 97; Wolff, *Levnetsefterretninger,* 19.

CHAPTER 4. A DREAM OF EMPIRE

1. Fisher, BV, 120–23; Gibson, "Supplying the Kamchatka Expeditions," in Frost, 111–12. The Austrian resident was Nikolai Sebastian von Hohenholz.

2. Fisher, BV, app. 2, 184–85.

3. Divin, GRN, 61; Fisher, BV, 110.

4. Gibson, "Supplying the Kamchatka Expeditions," 101.

5. Fisher, BV, app. 2, 186.

6. Black, *G.-F. Müller,* 53.

7. Waxell, AE, 65.

8. Divin, GRN, 68–71.

9. Fisher, BV, app. 2, 187.

10. RP, 96–100.

11. Ibid., 108.

12. Rasputin, *Siberia, Siberia,* 186, 198, 262.

13. RP, 112.

14. Concerning Ovtsin's misfortune, see Armstrong, "Siberian and Arctic Exploration," in Frost, 117–26.

15. Waxell, AE, 59–60.

CHAPTER 5. SET UP TO FAIL

1. Lind and Møller, KK, 51–52.

2. Gibson, "Supplying the Kamchatka Expeditions," in Frost, 104; Collins, "Subjugation and Settlement," in Wood, 47.

3. Forsyth, "Siberian Native Peoples," in Wood, 81.

4. The Itelmens (Kamchadals) called the Russians *brikhtatyn* or "men of fire" because of their use of firearms (Krasheninnikov, EK, 195).

5. RP, 118.

6. Waxell, AE, 51.

7. RP, 119.

8. V. Bering, "Report," in Pokrovskii, 132.

9. Ibid., 132–33.

10. Len'kov et al., KC, 126.

11. Ibid., 128–30.

12. Ibid., 133.

13. Black, *G.-F. Müller*, 67.

14. Stejneger, GWS, 110.

15. Ibid., 109.

16. Black, *G.-F. Müller*, 65.

17. Lind and Møller, KK, 63.

18. Krasheninnikov, EK, 351–52.

19. Ibid., 346.

20. Ibid., 350.

21. Divin, GRN, 105; Waxell, AE, 74.

22. Krasheninnikov, EK, 352–53.

23. V. Bering, "Report," 135.

24. Gibson, "Supplying the Kamchatka Expeditions," in Frost, 108–9, 113.

25. Waxell, AE, 69.

26. Steller, J, 56.

27. T. Fedorova, "Building of the *St. Peter* and *St. Paul*," in Frost, 160.

28. Waxell, AE, 91.

29. Lauridsen, VB, 101; Divin, GRN, 109.

30. Lauridsen, VB, 95; Kirilov's successor was Fedor I. Soimonov, a hydrographer.

31. Ibid., 94; Divin, GRN, 104.

32. Waxell, AE, 84.

33. Lensen, *Russian Push*, 53.

34. See Atavin, "Reconstructing," in Smith.

CHAPTER 6. LETTERS HOME

1. Lind and Møller's KK includes the letters in German with Danish translation.

2. Divin, GRN, 98, 102.

3. Lind and Møller, KK, 62.

4. Ibid., 64; italics added.

5. Ibid.; italics added.

6. Ibid.

7. Ibid., 66.

8. Ibid., 67, 68.

9. Ibid., 69.

10. Ibid., 72.

11. Ibid., 81–82.

12. Ibid., 73–77.

13. Ibid., 101.

14. Ibid.

15. Ibid.

16. Ibid., 102.

17. Ibid., 102–3.

18. Ibid., 97.

19. Belov, *Russians in the Bering Strait*, 33–34. Belov notes that Bering was related to the merchant Jacob Lund. The latter is Johann (Janeman) Lund's deceased father.

20. Lind and Møller, KK, 97–99.

21. Ibid., 100.

22. Ibid., 115.

23. Ibid., 125.

24. Belov, *Russians in the Bering Strait*, 34; Steller, J, 139.

25. Gibson, "Supplying the Kamchatka Expeditions," in Frost, 111–12.

CHAPTER 7. STELLER SIGNS ON WITH BERING

1. Steller, "Reisejournal," in Hintzsche, 146–47; Steller was wearing a *Sipun* (Russ. *ẓipun*), a loose outer smock commonly used by laborers, and a *Rockelor*, a raincoat.

2. Steller, J, 49.

3. Lind and Møller, KK, 109–10.

4. V. Bering, "Report," in Pokrovskii, 123.

5. Ibid., 126–27.

6. Ibid., 127.

7. Steller, "Reisejournal," 146.

8. Ibid., 146–47.

9. Waxell, AE, 93–95. Waxell does not mention any of Khitrovo's mishaps.

10. Ibid., 97–98 (Waxell uses the Dutch or German mile); Krasheninnikov, EK, 42.

11. V. Bering, "Report," 146. The reindeer had been purchased at Anadyr.

12. Ibid., 148.

13. Waxell, AE, 98.

14. Steller, "Most Respectful Report," in Pekarskii, 14.

15. Ibid., 15.

16. V. Bering, "Report," 141; Fisher, BV, 128.

17. Waxell, AE, 99.

18. Steller, J, 52; Steller, "Most Respectful Report," 15.

19. Divin, GRN, 109.

20. Steller, *Beschreibung*, 208–9; Stejneger, GWS, 248n48, and Gmelin to Müller, Oct. 13, 1742, quoted 244.

21. Steller, *Beschreibung*, 220, 233. Between 1697 and 1734 the Itelmen population declined from about 12,700 to 7,000 (Forsyth, "Siberian Native Peoples," in Wood, 139).

22. Stejneger, GWS, 230.

23. The map is reproduced in Müller, BV, 35. Müller's "Geographie und Verfässung von Kamtschatka" is included as an addendum in the 1774 edition of Steller's *Beschreibung*.

24. Steller, J, 105.

25. Ibid., 51; RP, 114.

26. Waxell, AE, 100-101; Urness, "Joseph Nicolas Delisle's Map," in Pierce, 90-92.

27. Chirikov, in Golder, BV, 1:312.

28. See Falk, "Maps of the North Pacific," in Frost, 127-38.

29. Golder, BV, 1:41.

CHAPTER 8. FROM KAMCHATKA TO NORTH AMERICA

1. RP, 115, 119.

2. Steller, J, 54, 58.

3. Ibid., 54; Golder, BV, 1:57.

4. Steller, J, 54-55.

5. Golder, BV, 1:289.

6. Waxell, AE, 104.

7. Steller, J, 59.

8. Kenyon, *Sea Otter in the Eastern Pacific Ocean*, 66-70. Steller's credibility concerning frequent appearances of sea animals has not previously been challenged, but Stejneger seems to raise questions in his observation that "Steller wastes many pages giving his reasons for insisting on the nearness of land" (Stejneger, GWS, 259).

9. Steller, J, 60.

10. Ibid., 58.

11. Waxell, AE, 103.

12. "Decision to Change Course," in Golder, BV, 1:90.

13. Steller, "Most Respectful Report," in Pekarskii, 17.

14. Golder, BV, 1:290.

15. Ibid., 291, 314.

16. The Delisle map that Chirikov refers to shows Cape Mendocino (at 40°25'N) and Cape Blanc, now Blanco (at 42°53'N).

17. Golder, BV, 1:295.

18. Ibid., 296.

19. Ibid.

20. Ibid., 297.

21. Bertholf, "Note," in Golder, BV, 1:344–46. Ellsworth Bertholf was an American hydrographer.

22. Imbert, "Bering and Chirikov," in Frost, 68–69. He is Bertrand C. Imbert.

23. Golder, BV, 1:293.

24. See Golder, "Note on the Loss of Chirikov's Men," ibid., 311. See also Barratt, "Afterlife of Chirikov's Lost Men," in Frost, 266–68.

25. Steller, J, 61.

26. Ibid., 64.

27. Ibid., 62.

28. Ibid., 63.

29. Ibid., 58.

30. Ibid.

31. Ibid., 56.

32. Ibid.

33. Golder, BV, 1:96. Golder's translation of the log reads, "bottom soft bluish clay." The Coast and Geodetic Survey map, no. 8513 (Controller Bay), 7th ed., 1963, shows "buM," or "blue mud."

CHAPTER 9. FIRST LANDING

1. Steller was displeased that "the outermost [island] had to be called Cape St. Elias" because "an island cannot be called a cape" (J, 63).

2. Steller Creek is almost certainly the source of the expedition's fresh water (see Frost, "Landing on Kayak Island," in Frost, 167–203).

3. Sources for the Bering–Steller dispute are Steller, J, 64–65, and his "Most Respectful Report," in Pekarskii, 18–19.

4. Concerning a "particular prayer," see Lauridsen, VB, 151; Golder, BV, 2:40n67; Stejneger, GWS, 265.

5. I am indebted to Jäger, "Die ersten Listen," 322, for this reasonable assumption.

6. The manuscript version of the ship's log reads, translated: "At the 11th hour the yawl came with water. [The men] said that they saw a fire site, human footprints, and several foxes running along the shore. Steller's assistant brought various herbs [plants]." This last statement corrects a mistranslation in Golder, BV, 1:96.

7. See Steller, J, 68, Fig. 9.

8. See ibid., 195n32.

9. In 1987 Susan Morton of the National Park Service, John F. C. Johnson of the Chugach Alaska Corporation, and I obtained dendrochronological samples (cores) from culturally altered trees. Results of analysis of cores suggest that trees at the site were stripped 100 to 400 years ago.

10. J. F. C. Johnson lists three uses of the bark by his people in former times: construction (roofs), food (the sweet inner cambium layer), and medicine. In 1778 Captain Cook's men saw Eskimos eating this inner bark in Prince William Sound. See Cook, *Journals*, 2:374.

11. Birket-Smith and De Laguna, *Eyak Indians*, 341–42; Krauss, *In Honor of Eyak*, 11–13.

12. Sauer, *Account of a Geographical and Astronomical Expedition*, 193–94.

13. Steller, J, 69.

14. Ibid.

15. Ibid.

16. Cook, *Journals*, 2:350.

17. Steller, J, 70–71.

18. Vancouver, *Voyage*, 3:218. It is here described as "a steep green point."

19. Steller, J, 71. Bering's reply through an intermediary, as reported by Steller, is as follows: "ich sollte mich nur geschwinde nach dem Fahrzeuge paken, oder man würde ohne zu warten, mich am Lande lassen" (*Steller's Journal: The Manuscript Text*, 160).

20. Steller, J, 72.

21. Ibid., 78.

22. Frost, "Getting the Record Straight," 115–22; Jäger, "Die ersten Listen," 357–65.

23. See Stejneger, GWS, 269; Ford, *Where the Sea Breaks Its Back*, 80–81.

24. John F. Thilenius Jr. made collections in 1981 and 1984, Walt Cunningham and Susan Stanford in 1997, and Ullrich Wannhoff in 1998.

25. Steller, J, 72.

26. Ibid.

27. Potap Zaikov anchored here on July 27, 1783. See Tikhmenev, *History*, 2:1.

28. Steller, J, 75.

29. Ibid., 77.

CHAPTER 10. SCURVY

1. Steller, J, 79.

2. Ibid., 61.

3. Waxell, AE, 107.

4. Golder, BV, 1:103.

5. Waxell, AE, 107–8.

6. Steller, J, 80; Golder, BV, 1:111; Waxell, AE, 108.

7. Golder, BV, 1:112n56.

8. Steller, J, 80.

9. Ibid., 82.

10. Ibid.
11. Ibid., 83.
12. Ibid., 82. For a picture of Gesner's sea ape, see ibid., 81.
13. Stejneger, GWS, 280.
14. Golder, BV, 1:120.
15. Ibid.
16. Steller, J, 85.
17. Golder, BV, 1:138.
18. Steller, J, 85.
19. Ibid.
20. Ibid., 86.
21. Ibid.
22. Ibid., 87.
23. Ibid., 89.
24. Ibid.
25. Lloyd, *Health of Seamen*, 20–21.
26. Steller, J, 89.
27. Ibid.
28. Ibid.
29. Ibid., 94; Golder, BV, 1:142.
30. Steller, J, 94.
31. Ibid.
32. Waxell, AE, 108–9.
33. Golder, BV, 1:142.
34. Waxell, AE, 108–9.
35. Steller, J, 89.
36. Waxell, AE, 199–200; Fortuine, "Scurvy," 21–22.
37. Lloyd, *Health of Seamen*, 8–11, 20–21.
38. Golder, BV, 1:143.
39. Steller, J, 94–95.

CHAPTER 11. NATIVE AMERICANS

1. Golder, BV, 1:142n85.
2. Ibid., 145n89.
3. Waxell, AE, 111.
4. Golder, BV, 1:143.
5. Waxell, AE, 111.
6. Steller, J, 95.
7. Waxell, AE, 111–12.
8. Golder, BV, 1:145.
9. Ibid.

10. Waxell, AE, 112.

11. Steller, J, 96.

12. Waxell, AE, 112; Steller, J, 96.

13. Steller, J, 95.

14. Ibid., 93. Steller also collected here seeds of 16–20 plants later described in his "Catalogus seminum anno 1741 in America Septemtrionali."

15. Steller, J, 93–94.

16. Ibid., 93; Waxell, AE, 142.

17. Steller, J, 97; Waxell, AE, 113.

18. Waxell, AE, 119; RP, 113.

19. Waxell, AE, 115.

20. Ibid.; Steller, J, 100.

21. Steller, J, 100.

22. Ibid.

23. Waxell, AE, 115.

24. Müller, BV, rightly states, "Lahontan does not belong among the conscientious and reliable travel writers" (109).

25. Steller, J, 100. Like Waxell, Steller did not realize that the Koryak and Aleut spoke different languages.

26. Waxell, AE, 116.

27. Steller, J, 101, 207n15.

28. Ibid., 102.

29. Ibid.

30. Ibid., 103.

31. Waxell, AE, 117.

32. Ibid., 118.

33. Steller, J, 102.

34. Waxell, AE, 117.

35. Steller, J, 103.

36. Sauer, *Account of a Geographical and Astronomical Expedition*, 157–59.

37. Steller, J, 103.

38. Olearius, *Vermehrt neue Beschreibung*, 173.

39. Steller, J, 105.

40. Waxell, AE, 118; Golder, BV, 1:149; Steller, J, 105–6.

41. Veniaminov, *Notes*, 250.

42. Waxell, AE, 118.

43. Steller, J, 107; Waxell, AE, 119.

44. Steller, J, 97.

45. Veniaminov, *Notes*, 219.

46. Jochelson, *History*, 15.

47. Wells, *Ipani Eskimos*, 97–99.

48. Veniaminov, *Notes*, 218–19.
49. Steller, J, 98–100.

CHAPTER 12. CRUEL WAVES

1. Waxell, AE, 121.
2. Golder, BV, 1:167.
3. Steller, J, 115.
4. Ibid., 112–13.
5. Golder, BV, 1:303.
6. Ibid., 304.
7. Ibid., 304–5.
8. Ibid., 305.
9. Ibid., 304.
10. Ibid., 320.
11. Steller, J, 113.
12. Ibid.; Steller, "Most Respectful Report," in Pekarskii, 22.
13. Steller, J, 114.
14. Ibid.
15. Ibid.
16. Ibid., 115.
17. Ibid., 117; Golder, BV, 1:192.
18. Steller, J, 115.
19. Golder, BV, 1:192–93, 195; Waxell, AE, 122.
20. Waxell, AE, 122.
21. Steller, J, 93.
22. Ibid.
23. Waxell, AE, 122.
24. Golder, BV, 1:196n108.
25. Ibid., 199n109.
26. Ibid., 201.
27. Steller, J, 120.
28. Ibid., 120–21.
29. Golder, BV, 1:201n115.
30. Ibid., 201–2.
31. Steller, J, 121.
32. Ibid.
33. Ibid., 122.
34. Golder, BV, 1:204, 206, 208–9.
35. Ibid., 206; Waxell, AE, 123.
36. Golder, BV, 1:208n121.
37. Steller, J, 123.

38. Ibid., 123–24.

39. Waxell, AE, 124.

CHAPTER 13. DECISION TO LAND

1. Steller, J, 124. Waxell gives the impression that the decision to "make for land" was unanimous (AE, 124–25). He is motivated to rewrite history. Steller's account is credible.

2. Steller, J, 124–25; Waxell, AE, 124.

3. Steller, J, 124.

4. Ibid.

5. Ibid., 125.

6. Ibid.

7. Ibid., 123.

8. Ibid., 125.

9. Ibid.

10. The subtitle of *Comandor* by Wannhoff and Törmer is *Leben am Ende der Welt*.

11. Golder, "Bering Island Tragedy," 3–4, is set on Bering and Copper islands; Len'kov et al., KC, 93–94.

12. Steller, J, 162.

13. Ibid., 125.

14. Ibid., 126; Waxell, AE, 125.

15. Steller, J, 126.

16. Ibid.

17. Ibid., 126–27.

18. Ibid., 126. Steller hints that the unnamed officer is Khitrovo.

19. Waxell, AE, 126.

CHAPTER 14. DEATH CAMP

1. Steller, J, 127.

2. Ibid., 128.

3. Ibid., 128–29. Bolshaya River is an early name for Bolsheretsk.

4. Ibid., 130. *Entale*, or tooth shell, is derived from the name of its genus, *Dentalium*.

5. Ibid.

6. Ibid., 131–32.

7. Ibid., 131.

8. Ibid., 135.

9. Ibid., 132.

10. Ibid., 133.

11. Müller, BV, 115.

12. Steller, J, 133.

13. Ibid., 141.

14. Ibid., 134.

15. Ibid.

16. Ibid.

17. Len'kov et al., KC, 9n18.

18. Steller, J, 135.

19. Ibid., 137–38. Steller laments that Hesselberg had been treated like "a silly child and idiot" by men who had neither his experience nor his skill.

20. Ibid., 136.

CHAPTER 15. BERING'S DEATH

1. Müller, BV, 115. Müller claims Bering "near the end . . . became distrustful." This view contradicts Steller's account of "a blissful end" (J, 141).

2. Waxell, AE, 135.

3. Steller, J, 141.

4. Ibid.

5. Ibid., 140.

6. Ibid., 140–41.

7. Ibid., 141.

8. Müller, BV, 115.

CHAPTER 16. HOW BERING'S MEN GOT OFF THE ISLAND

1. Golder, BV, 1:231.

2. Ibid., 231–32.

3. Ibid., 232.

4. Ibid.

5. Waxell, AE, 139.

6. Steller, J, 180.

7. Ibid., 147; Waxell, AE, 137–38.

8. Waxell, AE, 137.

9. Ibid., 138.

10. Steller, J, 143.

11. Waxell, AE, 142.

12. Steller, J, 144–45.

13. Ibid., 147–48.

14. Ibid., 148.

15. Ibid., 149–50.

16. Ibid., 143.

17. Ibid., 144.

18. Waxell, AE, 135–36.

19. Steller, J, 152–53. Steller's "other remedies"were tobacco and cubeb.

20. Ibid.

21. Ibid., 153–54.

22. Waxell, AE, 142–43.

23. Ibid., 143.

24. Ibid., 145.

25. Golder, BV, 1:233.

26. Waxell, AE, 147–48.

27. Ibid., 142.

28. Steller, J, 156.

29. Steller, *Beasts of the Sea*, 207.

30. Ibid., 201; Steller, J, 160.

31. Khitrovo's journal says "the cable was held by 20 men who were ashore" (Golder, BV, 1:238), but Steller speaks of "a very long rope . . . held on shore in the hands of the other forty men" (J, 159). No doubt the number varied from time to time.

32. Steller, J, 163.

33. Ibid.

34. Waxell, AE, 151; Steller, J, 164.

35. Steller, J, 165; Waxell, AE, 152.

36. Steller, J, 166.

37. Ibid., 167.

38. Ibid., 169; Waxell, AE, 158.

39. Divin, GRN, 186. Poludennyi Mys, just north of Steller's Arch, very possibly hid the entire northwest coast of Bering Island from Chirikov's view.

40. Bancroft, *History*, 92n19.

CONCLUSION

1. Lind and Møller, KK, 116.

2. Grey, *Romanovs*, 158.

3. Vernadsky, *Political and Diplomatic History*, 251.

4. Soloviev, *History of Russia*, 37:12–15.

5. Lind and Møller, KK, 125–27.

6. Ibid., 143. Also included with these items were Chinese fabrics and six kilos of Chinese beads. Lind and Møller surmise that Bering "reckoned seriously the chance for private barter with natives," for what other use would he have for such goods in his nine sea chests?

7. Ibid., 130. Anna makes a similar statement in her petition of Sept. 11, 1744.

8. Rogger, *National Consciousness*, 26.

9. Ibid., 32.

10. Amburger, "Vitus Berings Nachkommen," 36–38.

11. Ibid.

12. Urness reviews such news in "The Setting," in Müller, BV, 38–56.

13. Ibid., 39.

14. Ibid., 42.

15. Müller, *First Official Report from Russian Sources*, 15, 21, 26–27.

16. Urness, "The Setting," in Müller, BV, 50.

17. Müller, *Lettre d'un officier*, 11.

18. Müller, BV, 104.

19. Waxell, AE, 48.

20. Steller, J, 50.

21. Makarova lists many of the expeditions (*Russians on the Pacific*, 209–10).

22. Landes, *Wealth and Poverty of Nations*, 61–63, 71–72.

Bibliography

PRIMARY SOURCES

Andreev, A. I., ed. *Russian Discoveries in the Pacific and in North America in the Eighteenth and Nineteenth Centuries: A Collection of Materials*. Trans. C. Ginsburg. Ann Arbor, 1952.

Bergsland, K., and M. L. Dirks, eds. *Aleut Tales and Narratives: Collected 1909–1910 by Waldemar Jochelson*. Fairbanks, 1990.

Bering, V. J. "A Report from Captain-Commander Vitus Bering to Empress Anna Ivanovna concerning the Status of the Second Kamchatka Expedition." April 18, 1741. In Pokrovskii, *Bering's Expeditions*, 123–50. In Russian.

———. "Report of Fleet-Captain Bering on His Expedition to the Eastern Coast of Siberia." In F. Golder, *Bering's Voyages*, 1:9–20.

Bridge, C. A. G. *History of the Russian Fleet during the Reign of Peter the Great by a Contemporary Englishman*. London, 1899.

Catesby, M. *The Natural History of Carolina, Florida and the Bahama Islands*. London, 1731.

Chirikov, A. "Report on the Voyage of the 'St. Paul.' " In Golder, *Bering's Voyages*, 1:312–27, 341–48.

Cook, J. *The Journals of Captain James Cook on His Voyages of Discovery: The Voyage of the "Resolution" and "Discovery," 1776–1780*. Ed. J. C. Beaglehole. Cambridge, 1967.

Coxe, W. *Account of the Russian Discoveries between Asia and America.* 4th ed. London, 1803.

Dobell, P. *Travels in Kamchatka and Siberia.* 2 vols. London, 1830.

Efimov, A. V. *Atlas of the Geographical Discoveries in Siberia and Northwestern America in the Seventeenth and Eighteenth Centuries.* Moscow, 1964. In Russian.

Fisher, R. H., ed. *The Voyage of Semen Dezhnev in 1648: Bering's Precursor, with Selected Documents.* London, 1981.

Gilbert, M. *Atlas of Russian History from 800 B.C. to the Present Day.* New York, 1993.

Gmelin, J. G. *Reise durch Sibirien von dem Jahre 1733 bis 1743.* 4 vols. Göttingen, 1751–52.

Golder, F. "A Bering Island Tragedy." *Journal of American Folkore* 22 (1909): 3–4.

————. *Bering's Voyages: An Account of the Efforts of the Russians to Determine the Relation of Asia and America.* 2 vols. New York, 1922, 1925.

Hayes, D. *Historical Atlas of the North Pacific Ocean: Maps of Discovery and Scientific Exploration, 1500–2000.* Seattle, 2001.

Hintzsche, W., ed. *Reisetagebücher, 1735 bis 1743.* Halle, 2000.

Homann, J. B. *Grosser Atlas über die gantze Welt.* Nuremberg, 1725.

Jäger, E. J. "Die ersten Listen und Aufsammlungen von Pflanzen aus Alaska— Georg Wilhelm Stellers botanische Arbeiten in America." *Feddes Repertorium,* 2000, 321–68.

Johnson, J. F. C. *Chugach Legends: Stories and Photographs of the Chugach Region.* Anchorage, 1984.

Krasheninnikov, S. P. *Explorations of Kamchatka, 1735–1741.* Trans. E. A. P. Crownhart-Vaughan. Portland, Ore., 1972.

Lind, N., and P. U. Møller. *Kommandøren og Konen.* Copenhagen, 1997.

Lloyd, C., ed. *The Health of Seamen: Selections from the Works of Dr. James Lind, Sir Gilbert Blane and Dr. Thomas Trotter.* London, 1960.

Markov, S. F., ed. *Bering's Expeditions: Collections of Documents.* Moscow, 1941. In Russian.

Monumenta Sibiriae: Quellen zur Geschichte Sibiriens und Alaskas aus russischen Archiven. Gotha, n.d.

Müller, G. F. *Bering's Voyages: The Reports from Russia.* Trans. C. L. Urness. Fairbanks, 1986.

————. *The First Official Report from Russian Sources Concerning Bering's Voyage to America.* Trans. O. M. Griminger. Ed. O. Frost. Anchorage, 1986.

————. "Geographie und Verfüssung von Kamtschatka." Addendum to Steller, *Beschreibung von dem Lande Kamtschatka,* 1–58.

————. *Lettre d'un officier de la marine russienne à un seigneur de la cour concernant la carte des nouvelles découvertes au nord de la Mer du sud.* Berlin, 1753.

Olearius, A. *Vermehrt neue Beschreibung der muscowwitischen und Persischen Reysen.* Ed. D. Lohmeier. Tübingen, 1971.

Oleksa, M. J., ed. *Alaska Missionary Spirituality.* Mahwah, N.J., 1987.

Pekarskii, P., ed. *Archival Research Concerning Descriptions of the Previously Nonexistent Animal "Rhytina borealis."* St. Petersburg, 1869. In Russian.

Pokrovskii, A. A., ed. *Bering's Expeditions: Collection of Documents.* Moscow, 1941. In Russian.

Russian Penetration of the North Pacific Ocean: A Documentary Record, 1700–1797. Trans. B. Dmytryshyn, E. A. P. Crownhart-Vaughan, and T. Vaughan. Portland, Ore., 1988.

Russia's Conquest of Siberia: A Documentary Record, 1558–1700. Trans. B. Dmytryshyn et al. Portland, Ore., 1985.

Sarychev, G. A. *Account of a Voyage of Discovery to the North-East of Siberia, the Frozen Ocean, and the North-East Sea.* London, 1806.

Sauer, M. *An Account of a Geographical and Astronomical Expedition to the Northern Parts of Russia.* London, 1802.

Steller, G. W. "The Beasts of the Sea." Trans. W. Miller and J. E. Miller. In *The Fur Seals and Fur-Seal Islands of the North Pacific Ocean,* ed. D. S. Jordan, pt. 3, pp. 179–218. Washington, D.C., 1899.

————. *Beschreibung von dem Lande Kamtschatka.* Frankfurt and Leipzig, 1774.

————. "Catalogus plantarum intra sex horas in parte Americae septemtrionalis iuxta promontorium Eliae observatarum anno 1741 die 21 Iulii sub gradu latitudinis 59." Manuscripts Division, Library of Congress, Washington, D.C.

————. "Catalogus seminum anno 1741 in America septemtrionali sub gradu latitudinis 59 et 55 collectorum, quorum dimidia pars die 17 Novembris 1742 transmissa." Manuscripts Division, Library of Congress, Washington, D.C.

————. "De bestiis marinis." *Novi Commentarii Academiae Scientiarum Imperialis Petropolitanae* 2 (1751): 289–398.

————. *Journal of a Voyage with Bering, 1741–1742.* Ed. O. Frost. Trans. M. A. Engel and O. Frost. Stanford, 1988. This translation is made from *Steller's Journal: The Manuscript Text* (Anchorage, 1984).

————. "Mantissa plantarum minus aut plane incognitarum." Manuscripts Division, Library of Congress, Washington, D.C.

————. "Most Respectful Report to the High Senate about Occurrences on Kamchatka." November 16, 1742. In Pekarskii, *Archival Research,* 13–33. In Russian.

————. "Reisejournal von Irkuck nach Ochock und Kamchatka, 4 März 1740 bis 16 September 1740." In Hintzsche, *Reisetagebücher,* 77–216.

————. "Tagebuch 1741/1742 Beringinsel." Ed. W. Hintzsche. Forthcoming.

————. "Tagebuch seiner Seereise aus dem Petripauls Hafen in Kamtschatka bis an die westlichen Küsten von Amerika und seiner Begebenheiten auf der Rückreis." In P. S. Pallas, ed., *Neue Nordische Beyträge* 5 (1793): 129–236; 6 (1793): 1–26.

Strahlenberg, P. J. T. von. *An Historico-geographical Description of the North and Eastern Parts of Europe and Asia.* London, 1738.

Tikhmenev, P. A. *A History of the Russian-American Company.* Trans. D. Krenov. 2 vols. Kingston, Ont., 1979.

Vancouver, G. *A Voyage of Discovery in the North Pacific Ocean.* 4 vols. London, 1798.

Veniaminov, I. *Journals of the Priest Ioann Veniaminov in Alaska, 1823 to 1836.* Trans. J. Kisslinger. Fairbanks, 1993.

————. *Notes on the Islands of the Unalashka District.* Trans. L. T. Black and R. H. Geoghegan. Kingston, Ont., 1984.

Waxell, S. *The American Expedition.* Trans. M. A. Michael. London, 1952.

————. "Report on the Voyage of the *St. Peter.*" In Golder, *Bering's Voyages,* 1:270–82.

Wolff, O. *Levnetsefterretninger om den berømte Søemand og udødelige Landopdager Commandeur Vitus Jonassen Beering.* Copenhagen, 1822.

SECONDARY SOURCES

Albrethsen, S. E. "Vitus Bering's Second Kamchatka Expedition—The Journey to America and Archaeological Excavations on Bering Island." In Jacobsen, *Vitus Bering,* 66–96.

Alekseev, A. I. *The Destiny of Russian America.* Trans. M. Ramsey. Kingston, Ont., and Fairbanks, 1990.

Amburger, E. "Vitus Berings Nachkommen in Russland." In *Personalhistorisk Tidskrift.* Copenhagen, 1936.

Armstrong, T. "Bering's Expeditions." In J. H. Bater and R. A. French, eds., *Studies in Russian Historical Geography.* London and New York, 1983.

————. *Russian Settlement in the North.* Cambridge, 1965.

————. "Siberian and Arctic Exploration." In Frost, *Bering and Chirikov,* 117–26.

Atavin, G. A. "Reconstructing the Drawings [and] Building a Model of the 'St. Peter.' " In Smith, *Science under Sail.*

Bagrow, L. *A History of Russian Cartography up to 1800.* Ed. H. W. Castner. Wolfe Island, Ont., 1975.

Baikalov, A. V. "The Conquest and Colonization of Siberia." *Slavonic Review* 10 (1932): 557–71.

Bancroft, H. H. *History of Alaska, 1730–1885.* San Francisco, 1886.

Barratt, G. "The Afterlife of Chirikov's Lost Men." In Frost, *Bering and Chirikov*, 265–75.

————. *Russia in Pacific Waters, 1715–1825: A Survey of the Origins of Russia's Naval Presence in the North and South Pacific.* Vancouver, 1981.

Beaglehole, J. C. *The Life of Captain James Cook.* London, 1974.

Belov, M. I. "Denmark and Vitus Bering." In Belov, ed., *Journeys and Geographical Discoveries in the Fifteenth to Nineteenth Centuries* (Leningrad, 1965), 46–56. In Russian.

————. *Russians in the Bering Strait, 1648–1791.* Ed. J. L. Smith. Trans. K. Solovjova. Anchorage, 2000.

Berg, L. S. *The Discovery of Kamchatka and Bering's Expeditions, 1725–1742.* Moscow and Leningrad, 1946. In Russian.

————. "Russian Discoveries in the Pacific." In *The Pacific: Russian Scientific Investigations.* New York, 1969.

————. *Studies in the History of Russian Geographical Discoveries.* Moscow, 1946. In Russian.

Bering, O. "Bering-Slaeghten," *Horsens Social-Demokrat,* December 16, 1941.

Berkh, V. N. *A Chronological History of the Discovery of the Aleutian Islands; or The Exploits of Russian Merchants.* Trans. D. Krenov. Kingston, Ont., 1974.

Bertholf, E. "Note to Accompany the Chart of the Voyage of Bering and Chirikov from Kamchatka to the Alaskan Coast and Return, 1741." In Golder, *Bering's Voyages*, 1:330–48.

Billington, J. H. *The Icon and the Axe.* New York, 1966.

Birket-Smith, K., and F. De Laguna, *The Eyak Indians of the Copper River Delta, Alaska.* Copenhagen, 1938.

Black, J. L. *G.-F. Müller and the Imperial Russian Academy.* Kingston, Ont., and Montreal, 1986.

Black, L. T. *Aleut Art.* Anchorage, 1982.

————. *Atka: An Ethnohistory of the Western Aleutians.* Kingston, Ont., 1984.

————. *Glory Remembered: Wooden Headgear of Alaska Sea Hunters.* Juneau, 1991.

————. *A Good and Faithful Servant.* Fairbanks, 1997.

————. "Some Problems in Interpretation of Aleut Prehistory." *Arctic Anthropology* 20 (1983): 49–78.

Boas, F. *Relationships between North-west America and North-east Asia.* Toronto, 1933.

Bobrick, B. *East of the Sun: The Epic Conquest and Tragic History of Siberia.* New York, 1992.

Bondareva, N. A. *Seven Weeks on the Commanders.* Petropavlovsk-Kamchatka, 1966. In Russian.

Carpenter, K. J. *The History of Scurvy and Vitamin C.* Cambridge, 1986.

Chukovskii, N. K. *Bering: Biography.* Moscow, 1961. In Russian.

Collins, D. N. "Subjugation and Settlement in Seventeenth- and Eighteenth-Century Siberia." In Wood, *History of Siberia,* 37–56.

Cook, W. L. *Flood Tide of Empire: Spain and the Pacific Northwest, 1543–1819.* New Haven, 1973.

Cracraft, J. *The Church Reform of Peter the Great.* London, 1971.

———. "Feofan Prokopovich." In J. G. Garrard, ed., *The Eighteenth Century in Russia,* 75–105. Oxford, 1973.

Crass, B. A. "Vitus Bering, a Russian Columbus?" In Frost, *Bering and Chirikov,* 394–411.

Dall, W. H. "A Critical Review of Bering's First Expedition, 1725–1730." *National Geographic* 2 (1890): 111–66.

Dauenhauer, R. L. "Education in Russian America." In Smith and Barnett, *Russian America,* 155–64.

Davidson, G. *The Tracks and Landfalls of Bering and Chirikof on the Northwest Coast of America.* San Francisco, 1901.

Debenham, F. "Bering's Last Voyage." *Polar Record* 3 (1941): 421–26.

De Laguna, F. *Chugach Prehistory: The Archaeology of Prince William Sound, Alaska.* Seattle, 1956.

———. *Under Mount Saint Elias: The History and Culture of the Yakutat Tlingit.* 3 pts. Washington, D.C., 1972.

Demin, L. M. *Semen Dezhnev.* Moscow, 1990. In Russian.

Divin, V. A. *The Great Russian Navigator, A. I. Chirikov.* Trans. R. H. Fisher. Fairbanks, 1993.

Domning, D. P. "Sea Cow Family Reunion." *Natural History* 96 (1987): 64–71.

———. *Sirenian Evolution in the North Pacific Ocean.* Berkeley, 1978.

———. "Steller's Sea Cow and the Origin of North Pacific Aboriginal Whaling." *Syesis* 5 (1972): 187–89.

Donnert, E., ed. *Europa in der Frühen Neuzeit: Festschrift für Günter Mühlpfordt.* 5 vols. Cologne and Vienna, 1996–2001.

Dørflinger, J. "Die Namensgeschichte der Bering-Strasse." *Veröffentlichungen der Kommission für Geschichte der Mathematik, Naturwissenschaften und Medizin* 14 (1975): 128–46.

Dumond, D. E. *The Eskimos and Aleuts.* London, 1987.

Dyson, G. *Baidarka.* Edmonds, Wash., 1986.

Erickson, J. H. *Orthodox Christians in America.* New York and Oxford, 1999.

Falk, M. "Maps of the North Pacific to 1741." In Frost, *Bering and Chirikov,* 127–38.

———. "Vitus Bering." In A. Shalkop and R. L. Shalkop, eds., *Exploration in Alaska: Captain Cook Commemorative Lectures,* 103–7. Anchorage, 1980.

Fedorova, S. G. *The Russian Population in Alaska and California: Late 18th Century [to] 1867.* Trans. R. A. Pierce and A. S. Donnelly. Kingston, Ont., 1973.

Fedorova, T. S. "The Building of the *St. Peter* and *St. Paul.*" In Frost, *Bering and Chirikov,* 158–61.

Fernández-Armesto, F. *Columbus.* Oxford and New York, 1991.

Fisher, R. H. *Bering's Voyages: Whither and Why.* Seattle, 1977.

———. "The Early Cartography of the Bering Strait Region." *Arctic: Journal of the Arctic Institute of North America* 37 (December 1984): 574–89.

———. "Finding America." In Smith and Barnett, *Russian America,* 17–31.

———. *The Russian Fur Trade, 1550–1700.* Berkeley, 1943.

———. "To Give Chirikov His Due." In Frost, *Bering and Chirikov,* 37–50.

Fitzhugh, W. W., and A. Crowell, eds. *Crossroads of Continents: Cultures of Siberia and Alaska.* Washington, D.C., 1988.

Ford, C. *Where the Sea Breaks Its Back: The Epic Story of Early Naturalist Georg Steller and the Russian Exploration of Alaska.* Anchorage and Seattle, 1992.

Forsyth, J. *A History of the Peoples of Siberia: Russia's North Asian Colony, 1581–1990.* Cambridge, 1992.

———. "The Siberian Native Peoples Before and After the Russian Conquest." In Wood, *History of Siberia,* 69–91.

Fortuine, R. "Scurvy in the Early History of Alaska: The Haves and Have-Nots." *Alaska History* 3 (1988): 21–44.

Foust, C. M. "Russian Expansion to the East through the Eighteenth Century." *Journal of Economic History* 21 (1961): 469–83.

Frost, O. "Adam Olearius, the Greenland Eskimos, and the First Slaughter of Bering Island Sea Cows, 1742: An Elucidation of a Statement in Steller's Journal." In Pierce, *Russia in North America,* 123–28.

———. "Getting the Record Straight: Georg Steller's Plant Collecting on Kayak Island, Alaska, 1741." *Pacific Northwest Quarterly* 90 (1999): 115–22.

———. "The Landing on Kayak Island." In Frost, *Bering and Chirikov,* 167–203.

———. "Vitus Bering Resurrected: Recent Forensic Analysis and the Documentary Record." *Pacific Northwest Quarterly* 84 (1993): 91–97.

———. "Von Deutschland über Russland und Sibirien nach Nordamerika: Der Naturforscher Georg Wilhelm Steller." In Donnert, *Europa in der Frühen Neuzeit,* 2:515–38.

———, ed. *Bering and Chirikov: The American Voyages and Their Impact.* Anchorage, 1992.

Garrett, P. D. *St. Innocent: Apostle to America.* Crestwood, N.Y., 1979.

Geyer-Kordesch, J. "German Medical Education in the Eighteenth Century:

The Prussian Context and Its Influence." In W. F. Bynum and R. Porter, eds., *William Hunter and the Eighteenth-Century Medical World*, 177–205. Cambridge, 1985.

Gibson, J. R. *Feeding the Russian Fur Trade: Provisionment of the Okhotsk Seaboard and the Kamchatka Peninsula, 1639–1856*. Madison, 1969.

———. *Imperial Russia in Frontier America*. New York, 1976.

———. "Supplying the Kamchatka Expeditions, 1725–30 and 1733–42." In Frost, *Bering and Chirikov*, 90–116.

Goldenberg, L. A. *Gvozdev: The Russian Discovery of Alaska in 1732*. Trans. N. M. Phillips and A. M. Perminov. Anchorage, 1990.

Golder, F. *Russian Expansion on the Pacific, 1641–1850*. Gloucester, Mass., 1960.

Goodhue, C. *Journey into the Fog: The Story of Vitus Bering and the Bering Sea*. Garden City, N.Y., 1944.

Grebnitzky, N. A. *Commander Islands*. Trans. L. Woehlcke. St. Petersburg, 1902.

Grey, I. *The Romanovs: The Rise and Fall of a Dynasty*. New York, 1970.

Henry, J. F. *Early Maritime Artists of the Pacific Northwest Coast, 1741–1841*. Vancouver and Toronto, 1984.

Hintzsche, W., and T. Nickol. "Eine Topographie der Stadt *Tobol'sk* von Gerhard Friedrich Müller." In Donnert, *Europa in der Frühen Neuzeit*, 3:79–93.

———, eds. *Die Grosse Nordische Expedition: Georg Wilhelm Steller (1709–1746): Ein Lutheraner Erforscht Sibirien und Alaska*. Gotha, 1996.

Hopkins, D. M., ed. *The Bering Land Bridge*. Stanford, 1967.

Hrdlicka, A. *The Aleutian and Commander Islands and Their Inhabitants*. Philadelphia, 1945.

Hughes, L. *Peter the Great: A Biography* New Haven, 2002.

———. *Russia in the Age of Peter the Great*. New Haven, 1998.

Hultén, E. *Flora of Alaska and Neighboring Territories: A Manual of Vascular Plants*. Stanford, 1968.

———. "History of Botanical Exploration in Alaska and Yukon Territories from the Time of Their Discovery to 1940." *Botaniska Notiser* (1940): 289–346.

Imbert, B. C. "Bering and Chirikov: Pioneers of Siberian and North Pacific Geography." In Frost, *Bering and Chirikov*, 51–74.

Jacobsen, N. K., ed. *Vitus Bering, 1741–1991*. Copenhagen, 1993.

Jochelson, W. *History, Ethnology, and Anthropology of the Aleut*. Washington, D.C., 1933.

———. *Peoples of Asiatic Russia*. Washington, D.C., 1928.

Kan, S. "Recording Native Culture and Christianizing the Natives: Russian Orthodox Missionaries in Southeastern Alaska." In Pierce, *Russia in North America*, 298–313.

Kashevarov, A. P. "John Veniaminov Innocent, Metropolitan of Moscow and Kolomna." In Oleksa, *Alaska Missionary Spirituality*, 341–62.

Kenyon, K. W. *The Sea Otter in the Eastern Pacific Ocean*. Washington, D.C., 1969.

Kerner, R. J. *The Urge to Sea: The Course of Russian History*. Berkeley, 1942.

Keuning, J. "Nicolaas Witsen as a Cartographer." *Imago Mundi* 11 (1954): 95–110.

Krauss, M. E. "Alaska Native Languages in Russian America." In Smith and Barnett, *Russian America*, 205–13.

———. "Bering 1728 and Gvozdev 1732." In Smith, *Science under Sail*.

———, ed. *In Honor of Eyak: The Art of Anna Nelson Harry*. Fairbanks, 1982.

Kushnarev, E. G. *Bering's Search for the Strait: The First Kamchatka Expedition, 1725–1730*. Trans. E. A. P. Crownhart-Vaughan. Portland, Ore., 1990.

Landes, D. S. *The Wealth and Poverty of Nations: Why Some Are So Rich and Some So Poor*. New York and London, 1998.

Lantzeff, G. V. *Siberia in the Seventeenth Century: A Study of the Colonial Administration*. Berkeley, 1943.

Lantzeff, G. V., and R. H. Pierce. *Eastward the Empire: Exploration and Conquest on the Russian Open Frontier to 1750*. Montreal and London, 1973.

Laughlin, W. S. *Aleuts: Survivors of the Bering Land Bridge*. New York, 1980.

———. *The First Americans*. New York, 1979.

———. "Russian-American Bering Sea Relations: Research and Reciprocity." *American Anthropologist* 87 (1985): 775–92.

Lauridsen, P. *Vitus Bering: The Discoverer of Bering Strait*. Trans. J. E. Olson. Chicago, 1889.

Lebedev, D. M., and V. I. Grekov. "Geographical Exploration by the Russians." In H. R. Friis, ed., *The Pacific Basin: A History of Its Geographical Exploration*, 170–85. New York, 1967.

Len'kov, V. D., G. L. Silan'tev, and A. K. Staniukovich. *The Komandorskii Camp of the Bering Expedition*. Trans. K. L. Arndt. Ed. O. Frost. Anchorage, 1992.

Lensen, G. A. *The Russian Push toward Japan: Russo-Japanese Relations, 1697–1875*. Princeton, 1959.

Levin, M. G. *Physical Anthropology and Ethnogenetic Problems of the Peoples of the Far East*. Moscow, 1958.

Levin, M. G., and L. P. Potapov. *The Peoples of Siberia*. Chicago, 1964.

Liapunova, R. G. *Essays on the Ethnography of the Aleuts (at the End of the Eighteenth and the First Half of the Nineteenth Century)*. Trans. J. Shelest. Fairbanks, 1996.

Lincoln, W. B. *The Conquest of a Continent: Siberia and the Russians*. New York, 1994.

Lower, J. A. *Ocean of Destiny: A Concise History of the North Pacific, 1500–1918.* Vancouver, 1978.

Madsen, O. S., G. Petersen, and O. Schiørring. "Excavating Bering's Grave, Komandor Bay, Bering Island, August 1991: A Preliminary Report." In Frost, *Bering and Chirikov,* 229–47.

Makarova, R. V. *Russians on the Pacific, 1743–1799.* Trans. R. A. Pierce and A. S. Donnelly. Kingston, Ont., 1975.

Marker, Gary. *Publishing, Printing, and the Origins of Intellectual Life in Russia, 1700–1800.* Princeton, 1985.

Massie, R. K. *Peter the Great: His Life and World.* New York, 1980.

Masterson, J. R., and H. Brower, eds. *Bering's Successors, 1745–80: Contributions of Peter Simon Pallas to the History of Russian Exploration toward Alaska.* Seattle, 1948.

McDougall, W. A. *Let the Sea Make a Noise: A History of the North Pacific from Magellan to MacArthur.* New York, 1993.

Medushevskaya, O. M. "Cartographic Source for the History of Russian Geographical Discoveries in the Pacific Ocean in the Second Half of the Eighteenth Century." Trans. J. R. Gibson. *Canadian Cartographer* 9 (1972): 99–121.

Morton, H. A. *The Wind Commands: Sailors and Sailing Ships in the Pacific.* Middletown, Conn., 1975.

Mousalimas, S. A. "Russian Orthodox Missionaries and Southern Alaskan Shamans: Interactions and Analysis." In Pierce, *Russia in North America,* 314–21.

Murashko, O. "A Demographic History of the Kamchadal/Itelmen of the Kamchatka Peninsula." *Arctic Anthropology* 31 (1994): 16–30.

Murphy, R. *The Haunted Journey.* Garden City, N.Y., 1961.

Neatby, L. H. *Discovery in Russian and Siberian Waters.* Athens, Ohio, 1973.

Okladnikova, E. A. "Science and Education in Russian America." In Starr, *Russia's American Colony,* 218–48.

Oleksa, M. *Orthodox Alaska: A Theology of Mission.* Crestwood, N.Y., 1998.

Parkinson, C. L. "Variability of Arctic Sea Ice: The View from Space, an 18-Year Record." *Arctic: Journal of the Arctic Institute of North America* 53 (2000): 341–58.

Paseniuk, L. *The Commander Islands: Mine and Yours.* Moscow, 1989. In Russian.

Pasetskii, V. M. *Vitus Bering, 1681–1741.* Moscow, 1982. In Russian.

Petersen, J. *Vitus Bering, der Seefahrer.* Trans. H. Kurtzweil. Hamburg, 1947.

Petersen, S. G. "Vitus Bering's Second Kamchatka Expedition—the Journey to America and Archaeological Excavations on Bering Island." In Jacobsen, *Vitus Bering,* 66–93.

Petersen, S. G., and O. Schiørring. "Han Dóde 8. December." *Skalk*, no. 6 (1991): 3–8.

Pierce, R. A., ed. *Russia in North America*. Kingston, Ont., 1990.

Polevoi, B. P. "America in the Plans of Peter the Great." In Frost, *Bering and Chirikov*, 77–89.

———. "The Discovery of Russian America." In Starr, *Russia's American Colony*, 13–30.

Posselt, D. *Die Grosse Nordische Expedition von 1733 bis 1743*. Munich, 1990.

Postnikov, A. V. "The Russian Navy as Chartmaker in the Eighteenth Century." *Imago Mundi* 52 (2000): 79–95.

Raeff, M. "Seventeenth-Century Europe in Eighteenth-Century Russia." *Slavic Review* 41 (1982): 611–19.

Rasputin, V. *Siberia, Siberia*. Trans. M. Winchell and G. Mikkelson. Evanston, Ill., 1996.

Ray, D. J. *Aleut and Eskimo Art: Tradition and Innovation in South Alaska*. Seattle, 1981.

Rogger, H. *National Consciousness in Eighteenth-Century Russia*. Cambridge, Mass., 1960.

Rowell, M. "Early Russian Botanical Exploration in the North Pacific." *Episteme* 7 (1973): 165–85.

Sears, D. G. "Der Kolumbus des Zaren." *GEO*, no. 12 (1992): 106–25.

Sebald, W. G. *After Nature*. Trans. M. Hamburger. New York, 2002.

Semyonov, Y. *The Conquest of Siberia: An Epic of Human Passions*. Trans. E. W. Dickes. London, 1944.

Shalkop, A., and R. L. Shalkop, eds. *Exploration in Alaska: Captain Cook Commemorative Lectures*. Anchorage, 1980.

Sherwood, M. B. "Science in Russian America, 1741–1865." *Pacific Northwest Quarterly* 58 (1967): 33–39.

Siberia—Terra Incognita: The Role of German Scholars in the Early Exploration of Siberia in the 18th Century. Halle, 1999.

Smith, B. S. *Russian Orthodoxy in Alaska: A History, Inventory, and Analysis of the Church Archives in Alaska*. Anchorage, 1980.

———, ed. *Science under Sail: Russian Exploration in the North Pacific, 1728–1867*. Forthcoming.

Smith, B. S., and R. J. Barnett, eds. *Russian America: The Forgotten Frontier*. Tacoma, 1990.

Sokol, A. E. "Russian Expansion and Exploration in the Pacific." *American Slavic and East European Review* 11 (1952): 85–106.

Solovev, A. I. *Northern Expeditions, 1733–1743*. St. Petersburg, 1861. In Russian.

Soloviev, S. M. *History of Russia*. Vol. 34: *Empress Anna: Favorites, Policies, Campaigns*. Trans. W. J. Gleason Jr. Gulf Breeze, Fla., 1984.

————. *History of Russia*. Vol. 37: *Empress Elizabeth's Reign, 1741–1744*. Trans. P. J. O'Meara. Gulf Breeze, Fla., 1996.

Sopotsko, A. A. *History of the Voyage of V. Bering in the Boat "Sv. Gavriil" to the Arctic Ocean*. Moscow, 1983. In Russian.

Starr, S. F., ed. *Russia's American Colony*. Durham, N.C., 1987.

Stearn, W. T. *Botanical Latin: History, Grammar, Syntax, Terminology and Vocabulary*. London, 1983.

Stejneger, L. "Contributions to the History of the Commander Islands." *Proceedings of the U.S. National Museum* 6 (1883): 58–89; 7 (1884–85): 181–89, 529–38; 12 (1890): 83–94.

————. "An Early Account of Bering's Voyages." *Geographical Review* 24 (1934): 638–42.

————. *Georg Wilhelm Steller: The Pioneer of Alaskan Natural History*. Cambridge, Mass., 1936.

————. "On the Extermination of the Great Northern Sea-Cow." *Bulletin of the American Geographic Society* 18 (1886): 317–28.

————. "Witus Jonassen Bering." *American-Scandinavian Review* 29 (1941): 295–307.

Suvorov, E. K. *The Commander Islands and Fur-Hunting on Them*. St. Petersburg, 1912. In Russian.

Thiel, E. *The Soviet Far East: A Survey of Its Physical and Economic Geography*. Trans. A. Rookwood and R. M. Rookwood. New York, 1957.

Urness, C. L. *Bering's First Expedition: A Re-examination Based on Eighteenth-Century Books, Maps, and Manuscripts*. Ann Arbor, 1987.

————. "Captain-Commander Vitus Bering." In Frost, *Bering and Chirikov*, 11–36.

————. "Joseph Nicolas Delisle's Map for Bering's Second Kamchatka Expedition." In Pierce, *Russia in North America*, 79–101.

Vernadsky, G. *Political and Diplomatic History of Russia*. Boston, 1936.

Völker, A., ed. *Dixhuiteme: Zur Geschichte von Medizin und Naturwissenschaften im 18. Jahrhundert*. Halle-Wittenberg, 1988.

Vucinich, A. *Science in Russian Culture: A History to 1860*. Stanford, 1963.

Wagner, H. R. *The Cartography of the Northwest Coast of America to the Year 1800*. 2 vols. Berkeley, 1937.

Wannhoff, U., and K. Törmer, *Comandor: Leben am Ende der Welt*. Berlin, n.d.

Weber, F. C. *The Present State of Russia*. 2 vols. London, 1723.

Wells, J. *Ipani Eskimos: A Cycle of Life in Nature*. Anchorage, 1974.

Whitmore, F. C. Jr., and L. M. Gard Jr. *Steller's Sea Cow (Hydrodamalis gigas) of Late Pleistocene Age from Amchitka, Aleutian Islands, Alaska.* Geological Survey Professional Paper no. 1036. Washington, D.C., 1977.

Williams, G. *The British Search for the Northwest Passage in the Eighteenth Century.* London, 1962.

Wood, A., ed. *The History of Siberia: From the Russian Conquest to Revolution.* London and New York, 1991.

Zimmerly, D. W. *Qajaq, Kayaks of Siberia and Alaska.* Juneau, 1986.

Zolotarev, A. "The Ancient Culture of North Asia." *American Anthropologist* 40 (1938): 13–23.

Zviagin, V. N. "A Reconstruction of Vitus Bering Based on Skeletal Remains." In Frost, *Bering and Chirikov,* 248–64.

Zvyagin, V. N., Sh. M. Musayev, and A. K. Stanyukovich. *Vitus Jonassen Bering (1681–1741): A Portrait Developed by Forensic Methods.* Baku, 1995. In Russian and English.

Acknowledgments

My debts to individuals and institutions are enormous. In 1984, John F. Thilenius Jr. of the U.S. Forest Service introduced me to the natural wonders of remote Kayak Island. A grant from the Alaska Humanities Forum and National Endowment for the Humanities enabled me to make that first visit. In 1987, the National Park Service invited me to return to the island. Others who participated in these Kayak Island trips, John L. Mattson, Susan Morton, and John F. C. Johnson, have also been conscientious critics of a report I prepared for the Alaska Humanities Forum. In 1985, Edgar P. Bailey of the U.S. Fish and Wildlife Service led me to the outer Shumagin Islands. Subsequently I benefited as well from insights of the late Aleut historian Andrew Gronholdt, born in the Shumagins, and the anthropologist L. Lewis Johnson of Vassar College, who spent many summers with her students in the outer Shumagins. To Society Expeditions, Seattle, and its vice president, John D. Tillotson, I owe thanks for visits to Bering Island, Kayak Island, and the Shumagin Islands in 1997 and 1999 as lecturer aboard the *World Discoverer* and for the opportunity to serve again as lecturer in 2002 aboard the new *World Discoverer* during its maiden cruise around the Bering Sea, including the tour along Kamchatka and Chukotka coasts into Bering Strait.

Three individuals, each in his or her own way, know aspects of the subject of this book better than I, and I am indebted to them in many ways: Carol Urness, professor of history at the University of Minnesota, who reviewed my entire text and made invaluable recommendations; Wieland Hintzsche of the Francke Foundations, Halle, Germany, who shared precious Steller documents that he found in manuscript in Russian archives; and Peter Ulf Møller of the West European Institute, Copenhagen, Denmark, who graciously sent me a copy of his newly published work, *Kommandøren og Konen,* which he co-authored with Natasha Okhotina Lind. Three eminent scholars in various ways encouraged me: the late Raymond H. Fisher of the University of California, Los Angeles; Richard A. Pierce, founder of Limestone Press; and the late Terence Armstrong of the Scott Polar Institute, Cambridge University. The published works of long-deceased pioneers in the field of Bering studies continue to offer an accessible documentary record: Frank Golder of Stanford University, Leonhard Stejneger of the Smithsonian Institution, and Evgenii G. Kushnarev of the Central Naval Museum, Leningrad (now St. Petersburg).

I am grateful for the help of friends and colleagues who gave support to this project: Svend E. Albrethsen, Department of Archaeology, National Museum, Copenhagen; Wendy Baker, Anchorage, Alaska; Louie Bartos, sailmaker, Ketchikan, Alaska; Gudrun Bucher, Offenbach, Germany; Barbara A. Crass, University of Wisconsin, Milwaukee; Elena Creamer, Medford, Oregon; Molly Duryea, Medford, Oregon; Margritt A. Engel, University of Alaska, Anchorage; Tatiana S. Fedorova, Central Naval Archives, St. Petersburg; Olga Griminger, Highland Park, New Jersey; Gary H. Holthaus, formerly of the Alaska Humanities Forum, Anchorage; Bertrand C. Imbert, Centre d'études arctiques, Paris; E. J. Jäger, Institute of Geobotany, University of Halle; Angela Kay Kepler, Haiku, Maui, Hawaii; Amir A. Khisamutdinov, Far Eastern State University, Vladivostok; Vitalii A. Len'kov, Academy of Sciences, Vladivostok; William Lorch, Eagle River, Alaska; Vladimir Mann, Vladivostok; Jan Oelker, Dresden; Alix O'Grady, Victoria, British Columbia; the late Ole Schiørring, Horsens Museum, Denmark; Michael Schlosser, city library and archives, Bad Windsheim, Germany; David Sears, Copenhagen; G. L. Silant'ev, Vladivostok; A. K. Stanyukovich, International Society "Peace under Water," Moscow; Barbara Sweetland Smith, Anchorage; Richard and Roxie Templin, Medford, Oregon; Ullrich Wannhoff, Berlin; Karen E. Willmore, University of Alaska, Anchorage; and V. N. Zvyagin, Institute of Forensic Medicine, Moscow. None of these individuals is in any way responsible for deficiencies in this work.

I am indebted to Alaska Pacific University for granting me a full-year sabbatical in 1984–85, leaves without pay in 1986–91, and also travel and research funds to use archives and rare book collections of the British Library, Smithsonian Institution, Library of Congress, Hoover Institution, and the following universities: Yale, Harvard, Stanford, and Illinois (Urbana-Champaign). The Alaska Humanities Forum and the National Endowment for the Humanities provided funds for trips to Fairbanks and to Alaska coastal communities from Unalaska, in the Aleutian Islands, to Ketchikan, in southeastern Alaska, for discussion of public issues arising from the identification of the Bering expeditions' landing sites. Finally I am grateful to two superb editors: Lara Heimert, executive editor of Yale University Press, for her immediate interest in the subject of this book and her unfailing readiness to offer a kind word while promptly and efficiently moving my typescript through the initial editorial process; and Barbara Salazar, who saved me from much inadvertent use of the passive voice, no doubt a failing acquired during my years of ducking faculty fire as a college administrator.

Some observations that appear in this book have been published in slightly different form as "Georg Wilhelm Steller," *Alaska* 66 (2000): 48–55; "Vitus Bering Resurrected: Recent Forensic Analysis and the Documentary Record," *Pacific Northwest Quarterly* 84 (1993), 91–97; and "Vitus Bering and Georg Steller: Their Tragic Conflict during the American Expedition," *Pacific Northwest Quarterly* 86 (1994–95), 3–16. The following institutions kindly granted permission for publication of illustrations in this book: Alaska Historical Society, Anchorage; Anchorage Museum of History and Art; Horsens Museum, Denmark; James Ford Bell Library, University of Minnesota; and Leland Stanford Jr. University, Stanford, California. Most of the maps were produced by William L. Nelson, Accomac, Virginia.

My heaviest debt is to my wife, Mary, who has given me time, tea, and sympathy; allowed shared travels to be diverted to libraries and archives; and led me into amazing and helpful Internet searches. She reviewed drafts of the entire typescript. As always, she is my best critic.

Index